MOSES HESS
AND MODERN
JEWISH IDENTITY

Jewish Literature and Culture
Series Editor, Alvin H. Rosenfeld

MOSES HESS

AND MODERN

JEWISH IDENTITY

INDIANA UNIVERSITY PRESS
BLOOMINGTON & INDIANAPOLIS

Ken Koltun-Fromm

Publication of this book is made possible in part by generous support from the Koret Foundation.
This book is a publication of

Indiana University Press
601 North Morton Street
Bloomington, IN 47404-3797 USA

http://iupress.indiana.edu

Telephone orders 800-842-6796
Fax orders 812-855-7931
Orders by e-mail iuporder@indiana.edu

The paper used in this publication meets the minimum requirements of
American National Standard for Information Sciences—Permanence of
Paper for Printed Library Materials, ANSI Z39.48-1984.

Manufactured in the United States of America

Library of Congress Cataloging-in-Publication Data

Koltun-Fromm, Ken.
    Moses Hess and modern Jewish identity / Ken Koltun-Fromm.
        p. cm. — (Jewish literature and culture)
    Includes bibliographical references (p.   ) and index.
    ISBN 0-253-33934-0 (cl : alk. paper)
        1. Jews—Germany—Identity. 2. Hess, Moses, 1812–1875. 3. Jews—Cultural
assimilation—Germany. 4. Judaism—Germany—History—19th century. 5. Hess, Moses,
1812–1875. Rom und Jerusalem. I. Title. II. Series.

DS143 .K625 2001
305.892′4043—dc21   00-054097

1 2 3 4 5   06 05 04 03 02 01

For Naomi and Ariadne

CONTENTS

Acknowledgments

This book, like so many others, has strong roots, perhaps even deeper ones than I can even imagine. I first came across the works of Moses Hess in an independent reading course with my teacher and friend, Arnold Eisen. Those first moments of initial fascination and puzzlement continued throughout my dissertation project and this work. I learned how to approach texts with such critical absorption from Eisen, and for that (and for so much else), I am sincerely grateful. My other teachers at Stanford University encouraged and substantially contributed to this project from the start: Van Harvey, Lee Yearley, and Steven Zipperstein. So too my friends and colleagues there who continue to inspire: Avi Bernstein-Nahar, Steven Rappaport, and especially Zachary Braiterman who, in ever longer telephone conversations, always challenges my suspicious allegiance to theories of virtue. I am blessed with such friends and mentors, and their voices find their place in this book. Their support and nurture continue in colleagues at Haverford College who, drowned in their own work, still find the time and energy to further my own. Members of the religion department—David Dawson, Tracey Hucks, Naomi Koltun-Fromm, Anne McGuire, and Michael Sells—have read various drafts of this book, and all have provided a warm, caring, and intellectually aggressive atmosphere for its revisions. So too the Humanities Works in Progress group that read an early draft of the first chapter, and who helped shape the project in significant ways. Colleagues from afar have also encouraged my work, especially Allan Arkush, David Ellenson, Jonathan Frankel, and Susannah Heschel. Friends at Indiana University Press have been encouraging and responsive throughout the publication process. The help and support from Janet Rabinowitch, Dee Mortensen, Jane Lyle, and the wonderful editing by Joyce Rappaport significantly improved the focus and style of the work, and to them, indeed to many others at the Press, I owe a humble sense of gratitude. I have also received generous support at various and crucial times in developing this project from the Koret Foundation, Memorial Foundation, and Haverford College. Permission was kindly granted from Gordon and Breach Publishers and the Overseas Publishers Association to include parts of my article, "Public Religion in Samson Raphael Hirsch and Samuel Hirsch's Interpretation of Religious Symbolism" in chapter 5, and Oxford

University Press for allowing substantial portions of, "A Narrative Reading of Moses Hess's Return to Judaism," to appear in chapter 3.

I dedicate this book to two persons who have rooted my life, and this book, in subtle and lasting ways. Naomi is, as she well knows, more than friend, colleague, spouse, and mother to our two children. My sense of self and Jewish identity are integrally and lovingly connected to her own. My cousin Ariadne died too young to forge such an identity in this world, but lived long enough to help others struggle with theirs. She continues to live in many of us for our blessing. This dedication is but a reminder that we do not own our identities, much less our past, but stand eternally moved by the persons we cherish most.

MOSES HESS
AND MODERN
JEWISH IDENTITY

Oil painting of Moses Hess by Gustav Adolf Köttgen, 1845. By
permission of Stadtmuseum Düsseldorf.

Moses Hess and Modern Jewish Identity

1

In *Rome and Jerusalem* (1862), Moses Hess imagined a new Jewry, one progressive and traditional, religious and socialist, nationalist and humanitarian. But such a utopian vision would not go unchallenged. Hess's colleagues in Germany were the first to recognize the alarming tensions in his thought. Ludwig Philippson, the editor of the popular nineteenth-century German Jewish paper *Allgemeine Zeitung des Judentums*, complained in an unsigned article that Hess, who himself did not observe Jewish laws or customs, could demand from every Jew strict observance to the commandments and commitment to a Judaism unchanged in its traditional form: "What do we have here, dear reader?" chided Philippson. "This is the newest form of hypocrisy in Judaism."[1] Humiliated, Hess insisted that Philippson had missed his point about religious reform, and such personal attacks on his character would do nothing to reinforce Jewish national identity.

Hess's passionate and often conflicted views invited attacks on his works, and even on his character. Philippson, with obvious disdain for Hess's shallow display of piety, dismissed those conflicts as symptoms of a confused mind. But Philippson could not appreciate how those confusions addressed complex issues in modern Jewish identity. This was especially true in Hess's image of Jewish sacrificial worship as the beloved but hideous "scar":

> True love, the love that dominates spirit and mind, is in actuality *blind*. Blind because it does not desire, philosophically or aesthetically, the perfection of the beloved being, but rather loves it just as it is with all its excellences and faults. . . . The scar on the face of my beloved does not harm my love, but rather makes it even the more precious—who knows?—perhaps more precious than her beautiful eyes, which can be found in other beautiful women, while just this scar is characteristic of the individuality of my beloved.[2]

The face of Jewish tradition is scarred by ancient sacrificial worship, but loved all the more for its imperfections. Its appeal lies not in beauty but in individuality, not in perfection but in realism, not in reason but in passion. For Hess, modern Judaism, like the ancient sacrifices, must be unique, concrete, material, and meaningful. But it also must be connected to a past, however scarred. Hess's Judaism is a passionate commitment touched with doubt ("who knows?"), and so his appeal to a scarred past reveals profound tensions in modern Jewish identity. Rather than dismiss those tensions, as many scholars of Hess have done, we should embrace them as insightful reflections on identity. This book turns to Hess's passionate struggle for an authentic modern Judaism in order to grasp better the dynamics of modern

Jewish identity. The tensions in Hess's works, I want to argue, reveal in new ways the inescapable conflicts facing modern Jewry.

Contemporary scholars, following Philippson's lead, have criticized Hess for his lack of philosophical sophistication (though unlike Philippson, they still admire his character and commitment). Edmund Silberner, Hess's biographer, noticed the eccentric and erratic ordering of topics in *Rome and Jerusalem*. He responded by rewriting Hess's claims in a more "systematic" form.[3] Jonathan Frankel likened the "personal, fragmented, often emotional form" of *Rome and Jerusalem* to writing a confession.[4] Hess's work did not have the philosophical weight to be anything more. Even Isaiah Berlin, who fiercely defended Hess before his critics, complained that Hess's style was "sentimental, rhetorical, and at times merely flat; there are a good many digressions and references to issues now totally forgotten."[5] If, as I will argue in chapter 4, Berlin and Frankel poorly understood the rhetorical power of Hess's narrative style, others often dismissed Hess's religious thought entirely. In a book entitled *Moses Hess: Prophet of Communism and Zionism*, Shlomo Avineri ignored Hess's constructive proposals for modern Jewish religious identity, labeling Hess instead an "agnostic socialist" who did not want to get "bogged down in religious observance."[6] Hess was too passionate, unsystematic, conflicted, and secular to be taken seriously as a religious philosopher. Yet Hess's readers all maintained, with Berlin, that *Rome and Jerusalem* was indeed "a masterpiece."[7] So despite the confusing, passionate, and outdated jargon, *Rome and Jerusalem* still had something to offer.

The central claim in this book is that the confusions and tensions embedded throughout *Rome and Jerusalem* produce a meaningful testament and witness to the complexity of modern (and even post-modern) Jewish identity. The tensions abound in both the content and structure of the work. Composed as a series of twelve letters to Josephine Hirsch (whose sister Emilie married Hess's brother Samuel),[8] *Rome and Jerusalem* also includes an introductory preface, a concluding epilogue with six appendices, ten notes to the letters, and a postscript. *Rome and Jerusalem* is so clumsy and unyielding, loquacious and erratic, that Hess had difficulty publishing the work until Heinrich Graetz convinced a publisher in Leipzig to finance the project. But the work sold poorly when it appeared in 1862, and few of Hess's colleagues read the book or even took notice of it. No wonder, for one must jump from letter to note, sift through complex arguments and digressions in the epilogue, and again reread the letters to fully grasp Hess's claim that modern Jewish identity is rooted in a complex web of national and religious commitments. Yet Hess barely hints at this structural complexity in the preface, where he summarizes his work as a new account of national Jewish identity that evades the "illusions of the rationalists" (the Reformers) while also steering clear of the "dogmatic fanatics" (the Orthodox).[9] Throughout the letters, Hess paints a profound religious vision of Jewish history and the religious heritage that grounds Jewish political life and practice. He argues for the rebuilding of a Jewish state in Palestine that promotes religious, social, and political commitments. This proto-Zionist theme has received the most attention from scholars, but Hess also calls for critical

appraisal of modern Jewish identity, and for the religious and social goods associated with this self-awareness. Yet Hess does not guide us through this intricate
maze of commitments, emotional attachments, national ties, and religious practice.
We are left to pull the various fragments together. In so doing, readers of *Rome
and Jerusalem* reproduce Hess's very complex act of constructing identity out of
multiple and sometimes conflicting narrative strands. The complexity of *Rome and
Jerusalem* itself expresses the conflicting struggles of modern Jewish identity.

To be sure, *Rome and Jerusalem* is a scarred work of its own. Hess often confesses his own fears, ambitions, stubbornness, and hopes for the future. To take but
one example, it is clear from the letters to Josephine Hirsch that she represents
female Jewish piety. In Hess's reading, female piety displays a relentless and devoted
attachment to Jewish nationality. Through her faithfulness, Josephine Hirsch, and
others like her, are worthy of the redemptive return home to Jewish national existence. Indeed, she is more worthy than others of her generation, who change their
names and religious language to fit dominant cultural expectations. Hess suggests
that faithfulness to nationality, exhibited in part by the retention of the Hebrew
language and personal names, and a healthy distance from the dominant culture,
are necessary preconditions for the redemption of the Jewish people. This, by a
Jewish man married to a Christian woman, a man at home in European culture
and philosophy, fluent in both German and French, and a man who, with the singular exception of *Rome and Jerusalem,* signs his name M. Hess or Moritz Hess,
but never Moses Hess.[10] *Rome and Jerusalem* really does appear to be "the newest
form of hypocrisy in Judaism."

So even as he defended Jewish national identity, Hess was deeply ambivalent
about his own relationship to Judaism and the Jewish people, to mention nothing
of a "Jewish nation." Hess's ambivalence arises out of the religious and biological
imagery that informs his account of Jewish nationalism. The very term *nation* was
problematic in the context of nineteenth-century German debates on "the Jewish
question," for the term could imply a religious, racial, cultural or political community. Hess employed the word *nation* to signify all of these meanings. At times, the
Jewish nation identified a cultural and political legacy. In other texts, Hess described the nation as a religious community that continually re-evaluated (in ritual,
thought, and memory) the meaning of Jewish tradition.

Yet one cannot but notice the dissonance between Hess's defense of a Jewish
nation and his personal commitment to it.[11] Born the first of five children in 1812
in Bonn, Hess entered the world just three years before Prussia would reclaim the
Rhineland from France and once again restrict the rights of Jewish inhabitants-an
event, according to Shlomo Avineri, that influenced a great many radical German
Jewish thinkers, Hess among them.[12] Hess received a traditional Jewish education
until the age of fourteen, when, after his mother's death in 1825, he joined his
father's trade business in Cologne. Here, for the first time confronting the exhila-
rating world of German romantic and idealist philosophy, Hess felt ill-prepared
and groundless: *"Wo hatte [ich] studiert? Nirgend. Was? Nichts!!! [Where have I
studied? Nowhere. What? Nothing!!!]."*[13] He quickly devoured Schelling, Rous-

seau, Schiller, Kant, Hegel, and others in what appears to be an unsystematic study of the German philosophical tradition. Hess mentioned only two Jewish works: Mendelssohn's *Jerusalem* and Spinoza's *Tractatus,* texts that would later influence his understanding of Jewish identity. In 1835 Hess entered the University of Bonn, but again did not follow any systematic course of study, and never received a university degree. He would soon become a distinguished socialist revolutionary and writer, establishing close friendships with Karl Marx, Friedrich Engels, and Ferdinand Lassalle. But even as an influential and proud German socialist, Hess felt lost in the German culture surrounding him. His own socialist party members would desperately slander him with anti-Jewish epithets.[14] Yet he could not retreat to the more familiar environment of Jewish community or tradition. Hess was not an observant religious Jew, and his knowledge of Hebrew was minimal, though more proficient than his understanding of Jewish history. He had only contempt for Talmudic scholarship and education, and scornfully characterized his teachers as *"Unmenschen."*[15] As we shall see, Hess also detected the rift between his national claims and his personal commitments. He sought to mend the breach by appealing to nation as racial heritage. Even if he no longer embraced the Jewish religious and cultural legacy, Hess was still a Jew from birth, a product of what he called racial "integrity." Hess's racial theory offered the protection and promise of a stable and authentic Jewish identity. For Hess, so removed from the Jewish religious, political, and cultural heritage he endorsed but could not himself fully accept, race science became Jewish self-affirmation.[16]

The tensions are so clearly felt in Hess's appeal to Jewish tradition despite (or even because) of its scars; in his defense of Jewish national identity as an inescapable racial heritage; and finally, in his adopting the name "Moses" for *Rome and Jerusalem,* not as his birth name, but as his "old Testament name."[17] Jonathan Frankel has called *Rome and Jerusalem* Hess's most confessional work. In that confession Hess confronts the dilemmas of modern Jewish identity. The reader recognizes a Jew struggling to come to terms with the meaning of his conflicting commitments and impulses, a man at times religious, secular, socialist, and nationalist. But that struggle does not make *Rome and Jerusalem* any less philosophically rich or nuanced. Hess is witness to the conflicting appeals of modern goods, and reveals how one Jew negotiates their constraints and possibilities.

I read the texts that Silberner, Avineri, and Berlin find outdated and unconvincing as powerful resources for reconfiguring Jewish identity, modern and postmodern. In contrast to previous readings that narrowly focus on Hess's socialist or proto-Zionist concerns, this book stresses instead how Hess is a passionate *Jewish* thinker. Even as Hess highlights the specific and singular problems of nineteenth-century German Jewry, I want to claim that his dilemmas, conflicts, and tenuous solutions still confront modern Jews today. Where a previous generation discarded Hess's conflicts as bad philosophy, I reappropriate them to explore intractable dilemmas in modern Jewish identity. The goals of this book are thus two-fold: to offer a compelling and substantially new reading of Hess's corpus (especially *Rome and Jerusalem*), and to recommend Hess's works as rich resources for confronting the problems of modern Jewish identity.

Categories of Modern Identity

The concept of identity that informs my own thinking is taken from Charles Taylor's impressive work, *Sources of the Self.*[18] Much of the philosophical groundwork for Taylor's book was developed earlier, especially in his article, "What is Human Agency?"[19] In that article, Taylor distinguishes between the notion of a "self" and our understanding of "identity." He does this by appealing to the concept of "strong evaluation." A strong evaluator reflects about the kind of life worth living and the goods that make up this life. She reasons in terms of better and worse, and makes qualitative distinctions between baser and nobler kinds of action.[20] Taylor claims that this kind of qualitative judgment is an inescapable feature of human personhood. We simply could not imagine a well-developed human being bereft of this capacity to contrast and judge values and commitments qualitatively. Our identities, then, are defined by our strong evaluations:

> So my lineage is part of my identity because it is bound up with certain qualities I value, or because I believe that I must value these qualities since they are so integrally part of me that to disvalue them would be to reject myself. In either case, the concept of identity is bound up with that of certain strong evaluations which are inseparable from myself.[21]

Strong evaluation is a necessary formal characteristic of human agency. To be a self is to be a strong evaluator. Individual identity is determined by the content of particular strong evaluations. I am a self because I am a strong evaluator, but I am this and not that kind of person because of the strong evaluations I make. I employ the terms *identity, person,* and *agent* to refer to the kind of being imagined or described by strong evaluations. The word *self* I limit to the formal characteristics necessary to imagine or describe a recognizable human being.

Hess's works are full of strong evaluations that fit uneasily together. He appeals to moral sources that conflict, exposing the tensions in his own identity and the "national" Jews he describes. Taylor would not be surprised by these countervailing pressures. He believes such ambiguity is part of what it means to be a modern self. By the time Taylor writes *Sources of the Self* (1989), he suggests that the recovery of moral sources can reconcile conflicting commitments:

> The moral conflicts of modern culture rage within each of us. Unless, that is, our greater lucidity can help us to see our way to a reconciliation. If I may give expression to an even farther-out hunch, I will say that I see this as the potential goal and fruit of articulacy.[22]

Hess too yearns to reconcile his moral sources. Yet his works are littered with the strains of emotional and philosophical turmoil. If Taylor imagines a time when the moral conflicts finally abate, then I fear that his hermeneutics of reconciliation might suppress Hess's confusions. For it is precisely these confusions that make *Rome and Jerusalem* and Hess's other texts so profitable for modern persons. Moral conflicts certainly "rage" in Hess, and only a "greater lucidity" would lose sight of the tensions and compromises that inform and complicate modern Jewish identity. So reading Hess helps us to see the deficiencies in Taylor's approach to the modern self. Conflict and fragmentation should not be overcome by greater lucidity, but instead should be recognized as significant and constitutive features of modern life.

Hess speaks of a "national," "assimilated," or even "reform" Jew because these descriptive words impart normative claims about how to live and think in the world in ways that foster and shape Jewish identity. Hess's world is familiar to many Jews living in the contemporary West, where they (together with other peoples) often must choose among rival commitments, communities, and allegiances. These choices in part constitute and inform personal identity. *Rome and Jerusalem* exhibits modern commitments to national identity and social welfare goods, as well as post-modern struggles with conflict, insecurity, and fragmentation. Conflict is real for persons like Hess who experience competing obligations and commitments that cannot be ranked, unified, or displaced within a theory of the good.

Like many Jews today, Hess walks cautiously toward a theory of Jewish religious identity that promises to harmonize the commitments of both Orthodox and Reform traditions. He positions himself tenuously between the Orthodox defense of an oral tradition received from Sinai (and thus authoritative and divinely inspired), and the Reform critique that these rabbinic texts reflect a history of interpretive innovations. Even as he appeals to a flexible oral law (the Reform tradition), Hess recoils from the possible indeterminacy of interpretive license (the Orthodox fear). He therefore seeks a reform still sensitive to ritual, custom, Hebrew language, and the authority of rabbinic and medieval commentators. Yet Hess is not thoroughly successful. His critique of Reform and Orthodoxy is at times dismissive, callous, and misdirected; his positive agenda for Jewish renewal is often far too sweeping and vague. Yet there are moments (indeed moments that will occupy a significant part of this study) that reveal Hess's genuine ambivalence toward the Jewish tradition in general, and toward modern Jewish identity in particular. These flashes of insight and recognition are important to recover, for they illustrate the tensions that are still felt among many religious persons who are dedicated to an authoritative tradition, yet live uncomfortably with the inheritance from their past. Recovering Hess's religious polemic helps us to understand the multiple conflicts encountered by many contemporary Jews.

Hess's most distinguished biographer, Edmund Silberner, dismissed these religious concerns as thoroughly irrelevant to Hess's defense of Jewish identity.[23] Silberner was primarily concerned to free Hess from those who ridiculed his socialist "utopia." Indeed, the first biography on Hess focused on this very debate, and defended Hess from the Marxist attack.[24] But in reading Hess as a creative and independent socialist thinker, Silberner's corrective agenda came to dominate the project as a whole. Particular tropes and themes guided his reading, while others were relegated to the background or left unexplored. For a historian of socialism like Silberner, religion was a problematic feature of texts that promoted socialist principles. In the very first paragraph of his biography, Silberner quoted Hess's personal confession in 1849 or 1850 that "the socialist revolution is my religion." Silberner's biography would portray "the history of Moses Hess's life, the apostle of socialism."[25] During the 1950s and 60s, when Silberner researched and wrote his work, the meaning of the "socialist revolution" was still a pressing issue among many historians. Na'aman, Bloch, Lukács, Carlebach, Lademacher, and Mönke, to name just a few, have all contributed important studies concerning Hess's socialist thought and its place in the history of socialism.[26] Silberner's agenda, to be sure, shaped their concerns.[27] The vast majority of their scholarly research involved protracted debates concerning Hess's relationship to and influence upon Marx and Engels, his place within the left Hegelian movement and efforts in forming the German Socialist Party, his critique of capitalism, and his "true" or "utopian" socialism. Religious questions were tangential to their view of a socialist society, and therefore to Hess's as well. When scholars focus too narrowly on Hess's socialist or Zionist agenda, they only simplify the complex web of religious associations in Hess's works. We need to balance Silberner's corrective by refocusing our interpretive lenses, and we should ask different questions to see Hess's socialist and political thought from the perspective of modern Jewish religious identity.

New questions begin with a more expressive language for understanding identity in Hess's works. Hess's strong evaluations do not take shape in a vacuum, but among a complex fabric of relations. Language, community, and family are but the most obvious candidates that fashion Hess's reflective deliberations on identity. In this book, I want to focus on three other relations, or categories, that make possible a rich account of Jewish identity: *narrative, frameworks of meaning,* and *tradition.* All three are taken from Taylor, and each category helps to recover critical features of Jewish identity in Hess's texts. Though I disagree with Taylor's approach in significant ways, I still want to argue that Hess implicitly relies upon categories analogous to Taylor's in order to make sense of Jewish identity. In short, Hess operates with categories that Taylor later argues are inescapable for modern persons, but in doing so, Hess offers a more fragmented, ambiguous picture. Hess tells stories, recognizes limits, fixes borders, and situates persons within tradition(s), but unlike Taylor he constructs a modern identity in conflict. If we read Hess by asking how he imagines modern Jewish identity, then Hess's works offer potent challenges to Taylor's project.

Narratives, frameworks of meaning, and traditions are "spheres of human experience" in which "more or less any human being will have to make *some* choices rather than others, and act in *some* way rather than some other."[28] These spheres are inescapable in the sense that human agents draw upon them to make sense of their lives. Taylor argues that persons recognize who they are by the stories they tell. Persons affirm their identities in stories, and those stories in turn shape the kind of beings they are. Getting the narrative right is thus vital, for distorting narratives pervert a more lucid understanding of human agency. But whether clear or deforming, narratives shape identity. In this sense, stories are frameworks of meaning that help persons recognize value.

A framework is that in virtue of which persons recognize important moral, political, and religious goods that constitute identity. Moral ideals of autonomy and freedom, political goods of nationality and natural rights, and religious conceptions of human nature are all frameworks that inform how modern persons deliberate about value. Disagreements exist in politics, ethics, and religion because persons draw upon different frameworks to justify their claims. Frameworks, like narratives, inescapably fashion the way in which persons deliberate about the good, and thus about identity.

Traditions, whether political, religious, or ethical, are also frameworks of meaning that fashion modern identity. Persons act, reason, and imagine within some tradition(s), and they appeal to the values, languages, and arguments of those traditions to defend beliefs and choices. So narratives and traditions are inescapable frameworks for human agency, though such frameworks are not exhausted by them.

Let us return for a moment to Hess's discussion of the scar. Recall the text in which Hess discusses Temple sacrifices in ancient Judaism:

> True love, the love that dominates spirit and mind, is in actuality *blind*. Blind because it does not desire, philosophically or aesthetically, the perfection of the beloved being, but rather loves it just as it is with all its excellences and faults. . . . The scar on the face of my beloved does not harm my love, but rather makes it even the more precious—who knows?—perhaps more precious than her beautiful eyes, which can be found in other beautiful women, while just this scar is characteristic of the individuality of my beloved.[29]

Hess certainly appeals to the strong narrative of return in Jewish tradition to rebuild the Temple. But a second narrative of romantic love, with its blindness, passion, and particularity, interweaves with the Jewish one, and complicates how Hess understands the meaning of sacrificial worship. These narratives are frameworks that create meaning for Hess. He does not simply throw off the burdensome weight of a past, as some reformers had done before him, and appeal to historical progress in order to denounce sacrificial worship. Instead, he adopts that past as his own, even as he recognizes the scars. Therefore, love *must* be blind for Hess to embrace Jewish tradition. Love requires perfection, but blind love accepts it all, unconditionally and passionately. The narratives, frameworks, and tradition that Hess appeals to in this text all inform his understanding of modern Jewish identity. Modern Jews, for Hess, are burdened with a past that they can only accept blindly, and yet that blindness still reveals important scars. The face of Jewish tradition is a scarred one, and so too the modern Jews who welcome it.

Throughout his works, Hess tells stories that construct identity; he discusses frameworks within which identity is discovered and formed; and he describes traditions that ground and give substance to modern Jewish identity. I want to probe Hess's texts for the stories that fashion identity, and the traditions and frameworks that Hess draws upon to shape that identity. Reading Hess through these categories will not only enrich our understanding of his works; it will also help us evaluate features of modern Jewish identity. Hess's strong evaluations, I intend to show, are informed by traditions and are affirmed in stories that are inescapably rooted in multiple frameworks. Tradition, frameworks of meaning, and narratives are contested spaces within which Hess constructs a torn and scarred modern Jewish identity.

But Taylor has all but erased the scars of tradition. "Greater lucidity" means a complete and whole narrative identity: in short, an identity without scars, fissures, or conflicts. Taylor alleges that frameworks are inescapable only in a transcendental, formal sense, since we cannot take a stand on a whole range of ethical, political, and religious debates without implicitly drawing upon them. But despite his insistence, Taylor sneaks in the *substantive* claim that frameworks establish secure identities in the face of modern dislocation. Frameworks are, it turns out, necessary for maintaining a coherent identity. Without them, we would be "in the grip of an appalling identity crisis."[30] But this is special pleading. It is only "appalling" for those who believe that multiple frameworks, narratives, and traditions stretch identity beyond recognition and recovery. An identity in crisis is not incoherent nor episodic, but is an inescapable experience of modern life. Taylor silences conflicts with a more lucid, articulate hermeneutics of reconciliation. Reading Hess, however, shows us that a fragmented and scarred life is still meaningful, perhaps even necessary, for modern persons.

Outline of Chapters

The following chapters show how Hess's *Rome and Jerusalem*, read together with his many other works, fundamentally complicates, challenges, and revises contemporary accounts of modern Jewish identity. In chapter 2, I trace competing narratives that run through Hess's works. The one dominates Hess's early and middle works. Beginning with *Rome and Jerusalem*, however, there is a radical shift in Hess's underlying conception of self and Jewish identity; a shift, I want to emphasize, that does not entirely displace the earlier and competing account of identity. In his analysis of modern constraints and possibilities, Hess recognizes the contingent and open features of modern life. This new insight marks an important shift away from his previous studies on identity. Yet this novel view stands alongside a racial theory that grounds Jewish identity in the biological law of "our flesh and blood." In the former account, Hess appreciates the dynamic possibilities of modern Jewish identity. But in the latter theory, Jewish identity is rooted in an inescapable racial history. Thus, within the same text reside two conflicting visions of Jewish identity. These two competing narratives—the one open to ambiguity and contingency, the other hostile to new discoveries and sources of conflict—mark *Rome and Jerusalem* and later essays as distinctive and new works in Hess's literary career. The productive tension created by these two narratives is a peculiar feature of *Rome and Jerusalem* and modern Jewish identity.

Chapters 3, 4, and 5 discuss Hess's account of Jewish identity in *Rome and*

Jerusalem in relation to Taylor's categories. In each chapter, I bring contemporary discussions to bear on Hess's views, and draw Hess's arguments into conversation with current ethical philosophy. My concern in chapter 3 centers on Hess's reconstructed narrative of his literary corpus, and the various accounts of his "return" to Judaism. Hess presents two compelling though conflicting reports of his Jewish nationalism. The one recalls an emotional reaction to a bereaving relative, and its power to rekindle Hess's national passion; the other defends Jewish nationalism as a constant obsession in Hess's literary works. In this latter account, Hess insists that his return to Judaism is nothing more than a recovery of lost roots never completely abandoned. He describes his return as a "narrative quest" in which he is, at the very end of the journey, the very same kind of person throughout. This reconstructed narrative is historically inaccurate, and not only for the reasons presented in chapter 2, but also because *Rome and Jerusalem* provides the lens through which Hess interprets his earlier works. Even as Hess is open to conversionary moments, he continually softens them through stories of quest and return. This creative move to subsume discontinuous moments within a coherent and continuous narrative should be preserved (rather than ignored) in order to recognize how multiple and often discontinuous narratives inform both *Rome and Jerusalem* and modern Jewish identity.

In chapter 4, I discuss an often dismissed feature of *Rome and Jerusalem* and Hess's later essays: his racial theory. Many scholars deny its significance altogether, or translate Hess's racial terminology into less contested language (nation, ethnicity, culture). But these apologetic maneuvers overlook how Hess justifies his race science. He appeals to family and nation as emotional ties rooted in racial belonging, and describes Jewish racial "integrity" as an inescapable framework for Jewish identity. The emotional language so characteristic of *Rome and Jerusalem* is a rhetorical device that encourages readers to honor their racial attachments. Hess argues that a Jew who denies his national religious identity is a "traitor to his people, his race, and to his family." Jewish identity has become racial identity, a now inevitable feature of Jewish self-constitution. Taylor's analysis of inescapable frameworks helps explain the role that racial theory plays in Hess's account. Hess's racial theory builds upon his reconstructed narrative (discussed in chapter 3) to secure a Jewish identity beyond challenge. But more than this, it enables Hess to "return" to Jewish nationalism, because as an inescapable framework, racial "integrity" means that Hess had never really left his Jewish roots after all. If race science can affirm Jewish continuity, then a meaningful and coherent identity can still be fashioned despite modern dislocation. I conclude that Hess's racial theory is an important source for understanding the motivations behind Jewish identity politics.

Yet identity politics involves more than race science. For Hess, identity is always racial, national, *and* religious. The fifth chapter examines Hess's belief that Reform and Orthodox Jews fail to articulate the *religious* and moral commitments that in part constitute their Jewish identities. The Reformers, who zealously adopt the ideals of German *Bildung*, suppress features of their tradition that threaten social and political toleration. The Orthodox, however, restrict historical research and multiple interpretive schemes in order to safeguard the authority of revelation at Sinai. Yet in response, Hess offers two conflicting versions of tradition: the one is sensitive to historical contingency and hermeneutical creativity, the other appeals to Jewish unity and racial continuity. Hess is profoundly ambivalent about how to assess these divergent values. He qualitatively ranks different values (strong evaluation), even as he cannot reasonably justify that ranking. His ambivalence arises from a conflict of interpretation that eludes resolution. Hess's discussion reveals that for many modern Jews, negotiation and ambiguity are powerful features of the Jewish religious tradition. The conflicts embedded in tradition inform and complicate modern Jewish identity.

Rome and Jerusalem suggests that traditions are weighty but mired in contrasting visions of the good. Contrary to Taylor's theory, frameworks of meaning *conflict* and, moreover, are often *fragmentary* and thus *escapable*. Narratives, however, frequently secure identity beyond reflective critique and analysis (as they do for Hess in his racial theory). So even as Taylor's vocabulary helps us to understand Hess's notion of Jewish identity in a formal sense, Hess still constructs a substantially different picture of modern identity. Hess struggles to unite conflicting accounts of identity because he is mired in the Hegelian legacy that seeks unity, coherence, and reconciliation, even as he tries to revise that tradition by noting the fragmentary, ambiguous relations of modern persons. There are in Hess's works really two stories, two frameworks of meaning, and two traditions, and each exerts revisionary pressure upon the other. Narratives, frameworks of meaning, and traditions are affirmed, stretched, and challenged in Hess's works. It is this very quality of adoption and revision that makes Hess's thought so important for encountering the predicament of modern Jewish identity.

By exploring the problematics of Jewish identity, Moses Hess also contributes to our understanding of modern identity. Martha Nussbaum has alerted scholars to "features of humanness" or "spheres of experience" that "lie beneath all local traditions." Attending to local and specific qualities of a particular tradition can uncover aspects of many other human traditions. There is, she insists, "much family relatedness and much overlap among societies."[31] But "family relatedness" can only be discovered and appreciated through a thick, concentrated exploration into a local and particular tradition, and the specific problems confronting that tradition. In this book, the locality is nineteenth-century Germany, the tradition is Judaism, and the specific problem is Moses Hess's construction of Jewish identity. The particular dilemmas facing Hess and his Jewish contemporaries raise important questions for contemporary generations (Jews and non-Jews alike); a Judaism under siege by competing "plausibility structures," to adopt Peter Berger's phrase, is not alone among religious traditions coping with the challenges of the modern world; and the complexity of Jewish identity offers a dense and detailed picture of the uncertainty facing many modern persons. The problem of Jewish identity is not for and about Jews alone, but it implicates modern persons who struggle to unite and manage conflicting obligations and pressures. Jewish identity is but one localized variant of modern identity, and can offer important contributions to our understanding of "family relatedness."

The controlling thesis of this book is that Hess's struggle to unite conflicting commitments and allegiances offers intellectual and practical resources to reexamine the dilemmas of modern Jewish identity, and thereby enriches our understanding of modern identity. Hess's world of nineteenth-century German Jewry is certainly not our own, nor are his polemics or apologetics. But his commitments and ideals are still with us, if only because the conflicts of modern Jewish identity have not altogether disappeared. One would be remiss, and I think mistaken, to believe that nineteenth-century German Jewry, and the religious thought that developed from it, is a past well left behind.

To argue, as many do, that Hess prophetically warned of the racial conflicts that would soon develop in Germany, or that he saw further and more clearly than others of his generation, is to miss the most significant features of his texts. Hess could no more imagine the future than those who would live through it, nor could he anticipate the developments that would move European and Russian Jewry to a national revival. He was not a prophet, either of communism, Zionism, or modern racial theory. Hess was a Jew struggling to understand the meaning and significance of his life, and the lives of those he cared for. I conclude in the last chapter that in his struggle we have much to learn, for Hess reveals the kind of tensions, ambiguities, and conflicts that many contemporary Jews face. Modern Jewish identity is and should be scarred and fragmented among competing allegiances and narratives. This is so because identity is not something one owns, but an image that one struggles with, and often against. Hess's works are meaningful not as prophetic utterance, but as witness to the volatile and negotiated quality of modern Jewish identity.

Conceptions of Self and Identity in Hess's Early Works and *Rome and Jerusalem*

2

Hess delivered early copies of *Rome and Jerusalem* to his former publisher Otto Wigand and his good friend Berthold Auerbach. Hoping for critical assessments and honest praise, he instead received trenchant critique and contemptuous scorn. Both Wigand and Auerbach's response found their way into the fourth letter in *Rome and Jerusalem*.[1] Auerbach challenged Hess's already insecure position within the nineteenth-century German Jewish community: "Who," he asked, "has appointed you judge and ruler over us?"[2] The biblical allusion was surely intended, for the modern Moses appeared to Auerbach much like the biblical Moses: Hess's abrupt and mysterious return to Judaism was suspect. Hess had received a similar response from Phillipson, already noted in chapter 1. There, Phillipson accused Hess of hypocrisy. But Auerbach, a lifelong friend and defender of liberal Jewish observance, forced Hess to confront his ambiguous place within the Jewish tradition. He also brought to light an underlying theme in the very text he was criticizing: Hess's own relationship to the biblical Moses. We shall see in chapter 5 how Hess linked Moses, as an outsider to Jewish history and tradition, to the modern enlightened (*gebildete*) Jews in Germany. Both failed to acknowledge their deep Jewish ancestry and the commitments associated with it. As "people of Egypt," both the biblical Moses and the modern Jew were strangers to the Jewish tradition. Auerbach redirected Hess's critique, suggesting that Hess himself was far closer to the biblical Moses than he would care to admit. As if to stress this very point, Auerbach quoted Exodus 2:14 in Hebrew so that Hess could not possibly miss its biblical resonance.

It was thus both ironic and insightful that Auerbach, a German Reform Jew himself, had turned the tables on Hess. Not the Reform Jew, but the nationalist Hess had unjustly seized the mantle of Jewish leadership. Hess wanted European Jews to recognize their national history and to rebuild a Jewish homeland. Many reformers, Auerbach among them, were offended by Hess's claim that Reform Jewry sat complacent in a foreign land, lost from its traditional moorings and fat in European high culture. Who could blame them, for Hess had done little to win their respect, even less their allegiance. To Auerbach, Moses in Egypt had reappeared in the form of a modern Moses Hess. Perhaps Auerbach was not unaware that *Rome and Jerusalem* was the only text that appeared with Hess's first name *Moses*. In this light, Auerbach's critique threatened not only Hess's leadership but his integrity, not merely his stature but his authenticity, not just his vision but his Jewish identity.

Hess's "place" in the Jewish tradition is a central concern in the scholarly literature as well. But rarely, if at all, does a concern with "place" engage this deeper ambivalence about identity that Auerbach so astutely reveals. In this chapter, I will explore two texts that reveal, in productive ways, Hess's own ambivalent relation to the Jewish tradition. In the tenth letter of *Rome and Jerusalem*, Hess considers the restraints and creative possibilities of a human life, claiming there that identity is indeterminate and contingent. Yet Hess's defense of the Jewish tradition relies in part on racial imagery in both *Rome and Jerusalem* and in his later essays, suggesting that identity can be rooted (and thus secured) in a changeless, biological code that is "our flesh and bones." In the former account, Hess recognizes (and apparently endorses) indeterminate meanings and epistemological constraints for uncovering the sources of Jewish identity. But his racial language suggests that Jewish identity is only a linguistic cover for an inescapable attachment to a racial history. In the one, identity is problematic; in the other, identity is secure self-affirmation.

Before turning to these texts and the two accounts of identity and self they sustain, I will explore how scholars have generally situated *Rome and Jerusalem* within Hess's socialist and proto-Zionist thought. Although identity is an overriding concern in many of their debates, they still fail to consider how conceptions of identity inform Hess's sociology, philosophical anthropology, and political ideology. I will argue that *Rome and Jerusalem* is unique among Hess's works in its (unsuccessful) attempt to examine and unify two distinct visions of Jewish identity. Hess's account of an integrative and coherent identity dominates his literary corpus from 1837 until the writing of *Rome and Jerusalem*. But together with his "return" to Judaism, Hess recognizes the partial, fragmented, and dynamic features of identity in history. The uniform picture of identity in Hess's early works filters into *Rome and Jerusalem*, and stands in unresolved tension with this new account. The strategies employed by Hess to manage and control these tensions constitute the central problems and concerns of this book.

Rome and Jerusalem as Socialist and Zionist Manifesto

Hermeneutical concerns determine and constrain the kind of questions we pursue and ask of a text. Uncovering the interpretive questions reveals what is deemed valuable in a work, and this is certainly true in readings of *Rome and Jerusalem*. Two general questions dominate scholarly debate: how well does *Rome and Jerusalem* fit within Hess's literary corpus, and in what sense is this work a "return" to previously explored, but still undeveloped ideas? The various answers to these questions tend to fall into two opposing camps, which I will call the socialist and the Zionist readings.

Historians of socialism situated Hess's thought within the nineteenth-century German socialist tradition. Hess's stature as a leading socialist thinker was due to the influence of his second book, *The European Triarchy* (1841). In that work, Hess criticized Hegel's philosophy as a history of spirit that denied the equally spiritual characteristics of matter and activity. Hegel's was also a philosophy of the past. The left Hegelian movement was a transition, Hess argued, to the philosophy of action and represented the philosophy of the future. Socialist historians narrowly focused on Hess's critique of Hegel and its relation to Marx's dialectical materialism. Thus even *Rome and Jerusalem,* written some twenty years after Hess's *Triarchy,* was cited as a response to the "Jewish question" raised by Marx and Bauer in the 1840s. On this view, Hess's thought was valued only in how well (or more likely, how poorly) it illuminated Marx's analysis of social conflict.

Historians of Zionism, in part responding to this constricted Marxian picture, focused instead on the meaning of Hess's "return" to Judaism. After a career of socialist and scientific works that covered some twenty years of literary production, Hess suddenly recovered the Judaism of his youth in *Rome and Jerusalem.* Zionist commentators were interested in what motivated Hess to defend a Jewish national revival. Was *Rome and Jerusalem* a radical departure from his earlier works, or the mature answer to earlier, unsolved intellectual conflicts? Where the historians of socialism effaced Hess's Jewish concerns, the historians of Zionism emphasized them, hoping to find in Hess a "forerunner" to a movement that would begin almost forty years after the publication of *Rome and Jerusalem.* The Zionist and socialist approaches, read together, promoted two influential interpretive schemes: either we read Hess to illumine Marx's thought, or we understand Hess through modern Zionist preoccupations with the Jewish return to land, nation, and authenticity.

Zionist readings argue that *Rome and Jerusalem* is either a recovery and reworking of earlier strands of thought, and thus it incorporates earlier works within a more comprehensive Jewish vision, or a radically new work in its call for a Jewish state, and is therefore singular in its discussion of Jewish identity. Socialist approaches maintain either that *Rome and Jerusalem* is a response to the socialist dilemmas of the 1840s, and is thereby a return to Hess's socialist works of that period, or that the work is simply peripheral to the history of socialist thought (and thus not a return at all). This overly simplistic outline is not without its problems, for Shlomo Avineri draws socialist and Zionist strands together within his analysis of Hess. But the schema does help us to understand the questions and hence the concerns that preoccupy Hess's readers.

A review of the scholarly reception of *Rome and Jerusalem* is important, and this for two reasons: it helps situate my own approach to the text, and reveals how Zionist and socialist interests conceal what I think important in Hess's discussion of Jewish identity.

A dominant Zionist reading is Isaiah Berlin's account of *Rome and Jerusalem* as a return to Hess's earliest Jewish convictions, one that rivals and eventually prevails over Marx's historical determinism.[3] Highlighting the psychological turmoil apparent on almost every page of *Rome and Jerusalem,* Berlin claims that Hess "gives expression to a dominant conviction which he had for many years repressed, and which finally proves too strong to stifle, and feels at peace." Hess returns to earlier views in which "everything that had been suppressed by Hess for over twenty years now comes welling up."[4] Berlin's understanding is rooted in the very first lines of *Rome and Jerusalem*:

> Here I stand again, after some twenty years of estrangement, in the midst of my
> people, to take part in my people's joyous and mourning festivals, in its memories
> and hopes, in its spiritual struggles within its own house and with the cultured
> societies.[5]

The "twenty years" refers to Hess's socialist writings of the 1840s and his scientific
studies in the 1850s. *Rome and Jerusalem*, as a return to the ideas explored in Hess's
earliest works, is also, according to Berlin, the mature expression of his philosophy:

> Hess was, at any rate after 1848, an exceptionally penetrating and independent
> thinker who understood and formulated the problems with which he was dealing
> more clearly than the majority of his critics, whose rival diagnoses, admired for
> their wisdom in their own day, have stood up badly to the test of time.[6]

The "critics" that Berlin discusses are Marx and his followers, who crudely sati-
rized Hess's "utopian" socialism and his national ideology. It was clear to Berlin,
after he delivered his lecture on Hess in Israel, who won that debate! Certainly
Hess's appeal to justice as the proper grounding for a socialist society, and his claim
that national commitments generate more lasting conflicts than class differences,
have weathered "the test of time." Hess's return to suppressed Jewish national convictions, in Berlin's reading, transforms his Jewish thought into a sweeping indictment of Marxist ideology. Hess thought so too:

> The masses are never moved through abstract reasoning to progress, whose main-
> springs everywhere lie far deeper than even the socialist revolutionaries think. For
> the Jews, even more than nations that are oppressed on their own land, national
> independence must precede all political and social progress. A common native soil
> is for the Jews a first condition of healthy labor conditions.[7]

Hess re-evaluates his socialist and scientific works of the 1840s and 50s through a
return to a more original vision of Judaism that offers a penetrating critique of
socialism. Hess finds in his earliest childhood memories and scholarly achievements the inspirational sources for what Isaiah Berlin calls Hess's true masterpiece,
Rome and Jerusalem.

But surely Hess did not "return" to an early or nascent nationalism. How, then,
does his proto-Zionism fit within this picture of return? Jonathan Frankel believes
that the historical schema of Hess's first work, *The Sacred History* (*Die Heilige
Geschichte*, 1837), which traces historical periods marked by important political
events, lends itself quite easily to another great world-historical event: the rebirth
of a Jewish state. As Frankel sees it, once Hess predicts the rise of a Jewish state,
he "feels compelled to alter the historiographical scheme of *The Sacred History*,
even though surprisingly few basic changes are made."[8] The verb "compelled" further connects the basic substance of *Rome and Jerusalem* to Hess's earliest works, as
if *The Sacred History* defines and circumscribes the scope and vision of Hess's
thinking in 1862. Hess's proto-Zionist vision is lopped onto a historical schema
that remains as convincing for Hess in 1837 as it did in 1862. His call for the

rebirth of a Jewish state, for Frankel and Berlin, is but a reworking of Hess's earliest and most compelling attachments.

Not all Zionist thinkers agree, however, that Hess's nationalist program in 1862 harmonized well with his earlier works. Martin Buber's response is intriguing, for he interprets *Rome and Jerusalem* as a "beginning," a new adventure without precedent in Hess's earlier works.[9] As the first "religious socialist of Judaism,"[10] Hess's obsession with "land" and its implications for Jewish spiritual renewal literally begins here, with *Rome and Jerusalem*.[11] Buber's interests focus solely on Hess's demand for a Jewish state to provide a political framework for a vibrant Jewish life. Unfortunately, Buber rarely comments on Hess's religious vision, and we are left wondering whether political ideology alone takes the place of a more nuanced account of religious life and thought. But Buber's defense of Hess's revolutionary politics appeals to other Zionists who worship Hess as a prophet of modern Zionism. Samuel Blumenfield calls *Rome and Jerusalem* a "pre-Herzelian Zionist manifesto" (an obvious allusion to Marx's more famous pamphlet). Even as Blumenfield admits that Hess is a "dreamer, vague and immature" in his socialist writings of the 1840s, he defends Hess as a "keen and forceful thinker" in his Jewish writings.[12] Gershon Winer even claims that in the wake of *Rome and Jerusalem,* Hess's "other extensive political and historical writings, to which he had devoted the greater part of his life and talents, were relegated to oblivion."[13] Buber, Blumenfield, and Winer all distance Hess from his socialist works of the 1840s and position him within a movement that would not arise until after his death. They construct *Rome and Jerusalem* into the founding text of what would be the most powerful Jewish nationalist movement in the modern period. It is not, as Frankel and Berlin argue, a work that establishes ties to a period some twenty years earlier. Instead, *Rome and Jerusalem* is revolutionary, and revolutionary only in its concern for a Jewish state in Palestine.

For Zionist readers, *Rome and Jerusalem* is the pivotal text through which Hess's other works should be evaluated. Theirs is a response to socialist scholars who argue that Hess's writings in the 1840s provide the appropriate context for evaluating *Rome and Jerusalem*. The socialists, to the contrary, view Hess's "masterpiece" through the lens of socialist intellectual history. In Georg Lukács's view, *Rome and Jerusalem* emerged from Hess's tragic encounter with Marx in the 1840s and his inability to comprehend fully the significance of the material dialectic.[14] Lukács contends that Hess's socialist agenda collapsed into irreconcilable conflicts once it confronted Marx's material conception of history. Hess's socialist theory "led logically into the camp of reaction," and thus Marx and Engels were "completely correct," even mild, in their critique of utopian socialism in *The Communist Manifesto*.[15] Instead of moving beyond Hegel toward a Marxian critique of ideology and economics, Hess reversed course, and retrieved the insights of Feuerbach and Fichte.[16] Lukács astutely recognizes Feuerbach's influence upon Hess, for in personal correspondences and essays of the 1840s, it is clear that Feuerbach inspired Hess's socialist ideology and practice.[17] But for Lukács, it was Marx (and not

Feuerbach) who provided the yardstick for comparison: Hess was a tragic figure because, "of all idealist dialecticians, he occasionally came closest to the Marxian conception of the dialectic." Yet Hess continued to analyze "metaphysically, and not dialectically," for his socialism "was not the outcome of the contemporary concrete class struggle."[18]

Hess's theoretical failure in the face of Marxist economic theory in no way undermined his genuine revolutionary role as a socialist agitator. Hess should be remembered as "a honest thinker and revolutionary," but not as an intellectual giant of Jewish nationalism:

> Because Hess was unable to maintain his old standpoint, or to correctly under-
> stand and use the new one, his writing activity after his Marxist "conversion" is a
> helpless wandering among completely empty and abstract thought constructions,
> fantastic conceptions of a philosophy of nature, a foundation for Zionism contain-
> ing the elements of a racist theory and a history of philosophy, etc. As an honest
> revolutionary, he participated in the Lassallean worker's movement, and always
> remained in the rank and file of a fighting proletariat. As a theoretician, however,
> he was ruined in the collision with the materialist dialectic.[19]

Hess's theoretical failures in the 1840s haunted him throughout his literary career. Failing to appreciate and understand Marx's materialist critique fully, his nationalism was but another "helpless wandering" and fantastic illusion.

Bruno Frei, too, wants to free Hess from any serious Jewish national concerns, yet also defends Hess's socialist ideology in the face of Lukács's criticism.[20] Frei asks whether *Rome and Jerusalem* is a "return" and thus an integral part of Hess's entire life's work, or merely an "episode" in Hess's life. It is neither episodic nor central, Frei insists, but an original attempt "to translate his philosophy into action." And what is this philosophy? Hess's vision of a Jewish state emerges out of his "maturing understanding of socialism." For both Frei and Lukács, *Rome and Jerusalem* is not an inspired Zionist treatise nor one deeply concerned with Judaism. But Frei insists that it is a profound socialist work of manipulation: Jews and the Jewish state are merely vehicles for a grander socialist vision. Thus Frei will brand Heinrich Graetz a "Jewish historian," but Hess a "German Socialist."[21] *Rome and Jerusalem* is now claimed as a great socialist work inspired by the revolutionary German political movements of the 1840s.

Frei is certainly not alone among socialist scholars who regard *Rome and Jerusalem* as a reworking of Hess's socialist ideals in the 1840s. Horst Lademacher, the distinguished editor and compiler of Hess's socialist and religious essays, has written extensively on Hess's socialist thought. He is also, to his credit, aware of the Jewish and national commitments in *Rome and Jerusalem*. In his introduction to Hess's *Ausgewählte Schriften*, a collection of early works as well as *Rome and Jerusalem*, Lademacher claims that *Philosophie der Tat* (1843) encapsulates Hess's entire socialist agenda.[22] We soon learn that this work *is* Hess's agenda, and not just his socialist one. The philosophy of action, says Lademacher, is a philosophy of the future that moves beyond a simple critique of the past and present. But the Zionism of the 1860s corresponds precisely to Hess's "Gedankenwelt" of the 1840s. It is the same idea "in another terminology":[23]

> The concept of Judaism, the starting point of Zionism, fits thoroughly in the space of Hess's philosophical and social world of thought as we know it from the 40s and 50s.

> The justification for the anticipated Jewish state rests not only on the national desire of the time, but even more so on the philosophical and social basis of the worker's movement in the 40s.[24]

Hess's works of the 1850s, Lademacher notes, is but another language, a natural scientific language, for his socialist agenda.[25] The frame of reference is clearly Hess's socialism of the 1840s. And so Lademacher too will call Graetz first a Jew, but Hess a "socialist, then Jew and Zionist."[26]

Frei and Lademacher struggle to position *Rome and Jerusalem* within the socialist debates of the 1840s. But Lukács's critique tends to relegate *Rome and Jerusalem* beyond serious academic discussion of nineteenth-century German socialism. Lademacher certainly expresses tendencies in this direction. In an essay entitled, "The Political and Social Thought of Moses Hess," only once does he mention *Rome and Jerusalem,* and here only for biographical information.[27] One would expect, given the title, a more lengthy discussion. Or witness John Weiss's book entitled, *Moses Hess, Utopian Socialist.* In his chapter on Hess's life and thought between 1846–1875, *Rome and Jerusalem* is never mentioned. Even Sidney Hook, in an otherwise excellent essay on Hess's socialism, passes by *Rome and Jerusalem* entirely in his discussion of "Communism and Nationalism."[28] Some might get the impression that Hess had never written such a work.

This bias is most pronounced in Irma Goitein's critique of Hess's socialist and national thought.[29] Her stated objective is to substantiate Lukács's thesis further by examining several obscure works not cited by Lukács. Interested in the development of Hess's socialist thought, Goitein continually distances Hess's socialism from Marx's material dialectic. For a book entitled *Problems of Society and State in Moses Hess,* one would naturally assume that Goitein would find *Rome and Jerusalem* an interesting study for her survey. But this work remains outside her purview. She focuses instead on the works published between 1837–1851. Again, we see how the 1840s dominate the approach to *Rome and Jerusalem.* Auguste Cornu and Wolfgang Mönke, the editors of Hess's philosophical and socialist works from 1837 to 1850, claim that in *Rome and Jerusalem* Hess returns "to the representational world of his childhood and youth." But lest you think that such a return has the significance that Berlin attributes to it, *Rome and Jerusalem* is instead labeled a deeply confused work. It assumes that Jews can escape their economic and class situation and identify with a nation. This, of course, is inconsistent (*unverträglich*) with Marx's material approach to history.[30] Their analysis, inspired by Lukács's reading, explains why Goitein need not analyze *Rome and Jerusalem* in her discussion of society and state. Marx is the standard bearer, and *Rome and Jerusalem* simply fails to live up to this standard. *Rome and Jerusalem* is more than just insignificant, it is also peripheral to an understanding of socialism in the nineteenth century.

Rome and Jerusalem has thus been read as a reworking of Hess's socialist agenda of the 1840s, or as an unimportant failure in socialist political theory. It has also been considered a return to Hess's early childhood or first work of 1837, and as a beginning to a Zionist movement that would surface some thirty years after its publication. Both the socialist and Zionist readings implicate the other. Each wants to claim (or disclaim) this work within the history of German socialist or Zionist thought, and doing so leads to intractable disagreements over Hess's political ideology. Shlomo Avineri, recognizing this problem, attempts to overcome it in the very title of his book, *Moses Hess: Prophet of Communism and Zionism.*

What is lost in this truncated debate is the reconfiguring of Jewish identity in *Rome and Jerusalem*. With this text, there is a dramatic change in Hess's account of identity, but one that is coupled with earlier views that conflict with his new approach. Indeed, Hess's socialist and scientific theories of the 1840s and '50s continue to govern much of his thinking in *Rome and Jerusalem*. The significance of *Rome and Jerusalem* lies in the conflict produced by two divergent accounts of Jewish identity and the self, and this tension alters dramatically the "place" of *Rome and Jerusalem* within socialist and Zionist history. The core of my book (chapters 3, 4, and 5) examines how these tensions in narrative, inescapable frameworks, and tradition provoke insightful debates about the complexity of modern Jewish identity. It is thus far too simplistic to argue that Hess has "returned" to the Judaism of his youth. Similarly, viewing *Rome and Jerusalem* through the lenses of the 1840s not only defaces it of all ingenuity, but radically misinterprets the force of Hess's new approach to Jewish identity. If we can speak of a "return" at all in *Rome and Jerusalem,* it will be a return to a previous conception of identity that is moderated, complicated, and at times undermined by Hess's new perspective. We need to refocus our interpretive lenses if we are to see Hess's account of the self and identity as significant issues that move beyond, but also reconfigure socialist and Zionist polemics.

Conceptions of Self and Identity in Hess's Socialist and Scientific Works

Before turning to the conflicts generated by two alternative views of Jewish identity in the next three chapters, I will examine what is new about the self and identity in *Rome and Jerusalem* by comparing it to Hess's socialist and scientific works of the 1840s and '50s. Earlier, I followed Taylor in distinguishing theories of the self from conceptions of identity. I limit the term *self* to the formal characteristics required to imagine or describe a human being. Identity refers to the kind of being imagined or described by strong evaluations of worth and commitment. Discussions about identity presuppose a particular conception of self. Hess's account of tradition, history, and philosophy in *Rome and Jerusalem,* I will argue, presupposes two divergent conceptions of the self and identity. With *Rome and*

Jerusalem, Hess appreciates the self's contingency and ambiguity, but he is still captivated by earlier views in which the self is complete and clearly definable.

I begin by analyzing Hess's two earliest books, *The Holy History* and *The European Triarchy,* then move to his critical socialist essays of the 1840s, examine a typical essay written in 1855 on natural science, and finally explore texts in *Rome and Jerusalem* that reflect Hess's "new" and "old" approach to the self. The analysis will focus on three interrelated issues: 1) the accessibility or clarity possible in understanding the self, 2) the simplicity or complexity of the self, and 3) the possibility that identity can be complete and whole. I claim that before 1862, Hess imagined the self as accessible and simple, and identity as complete. An accessible self is one fully open to rational analysis and exact linguistic description. One can capture the self in a still-life photograph, analyzing and dissecting it with clarity, confidence, and precision. Such accessibility requires a simple or unencumbered self, one that is unattached to transient concerns, emotions, or conflicting commitments. Only a simple and accessible self can claim to be a complete person. By a complete person or identity, I refer to a human being who is potentially capable of living a life without regret, undeveloped virtues, or character deformations. In *Rome and Jerusalem,* however, the self is mysterious and complex, and identity is negotiated and fragmented. If before 1862 Hess could describe, with perfect clarity, the situation of the self in world history, after 1862 the self is far more concealed from his inquisitive gaze. If earlier he imagined a simple, non-conflicted self, in *Rome and Jerusalem* this seems hardly possible. In *The Holy History* and in his socialist and scientific studies of the 1840s and '50s, identity is rooted in a structured history and an unchanging nature. But by 1862 that identity is far more partial and limited. Yet the power of Hess's earlier account of the self still dominates his construction of Jewish identity in *Rome and Jerusalem.* It is this tension that proves so fruitful in understanding the complexity of modern Jewish identity.

The very title of Hess's first work, *The Holy History of Mankind* (1837), reveals a great deal about his approach to the self. History is open to Hess's analysis, and he can determine its profane and holy character. As a breathtaking panorama of the human drama, *The Holy History* is a Hegelian mapping of the past, present, and future manifestations of Spirit as it marches toward ultimate fulfillment. Moving with apparent ease through biblical history, to the Greek and Roman periods, then to the Middle Ages, and finally into the modern era inaugurated by the French Revolution, Hess exudes the confidence that he has accurately and completely diagnosed the movement of history. Within this history an open, complete self and identity fit easily and comfortably. Indeed, Hess's philosophy of history betrays a philosophy of the self. *The Holy History* is a sustained argument for a simple and accessible self that achieves a complete and unified identity in human history. Holy history has become human history.

Hess divides his holy history into "periods" in which Spirit realizes itself in a movement toward complete wholeness. In its Trinitarian format[31] and its Hegelian terminology, Hess has assimilated much of the German culture around him.[32] His history is precise, articulate, and all too easy:

When Jesus Christ appeared, Rome ruled the ancient world. The ancient world, that is, the history of the revelation of God the father or the knowledge of God in the images of fantasy, which up until this point prevailed throughout the world and found its holy root in the Jewish nation, was now completed. With Christ a new era had been inaugurated, the history of revelation of God the son, or the knowledge of God in a disposition of feeling.[33]

The patterns are clear and distinct, and Hess clarifies the movement of history with relative simplicity. Holy History is patterned history, and Hess becomes the ideal observer as finite spirits move from "fantasy" to "feeling." Each "new era" cancels without denying the previous one, just as knowledge rooted in feeling overcomes but still preserves fantastical images. It is a seamless history in which God and Christ remain distinct yet unified.[34] Hess claims that the "foundation of God's kingdom has been discovered [*die Grundlage des Gottesreiches entdeckt*]."[35] Definitive accounts of holy history and the self within it are possible because the rules of the game are known to us.

But if Hess absorbs the Hegelian terminology to describe his holy history, his thought certainly lacks the complexity and sophistication of Hegel's dialectic. Hess offers a rather facile account of how Spirit overcomes its negative opposition:

It is clear that reality does not abolish or cancel [*aufhebt*] what is true or positive in erroneous ideas, but it rather disregards that which is only false through the knowledge of reality so that erroneous ideas are purified without being completely nullified.[36]

"Reality" continually overcomes its negative (false ideas) through clearer and clearer accounts of the meaning of history. But conflict is not fundamental to Hess's picture of Spirit's progress. History and the Spirit that guides it move toward increasing clarity, purity, and truth, and so too the self as the carrier of Spirit in this history. Spirit overcomes and ultimately cleanses itself from conflict. The movement of Spirit is thus progressive and teleological: it is unified history that draws God's kingdom within human history and struggle. Adam, Hess claims, is the prototype of the first period (God the father), and Jesus the prototype of the second (God the son). But Spirit has moved beyond these historical figures and "erroneous ideas." We now live in the third and final period of Spirit's ascendancy, the period of "pure human being [*reine Menschen*]."[37] Spinoza is the prototype for modern persons, Hess concludes, because he fulfills the possibility within each of us: the possibility to live a complete and non-conflicted life.

Despite its appearance as unified and harmonious history, *The Holy History* exhibits important ambiguities and tensions. Two such strains in the text are important for our concerns: Hess's attitude toward Judaism and Islam. In his description of the "new Jerusalem" in the last section of the book, Hess glorifies and defends the Jewish tradition:

The Mosaic law related as much to the inner as the outer person. Religion and politics, church and state were intimately fused together, for they had one root, and bore one fruit. The Jews cannot distinguish between religious and political laws, between duties toward God and Caesar.[38]

Judaism mirrors the wholeness and integrity of Jewish identity, for the Jews unify private and public commitments. Yet on the very next page Hess describes the Jewish people as a "spirit without a body." And in a previous chapter, Hess proposed that just as the animal kingdom had overcome the plant kingdom, so too will the Christian overcome the Jewish kingdom.[39] The irony is striking: the Mosaic law is holy because it unifies church and state, but the Jewish "period" is subverted by the self-purifying Spirit. What relations exist among Jews, the Mosaic law, and Jewish history?

Jonathan Frankel argues that we must distinguish between Jews and Jewish history to make sense of Hess's historical schema. Hess appreciates Jewish history and its role within holy history, but he is less kind to Jews themselves, viewing them instead as living corpses. He can therefore praise the Mosaic law while denying Jews any redemptive role in the present or future holy history.[40] But Frankel constructs a false dualism. Hess does not divorce history from its actors. To the contrary, he believes them to be inseparable. The answer lies not in divorcing Jews from their history, but in separating both people and history from the Mosaic law. Hess describes Judaism as the prototype of unity and wholeness, a model for a "new Jerusalem." Yet in Hess's historical scheme, this same Judaism occupies a past and ultimately problematic movement of Spirit. The difficulty for Hess lies not in the difference between Jews and Jewish history, but in his interpretation of Judaism. Jews and their history were defeated by the birth of Jesus. Holy history has thus moved beyond Jewish history. But the "truth" in Judaism—its conflation of private and public life—has been appropriated by Spirit to become the guiding principle for the future. Hess's Judaism is one without a history and a people. It has given history only an idea (the Mosaic law). No wonder, then, that Hess describes the Jews as a "spirit without a body." The Jews only reflect the paradox inherent in Jewish tradition: the spirit of unity and fulfillment without a body to carry its message forward.

Hess seeks to preserve the Jewish idea of harmony without its embodied expression in a Jewish people or history. With Islam, Hess can only see *Irrthum*, a passive and feminine principle, the very opposite of Christian teaching.[41] While Judaism fits uneasily in Hess's vision of progress, Islam is radically discontinuous with the movement of Spirit. Islam, to him, is profane history, marked off and separated from holiness. As unqualified error, Islamic "ideas" are not purified but ignored. Islam signifies a potentially damaging historical moment hostile to Hess's prescribed pattern. He can only overcome it through abrupt dismissal. Unresolved conflicts are dangerous, for such discontinuity would radically challenge Hess's notion of a coherent and holy narrative. There is much at stake here, not only for understanding the holy in history, but also for evaluating the kind of human beings Hess imagines we are and should become.

The implicit account of self in Hess's philosophy of history becomes explicit in his discussion of Adam and the fall from the Garden of Eden. Just as Hess can accurately and clearly delineate the periods of history, so too he unveils the deep significance of Adam's sin in paradise. Clearly Hess's is a very Hegelian reading of the fall (at times he even adopts specific Hegelian terminology), in which Adam moves to a higher conception of Spirit through a process of self-consciousness.[42] But Hess does more than offer a Hegelian interpretation of the biblical text. He reads Genesis 1–3 as a mirror to the self in history. Textual reading (meaning) and historical reality (truth) are conflated in Hess's *Holy History*. Adam's fall is a necessary one, in which he recognizes himself as embodied Spirit through relations with an other (Eve). This movement from unconscious innocence to the recognition of embodied Spirit is a progressive movement forward in order to become a more fully conscious Spirit. As an "embryo of Spirit," Adam lives in Eden in innocence (*Unschuld*) and complete contentment. But he soon feels a profound cleavage (*Zwiespalt*) that divides himself against himself. One-sided instincts (*Triebe*) provoke this initial rupture and drive Adam from a state of innocence and Eden. He now searches restlessly after his lost good.[43] Separation, Hess claims, "was and remains the original sin."[44] Adam's sin is the rupture of the original unified self. It is a disobedience against oneself and God. As an embodiment of Spirit, Adam *ought* to be whole, undivided and perfectly content in his innocence and purity. But Adam's sin is ours as well. We continually sin in each moment of rupture, at the moment of tension in which our instincts or desires overcome the quest toward wholeness and integrity. The original sin "remains" because it now identifies our selves as descendants of Adam. We too search after a lost good that remains beyond our grasp.

But a fall from innocence is necessary for Spirit's full self-consciousness. In Eden, Adam lives in purity but also in a state of unconsciousness. For Spirit to fully realize itself as self-conscious Spirit, Adam must overcome his inner conflict through conscious appropriation of what Hess calls "knowledge of God."[45]

> After Adam had tasted the forbidden fruit, he saw more than all the creatures that came before him and all those living with him because he was then only a unity or holy oneness, and thus would know only himself.[46]

Adam's desires initiate an inner rupture that now unfolds into a public act. The tasting of the tree of good and evil is more than a symbolic gesture of Adam's previous inner disobedience. The initial inner cleavage damages the self; the public act reveals, in addition, that injury to self damages God as well. Knowledge of God, in Hess's peculiar use of the term, implicates knowledge of self. The disobedience against God is a public and necessary expression of a previous inner disobedience against self. But such failure is necessary for Adam to achieve full self-consciousness. Hess describes a pre-lapsarian Adam as self-enclosed and absorbed in his own uniqueness. Only after the inner and outer disobedience will Adam observe his surroundings and his fellow creatures. Suddenly, Adam can see and know an other. Consciousness, as described here, is a process of discovery through difference. While conflict propels Adam from a state of innocence, it is also the medium through which Adam achieves full self-consciousness.

Hess describes a deeply divided and split self, but in and through this division comes the possibility for spiritual harmony. Indeed, the central claim that human history *is* holy history implies that a complete and fully self-conscious identity is not only possible within a human life, but is necessary if this life is to count as a good one. A partial and conflicted life would be part of profane, not holy, history. The utopia envisioned in a later chapter ("Das neue Jerusalem und die letzten Zeiten"), one firmly entrenched in human/holy history, is a return to a higher, more conscious life of innocence:

> When the time has come when humanity no longer lives under an external law because everyone carries the law within, and when the original innocence of humanity is overcome in time through self-consciousness, then it will be possible, as in the beginning, to build one's own state for every couple.[47]

The Garden of Eden clearly provides the blueprint for a more pure, because more conscious, family and state life. But Adam's predicament is our own. Both his and our education in self-consciousness mirror the movement of Spirit in history. Jonathan Frankel observes that "only in the Old Testament, he [Hess] argued, could be seen—albeit in embryonic, partial and instinctive form—an example of what mankind was about to experience universally, totally, and consciously."[48] Hess's conception of past innocence provides the model for the self-conscious messianic future. To be human is to be a self-reflective and self-conscious Adam in Eden; or, to be more precise, in an Eden now transposed into the messianic age. The conflicted, torn, and lost post-lapsarian Adam is less human, less of a self. This self lives in the animal world (*Tierwelt*), a profane existence in human/holy history. A new Jerusalem, and a self in the conscious image of Adam in Eden, is indeed possible in human history, for complete contentment remains an achievable and appropriate good for self-conscious beings.

Although Hess follows Hegel closely in his interpretation of the fall, there remains a significant difference between their two accounts. Hegel emphasizes the implicit movement within the pre-lapsarian Adam to "step forth" out of his natural state. Adam, from the very beginning, is already falling away from simple immediacy.[49] But this complex movement is not found in Hess's description. For Hess, Adam's "soul is one" before the falling away. Adam lives completely in "innocence and happiness," and there is no mention of an implicit cleavage or contradiction. If for Hegel the pre-lapsarian Adam is by nature evil because his implicit being is evil, for Hess this Adam is undifferentiated goodness. The good life in Eden, according to Hess, is not complex nor implicitly divided, but whole and unified. Even more, this unity is a possible one for human beings after the fall. Religion and politics are unified in a holy history embedded in a human narrative.

The laws of history and structure of the self lay open before Hess's philosophical gaze. He observes a simple, undivided self that continuously falls into rupture and division. But conflict is not final nor fundamental to Hess's conception of the self. It is certainly true that only through struggle and division can unity and fulfillment be achieved. But conflict is neither essential nor abiding in this picture, for it must be overcome, and indeed is defeated in the new, earthly Jerusalem. We will see that Hess's conception of self, identity, and history in *The Holy History* re-appears in his works on socialism and the natural sciences in the 1840s and '50s. It is a pattern that Hess returns to again and again.

Hess's second work, *The European Triarchy* (1841), is far more incisive and critical than his first, and yet it continues the same pattern of thought in its account of the self.[50] Here again Adam, the "man of nature," is the prototype of the ancient world, while Christ, "the God-man," is the prototype of the Middle Ages. Spinoza, the "complete human being," is the prototype of the new age.[51] Each historical person represents the abiding characteristics of an age. A particular identity becomes the symbol of a historical period: a philosophy of history reveals a philosophy of self.

As in his first book, Hess slices up history into definite and clear periods, each laden with meaning, each overcome by the advances of the new age. Hess's clarity of vision—his capacity to dissect historical movements and to confine their significance to great men—exudes a confidence rarely matched in his earlier work. As history is an open book, so too is God's revelation, and thus human redemption:

> The relationship between humanity and God is known. God's revelation through the son of man, the teaching of Christ, is no longer something external to us. We have received it in flesh and blood. God has become Christ in flesh, Christ is in us, and God is in us through Christ.

That Hess could write such overtly Christian theology is stunning, and yet this follows the model set in his *Holy History*. Judaism in *Holy History* has been replaced by Adam (the natural being), and Christianity has become Christ in flesh and blood. Both are overcome by the new human being, Spinoza, whom Hess calls "the ideal foundation [*Grundlage*] of modern times."[52] Where the Jewish idea of wholeness provided the blueprint for the messianic age in Hess's first work, here it is Christianity and the revelation of the God-man that prepares the new age and the new human being. But the tension still exists here as before: Christianity offers merely an idea, while its personal and historical roots are suppressed in the new period. Christianity, like Judaism in *The Holy History*, fits uneasily in the progressive achievements of Adam, Christ, and Spinoza. The ambiguity can be seen in Hess's move from the "Christ in flesh" to the "Christ in us." The inner Christ is an ideal without a history or community. So too Spinoza, for he also represents a disembodied idea (a foundation), one without historical connections or social location. The *idea* of Spinoza is significant, not the Spinoza of flesh and blood. And because it is an idea, Hess can quite easily describe, analyze, and reify it. The holy history of mankind is really a holy history of the self, and a disembodied one at that.

When Hess actually turns to history, that history mimics the disembodied ideal of the self. Hess describes the European triarchy of Germany, France, and England as an ideal picture of world domination. He compares this *"Dreibund"* to an organic unity naturally related as a unified family of people.[53] Germany represents the "social-spiritual freedom" in its rich philosophical heritage. France embodies the "social-ethical freedom" characteristic of its revolutionary tradition. England expresses the "social-political freedom" evident in its practical and legislative government. Together these three countries will produce a new order that prefigures messianic redemption. Each alone, however, will never achieve power or influence, and so each must learn from and act with the other.[54] Yet there exists a hierarchy within this unity. The distinctions are progressively revealed in a history that begins with the German reformation, continues to the French revolution, and finally culminates in the much anticipated English industrial revolution. Just as Spinoza overcomes yet preserves the character of Adam and Christ, so too does England embody and prosper from the triumphs of Germany and France. Surely the new Jerusalem and the chosen people will reside in a now unified Europe:

> A Roman-German Europe is a chosen part of the world which stands under God's special protection. . . . What the holy Jewish state was in the ancient world, and the holy Roman empire was in the middle ages, a Roman-German Europe will be of the future: the apple of God's eye, the center from which the destiny of the world will be guided.

This new Jerusalem represents unified world leadership and prosperity in human history. German philosophy, French ethics, and English industry will effortlessly combine to form a "holy sanctuary" (*ein Heiligtum*) where complete and non-conflicted selves can flourish.[55] Neither Adam in the ancient world, nor Christ in the medieval could fully be at home in this new holy trinity. Only Spinoza fits here: he represents the new whole and unencumbered human being.

Despite his own religious politics, Hess soon realized that public policy guided by religious convictions would undermine human freedom. He therefore isolated religious ideology from public, political ethical life, as is evident in his article *Religion und Sittlichkeit* (1842), published in the radical journal *Rheinische Zeitung* only one year after *The European Triarchy*.[56] Recall that in his first work, *The Holy History*, Hess had praised the Jewish tradition for joining public politics with private religion. But by 1842, Hess recognized the need to frustrate religious motives in order to save human freedom and political toleration. He turned to philosophical anthropology to justify these political objectives. Human activity, Hess claimed, is forever split between the ethical and religious life; the one is public, unified and rational, the other private, dualistic and emotional.[57] Separating public and private lives into two "spheres" (*Gebiete*) would allow both to co-exist in tensionless harmony. Religion would disappear from public political discussion and policy making, but still develop "in its purity" in its own, private domain.[58] A public religion would only create discord and human frailty before an otherworldly God. Politics and religion exposed the abiding human characteristics of a self both capable and frail, rational and emotional, political and personal.

Hess endorsed an identity divided between private and emotional drives (*Religion*) and the political life of healthy, vibrant, rational and dignified political creatures (*Sittlichkeit*). The ethical must be distinguished from the religious to insure that public and private identity develop in their purity and integrity. Hatred and war, so Hess argues, evolve from the inappropriate mixture of the two spheres. Separating the private from the public realm guarantees human freedom and is confirmed by philosophical anthropology. Hess believes one can seamlessly move back and forth between a public and private life without loss of identity. The self remains unified despite the sharp division and conflict between the two realms of human activity. There is no seepage or estrangement: emotions remain intact and healthy in the inner life, while rational arguments dominate without obstruction in the public. The self is neatly and precisely catalogued and divided into transparent and articulate domains. It has no depth nor elasticity. Allotted to two separate compartments, the self is whole despite partition. The agenda in *The Holy History* guides the conception of self and identity even here.

In another article on state and religion, published in 1842, Hess describes the *Rheinische Zeitung* as a "*political* Journal" in which every religious or theological question "as such" remains outside its critical scope.[59] The argument here, as in *Religion und Sittlichkeit*, targets the proponents of a Christian state. Hess notes that the adjective *Christian* will lead to intractable debates on the very character of a "Christian state." Again, religious issues are best left at home.[60] But if in 1842 Hess divided religion from politics for the benefit of both, by 1843 he no longer believes in this functional dualism. The year 1843 marks a turning point in which Hess's criticisms against religion *and* politics are trenchant and derisive.[61] Overcoming both religion and state, rather than merely separating them, would solve what increasingly appear to him as intractable conflicts. Not reform but revolution would turn human subjugation to state and religion into the radical freedom promised by a socialist society. In 1842, religion still found a receptive place for Hess in the inner life of human development (although he clearly preferred the ethical life as more rewarding, even more human than the religious life). But in the 1843 essay, *Die eine und ganze Freiheit!*, Hess can speak of "only one freedom," a freedom that precludes religious activity and belief. Religious life is animal, passive existence: the once protective sphere of religion in *Religion und Sittlichkeit* is now the domain of human enslavement.[62] But such inner slavery only reflects the outer bondage in the social and political spheres. In another essay published in 1843, Hess calls religion "heavenly politics," a mirror image of earthly political servitude: "Religion and politics stand and fall with each other, for the inner enslavement of Spirit, heavenly politics, supports the outer, which again only sustains and nourishes the inner."[63] The Hess of 1842 defended private religion and public politics as two healthy and viable spheres of human flourishing. But by 1843 Hess could only portray the state and religion as prisons for human bondage.[64] Hegel's *Sittlichkeit*—the social and political sphere in which Spirit recognizes itself as embodied Spirit —no longer holds the promise of genuine human freedom, nor can religion fulfill private emotional needs.

It becomes increasingly clear in *Über das Geldwesen* ["On Money"], an article completed in 1843, though not published until 1845,[65] that a social conception of self and identity underlies Hess's critique of politics and religion. Marx and his followers would soon criticize Hess's appeal to ethical norms or utopian visions in defending his socialist agenda. But in *Über das Geldwesen,* Hess's ethical claims develop out of his account of the self. His argument moves from an understanding of the self as a being inextricably connected to and created by others, to a critique of subjective, egotistical worship of an inorganic god called money. Humans have become beings who worship money rather than beings who honor each other. We are social selves in the sense that every human act expresses human characteristics and possibilities. As selves that come to consciousness in and through the social, we literally find our selves in this shared activity. Every *Gattungsact* is a shared act because it reveals a distinctive human quality that each *Gattungswesen* participates in as a member of the human species. To be removed from this collective activity of human flourishing would necessarily deprive our selves of those very characteristics that make a flourishing life possible. Thus Hess can claim that "human association does not *originate* as something foreign to your being; it *is* your *true* being."[66] The private, religious life of *Religion und Sittlichkeit* has disappeared altogether. In its place is an expressive social self embedded in collective activity (*Zusammenwirken*).

Hess reinterprets original sin as the exile from the organic whole of community life. Recall that in *The Holy History*, Adam's fall betrays a prior *Trennung* within the self, an inner disobedience that would repeat itself in every generation as the sin of division and conflict. The post-lapsarian Adam now must search for the lost good outside himself, yearning to regain that inner harmony and peace. We find a similar picture in *Über das Geldwesen*. As essentially social beings, we nonetheless continually remove our selves from social activity in order to satisfy subjective, egotistical desires. We therefore look within for the lost good. But as beings who are essentially social, we cannot discover that lost good within. The *Trennung* or tension arises when a social self directs its activity toward individual self-fulfillment rather than toward communal achievements. But self-fulfillment is possible, Hess argues, only within a communal context. Requiring a good that exists outside the self, yet unwilling to find that good in the collective activity of social interaction, the modern Adam worships the only god of value in modern industrial society: money, our "flesh and blood."[67] Money usurps the place of the *Christuslehre* in *The European Triarchy,* and self-worth translates into market value: "what cannot be exchanged or sold has no worth. So far as human beings can no longer be sold, they are not even worth a single penny."[68] Human identity is assessed only in terms of monetary value, earnings capacity, and labor. But this reflects a profound alienation from true *Gattungswesen*, and exposes an *entmenschte Mensch* (a dehumanized being) that is isolated, private and egotistical.[69] Money has become the false god, the unnatural because inhuman good that develops from a prior separation from communal commitments and activity. As *Monaden*, we seek only that which will increase our market value, and judge human flourishing in terms of individual earnings capacity. The *Privatmensch*, the self-absorbed seeker and seller of *Geldwesen*, mirrors a modern economy and society that prizes individual fulfillment through the acquisition and sale of labor.[70]

Hess had previously described the good society in his 1842 essay, *Religion und Sittlichkeit*, as one that separated private and public attachments. An admirable community would honor private religious commitments and support public rational discussion in directing social policy. But in *Über das Geldwesen*, Hess contends that the private, self-serving life mirrors an equally narrow and shallow public life. Both private and public spheres, the heavenly and earthly politics, enslave identity by dehumanizing it. The social self, the *Gattungswesen*, cannot flourish in what Hess calls a *Lügenwelt*—a world of lies.[71] But by evoking such descriptions of the social self as true, natural, and real, and the individual, egotistical self as foreign, unnatural, and illusory, Hess confesses a strong commitment to the pattern set forth in *The Holy History*. The discrepancy between who we really are (social beings) and who we appear to be (individual consumers) motivates Hess's attack on modern conceptions of identity and the value of human activity. In the modern *Krämerwelt*, we simply appear as something other than ourselves, as an *entmenschte Mensch*. But private life is not "real" life, nor is the commercial world of *Geldwesen* the "essence" of human activity. All of this is *Lügenwelt*. While the conflict or *Trennung* exists between who we are and who we claim to be, its validity depends only on a false conception of self and identity. Once we again recognize the self as essentially social, such that human identity flourishes only in communal activity, private life will disappear together with its god. Money loses its value because we no longer appraise identity in terms of it. Hess denies the ultimate reality of a private life in conflict with the good of public activity.

In the years between the revolutionary upheavals in 1848 and the publication of *Rome and Jerusalem* in 1862, Hess continued to write on socialist issues, yet devoted more time to the study of natural science. He wrote numerous articles on this burgeoning field in the 1850s, many of which were deemed immature and wild by his contemporaries.[72] Unlike Engels (who, like Hess, was fascinated by natural science), Hess found no mentor to guide him, and in the pattern of his younger days, read eclectically on physics, chemistry, geology, and racial studies. Edmund Silberner characterized Hess's scholarly interest in the natural sciences as an attempt to ground his ethical and socialist agenda of the 1840s in the modern scientific research of the 1850s.[73]

Hess defends his socialist ideology in scientific articles that appeal to the same undivided self and whole identity found in his essays of the 1840s. In one characteristic paper on the natural sciences,[74] Hess describes scientific research as the discovery of nature's objective law. Through archeology, cultural studies, and social economics, the scientific researcher can expose "the secrets of our history of development," a logic now open to his scientific gaze. The original law (*Urgesetz*) shapes and reshapes the cosmic, organic and social realms.[75] This "eternal law of nature" is at the same time the law of reason (*Vernunftgesetz*), "the alpha and omega of all thinking": "We have therefore a touchstone for that which is truly logically necessary in our future."[76] We understand who we are by discovering the basic laws that underwrite existence and development. Once these laws are fully articulated, we recognize the seamless integration of all three life spheres—the cosmic, organic, and social kingdoms. The *Urgesetz* (the law of equilibrium) unifies all three spheres. The self is but one, well-defined entity among this tripartite constellation. It is located within the social realm, completely open to rational articulation and exploration because the law of nature is also the law of reason. The development of identity is not beyond science but within its grasp and vision.

Hess connects this identity to an idealist philosophy that, together with scientific research, promotes a socialist utopia of human flourishing. The philosopher's concepts are too abstract if not grounded in experience, but the scientist must base observations on "positive knowledge" in order to discover "the great secret of life." Philosophy and science join to unveil (*enthüllen*) the underlying *Logik* of human development.[77] Hess synthesizes materialism and idealism in order to unify life itself in a socialist utopia. In an essay written a year later, Hess draws on the confidence so reminiscent of his earlier works to articulate the grand vision and challenge of science: "The secret laws of nature are everywhere present. The past and the future lie before us. Nothing is hidden that cannot be revealed through research."[78] Like the holy history of his first work, "nothing is hidden" from philosophical and scientific research. And like his *Holy History*, Hess's philosophy of history reveals and sustains the conception of self and identity now so familiar to us, one that runs through Hess's various works on history, ethics, socialism, and the natural sciences. Identity is complete, unencumbered by ambiguous attachments, and open to philosophical and scientific scrutiny. As we turn to *Rome and Jerusalem*, we will notice an important shift in Hess's account of self and identity, one that emerges in conflict with this entrenched view.

Conceptions of Self and Identity in *Rome and Jerusalem*

In the tenth letter of *Rome and Jerusalem*, Hess discusses the limitations, possibilities, and historical contingencies that inform the most basic human concerns and commitments. His analysis of human flourishing also reveals a significant shift in his underlying conception of self and identity. He no longer unmasks the inner workings of self-development: its transparency is replaced by a murky glass less hospitable to the observer's inquisitive gaze. The laws of nature and the self are now replaced by a "belief" in a providential "plan." Rather than accessing the inner logic of human development, Hess maintains only a healthy confidence in the ultimate meaning of human existence. If Hess's scientific studies reveal the "secret laws of nature," trust in providence accepts those secrets as forever mysterious. This shift from "law" to "belief" marks a notable turn in Hess's understanding of the self and human identity.

Faith in a "cognizable divine law" is a belief, Hess claims, "in a divine Providence, a plan of creation."[79] Hess immediately redirects, indeed alters drastically, the meaning of *Gesetz*. In his scientific and socialist writings, a law revealed the inner logic of history and human behavior. As rational beings, we could discover those fundamental laws that guide and determine human conduct. With such axiomatic laws in hand, the socialist utopia would speedily arrive. But law in *Rome and Jerusalem* points to a reality far different than an essential rule of history. Law has come to mean "divine law," and divine law informs a divine history, or *Heilsgeschichte*. As a plan and not a logical rule, divine law is purposeful but mysterious. To believe in divine fate, Hess continues, is not to have a "fatalistic, blind faith in an inconceivable blind destiny." Having altered the meaning of *Gesetz* from law to mysterious divine plan, Hess must defend a notion of divine plan that does not deteriorate into a passive fatalism. To do so, he distinguishes his account of divine purpose from material views of history:

> I do not claim with the materialists that the organic and spiritual world, like the inorganic world, stands under the same laws [*Gesetze*] as an external mechanism. I claim the very opposite: the cosmic, mechanical phenomena have the same plan [*Plan*], the same purposefulness [*Zweckmässigkeit*], which springs out of the same holy life as the organic and spiritual phenomena. Nature and humanity are subordinated to the same holy laws [*göttlichen Gesetze*].[80]

Hess appears confused. He first opposes *Gesetze* and *Plan* only to re-enforce an apparently materialist view that humanity, like nature, is subject to *Gesetze*. This kind of philosophical confusion lends credence to the scholarly consensus that, as Jonathan Frankel argues, "philosophically, the book is highly old-fashioned."[81] Such a verdict would, at least in this case, miss Hess's more sophisticated point. The materialists claim that human activity is determined by mechanistic laws, a logic clearly establishing the limits and possibilities of human agency. Let us call this view *goal-determined activity*—agency limited and determined by fixed laws, in which identity fits into programmatic activity. But Hess's conception of *Gesetz* and identity is very different. *Gesetz* as *Plan* leads to goal-directed activity rather than belief in blind destiny. History is teleological, for it has meaning and purpose that directs, rather than determines, human activity. Human agency is not defined by mechanistic laws, but stands instead under "holy laws": laws that reveal an inner (yet mysterious) meaning to the movement of history. The materialist belief in mechanistic laws sacrifices human freedom in order to re-enforce determined and necessary human action. "Holy" laws, rather than "mechanistic" ones, lend only purpose and direction to human agency. Under this schema, identity is more capricious and less confined than the materialists imagine. Hess's belief in a divine providence is not blind, but is rooted in a commitment to human freedom. Skeptical that the materialists can discover laws of human behavior, he trusts instead in a divine plan that confers meaning and freedom to human agency.

But freedom is not unlimited. While human beings and nature follow the same plan or divine laws, Hess makes two important distinctions. Nature conforms blindly, but humanity, "if perfectly developed, follows it [the plan] consciously and willfully."[82] Nature is subsumed under the materialist conception of law, one that binds and determines activity. Hess's point seems to be that divine law appears as mechanistic law if followed blindly, for the underlying purpose and meaning is never consciously recognized. Human beings, however, are capable of following the divine laws consciously and deliberately. But they can only consciously and resolutely observe divine laws "if perfectly developed." Freedom is fragile, for human beings can always fail to recognize the meanings encoded in divine history. If humanity is singular in its capacity to knowingly and willfully move toward that which moves it, then it can fall short and fail to decode the divine laws. In its failure, humanity becomes more like nature in its blind and fatalistic conformity to the divine plan. But are human beings "perfectly developed?" Hess's second distinction, which draws a "still more important difference" between nature and humanity, shows that while nature has been perfected, humans are still beings toward perfection: "humanity is still in the process of its development, in the creation of its life."[83] A "fully developed" human being is the essential good of a divine process still in formation. Belief in a divine plan, therefore, marks a healthy confidence that a "fully developed" person will result from historical progress and human agency. But while in the midst of development, identity is not whole, and freedom in human activity is not absolute. It is a limited but noble freedom that distinguishes human beings as more than blind nature, but less than perfect gods.

The human predicament between nature and the gods emerges from Hess's conception of history and historical beings. History, as suggested above, is teleological: it moves toward some end that, according to Hess, originally moved it. This end (the divine laws or divine plan) confers meaning to seemingly unconnected or tragic events. Human beings, situated within this trajectory, can either consciously further the development of the divine plan or blindly follow it. But to yield to such fatalism would in fact work against the purpose of the plan. According to Hess, human development is an essential good worked out in historical progress. There exists a divine plan, but its force comes to the fore only if fully recognized and knowingly followed. Yet this can only be achieved at the end of historical development. The problem is one of recognition:

> We do not yet know the law [*Gesetz*] of the development of social life, its final goal and purpose, and we cannot yet know this law from experience because we are still in the process of development.[84]

One can only maintain a healthy confidence that such a law or divine plan informs human history.

In significant ways, the account in *Rome and Jerusalem* shares much with

Hess's earlier discussion of Spirit in *The Holy History*. In both texts, human beings become progressively more self-conscious and recognize patterns in history. In both texts, agents move toward that which moves them (Spirit in *Holy History*, divine plan in *Rome and Jerusalem*). But the confidence, clarity, and future movements of Spirit in Hess's *Holy History* are missing in *Rome and Jerusalem*, and it is this lack of precision and logic that I want to stress. By 1862 human history for Hess conceals the holy; and philosophical and scientific analysis can no longer recover hidden laws of development. Holy history is obscured by historical contingency. Since all three spheres of life (the cosmic, organic, and social) are integral features of the divine plan, Hess cannot fully recognize the law of development in any one of these spheres. As a historical being, Hess's capacity to uncover the meaning and purpose of development is severely curtailed and weakened. In the midst of development, historical beings must look through a glass darkly:

> The law of the world is the law of origination and development or, to use a customary expression, the law of "progress." This law is not yet completely known in all three life spheres. For complete knowledge, we still require a missing part: the conclusion of social life. The law of history can thus today not yet be scientifically [*wissenschaftlich*] known: the ways of providence are still dark for us.[85]

The materialists are deeply mistaken in their search for a logic that can be uncovered, recognized, and exploited. Indeed, Hess's critique of material views of history describes well his own theory of history in his early works. Not until *Rome and Jerusalem* will he argue that the laws of history and the structure of the self are still mysterious to historical beings like ourselves.

Hess's discussion moves in two directions: 1) criticism of the materialist conception of law, and 2) recognition of epistemological constraints. He criticizes the materialists by challenging their conception of law as *Gesetz*. Hess prefers to understand *Gesetz* as "Plan"—a meaningful direction in history toward an unknown divine end or good. *Gesetz* as mechanistic law undermines human agency and its place within the divine plan. But law as purposeful order concedes human insight and deliberation a role in historical progress. Yet as the argument proceeds, the problem of knowledge becomes Hess's central concern. Even if mechanistic laws do in fact exist, they nonetheless lie beyond the human capacity to know them. There are indeed epistemological constraints upon historical beings. The motives that inform human activity, and the meaning of history, are far murkier to Hess than to the author of *The Holy History*, or even to the Hess of the scientific writings in the 1850s. The clarity has been fogged over by a precarious faith in a divine history, in a *heilige Geschichte* that forever remains beyond the human capacity to fully articulate it.

This shift in confidence and loss of clarity is most clearly expressed in Hess's reading of the biblical account of creation. When God's creation of Adam completed the natural world, and the creator celebrated the natural Sabbath (*Natursabbath*), then began the creation of the social world, which will celebrate its Sabbath (*Geschichtssabbath*) at the completion of its "world historical labor," the messianic age.[86] This account differs significantly from Hess's analysis of the fall from Eden in his *Holy History*. Recall that in this earlier version, the pre-lapsarian Adam is the model self that prefigures more fully conscious beings in the new Jerusalem, and the fallen Adam depicts the human condition divorced from its "true" self. But in Hess's reworked version in *Rome and Jerusalem*, the pre-lapsarian Adam completes the natural creation of the world. This Adam has already celebrated his Sabbath. But the social world, our world, only *begins* with the fall from Eden. Hess emphasizes this point when he equates the completion of labor with the messianic age, for human labor begins only after Adam and Eve's disobedience. History begins with the expulsion from Eden. Our ancestry goes back to the conflicted, torn and lost Adam, not to the pre-lapsarian unified Adam. To be human is to be conflicted and torn. Yet in Hess's *Holy History*, conflict reveals a less human, because less full and complete, life. We should not be *those* kinds of beings, Hess warns. But if the messianic age is indeed a return to the wholeness and simplicity of the Adam in Eden, then in *Rome and Jerusalem* it would mean a return to a distinctly non-human life. Human life is historical, fragmented, and partial; these are constitutive features of being human. But Hess tells us later that creation is told only for the sake of the Sabbath. Historical human beings will celebrate their Sabbath too, like Adam before them: this shows belief in the divine plan. But the clarity, harmony, and wholeness achieved by Adam in Eden is not part of human experience while in the midst of historical development. From the perspective formed in *Rome and Jerusalem*, the pre-lapsarian Adam, as well as Christ and Spinoza in *Holy History*, are more like gods than human beings. For selves in history, the Sabbath—a symbol of harmony, wholeness, and perfection—is the completion, indeed the overcoming of human history and the selves embedded in it. Holy history still remains beyond human history.

The notion of a self limited by historical contingency remains a feature of Hess's works published after *Rome and Jerusalem*. In his essays concerned with Jewish history, Hess reiterates his account of creation and faith in a historical Sabbath. He also speaks more poetically about his messianic belief, now regarded as the end of human history that paradoxically overcomes historical reality and historical selves.[87] But perhaps the most surprising analysis of human limitations arises in Hess's posthumous work on the natural sciences, *Dynamische Stofflehre* ("The Dynamic Theory of Matter").[88] Hess's critical epistemology resurfaces here when he returns to the debate on freedom and necessity found in *Rome and Jerusalem*. Human spirits, like unconscious nature, are limited beings (*das Begrenzte*). As such, the universal or the limitless can only be known, and only exist at the "Summa" of historical activity.[89] Hess distinguishes between "real progress" and "unlimited progress" in history. As limited *Geiste*, human beings can only aspire to *wirkliche* progress and not what Hess calls an illusionary belief (*Wahnglaube*) in eternal progress. To yearn for the unlimited would only be proper for gods. But as finite spirits, human beings must acknowledge the limits both to human knowledge and human activity. To want more is to be like a god; to want less is to be barely human. But human spirit, while limited, is nonetheless open and "dynamic." Limited in scope, human history still retains an unlimited sense of open possibilities, even if its final limits remain beyond human comprehension. Hess recognizes human limitations while broadening human possibilities. This is the force of the *dynamische* in the *Stofflehre*, for Hess explicitly opposes his account of dynamic history to the mechanical ideal.[90] Hess's dynamic model limits human agency while opening history to unlimited possibilities.

All this shows that Hess's confidence has shifted from knowing the laws of social development to a belief in a meaningful and directed history. Skeptical that we can gain sufficient clarity into the path or end of social development, Hess is nonetheless assured of the openness of history, and forges a space for creative human agency. Human beings are limited, historical beings, embedded in an unrecognizable point of human development. We simply do not possess the kind of clarity into our "selves" that we would like, or that Hess once thought we could achieve. Our lives are partial lives, and must be, so long as we are recognizably human beings. But Hess fears that a philosophical anthropology that defines an agent full of unrealized and unknown potential would undermine Hess's own national and religious commitments. For how could Hess defend the national and religious features of a people if their character is mysterious, contingent, and radically indeterminate? To justify his national struggle, Hess does not merely situate the self in history, but also roots it in a *Kultus* (tradition). This move from historical contingency to tradition marks a partial return to the conception of self and identity that dominated Hess's essays from the 1840s and '50s.

Hess's most articulate account of the Jewish *Kultus* appears within the preface to *Rome and Jerusalem*. By the end of 1861 or early 1862, Hess actively seeks a publisher for his new work. He asks Leopold Löw, the well-known rabbi of Hungary and editor of the journal *Ben Chananja*, if he could find an interested publisher for *Rome and Jerusalem*. Löw requests a synopsis of the general "tendency and scope" of the work.[91] Hess responds by sending Löw the preface, stating that Löw could gather the tendency of his work "completely" from his *Vorrede*.[92] We therefore have, on Hess's own account, a short summary (only four pages) of *Rome and Jerusalem* in the form of a preface. Hess's discussion of the Jewish tradition represents one significant (though concise) part of this introductory chapter.

Hess begins the preface by appealing to the *Auferstehung*, the resurrection or rebirth, of Israel. In the wake of European nationalism, Israel too will participate in its own national rebirth. It is a claim that, on the one hand, fits Jewish history squarely within European history. But it is also a demand that Jews, who have for so long been denied the goods of European society, now take full advantage of the national movements engulfing Europe. Rather than fear modern nationalism, Jews should recognize the goods associated with it. National movements reveal the divine plan in history, and Jews should consciously and resolutely recapture their national heritage. When Jews regain their historical consciousness (*Bewußtsein*), they will struggle for their national rights.[93] This is as much an appeal to a new Jewish awareness as it is a judgment upon Europe. As Jews return to their national roots, both Jews *and* Europeans should recognize the divine plan guiding modern nationalist sentiment. European and Jewish history have conflated to become *heilige Geschichte*. The modern world is not hostile to Jewish life because holy history, as it was in Hess's earlier works, has now become human history.

The Jewish people are distinctive in their capacity to conserve national sentiments within religious expression. Jews, on the face of it, do not possess the characteristics appropriate to a nation: land, common language, and a collective political history.[94] All the more need, then, for Hess to claim a special significance for Jewish nationality. It only *appears* that Jews lack the required land, language, and political history of a nation. But Jews sustain a messianic hope for a return to Palestine, pray in the common language of Hebrew, and preserve a political awareness in their religious commandments and communal identity. As before, Hess claims that in Judaism both religion and nationality "are inseparably united [*untrennbar verbunden*] in the inalienable land of the fathers."[95] Hess recognized that religious commitments often justify political policy in many of his socialist writings of the 1840s. In 1842, he tried to limit religious discourse within the private sphere in order to secure a just society. Yet only a year later he would acknowledge that religion is but a heavenly politics.

In *Rome and Jerusalem,* Hess continues to believe that religion and politics are closely linked. But he now eagerly adopts this claim to articulate a distinctive Jewish national identity. To defend Jewish nationality, Hess embraces the character and scope of Jewish religion. Those who attempt to separate Hess's analysis of nationality from religion simply ignore his warnings that such a rupture is foreign to the Jewish tradition. Moreover, the religious and national awakening Hess envisions is deeply rooted in the "land of the fathers." A national rebirth binds memories of an "inalienable" land—a land not "alien" to Jewish aspirations. The *Auferstehung* announced by Hess calls European Jews to recognize the depth of their religious and political heritage in Jerusalem. A national rebirth requires, then, a religious rebirth as well. Hess weaves together collective memories, history, nationality, and religion as integral features of modern Jewish identity. Severing national commitments from religious hopes, memories, and history is "alien" to Jewish identity and tradition.

But according to Hess, the *Kulturjuden* (Reform German Jews) try to do just that. In order to acquire civil and political rights, they abandon their Jewish national attachments.[96] Those Jews who distinguish their national from religious identity reject what Hess calls their *Nationalkultus*. The term *Kultus* can best be captured by the English word *tradition*. The *Nationalkultus* incorporates the memories, history, and political aspirations all tied to the "land of the fathers." Jewish identity is integrally rooted in a tradition that comprises Jewish memories and hopes, history and politics, texts and interpretation. The *Kultus* is a carrier of meaning for Jews who affirm their identity only within this complex pattern of values. The reform Jews believe they can be both German nationals and religious Jews. They filter out the political commitments from the German national tradition and unite them with the religious heritage of the Jewish tradition. Hess tries to undermine this account of identity by affirming the unique Jewish capacity to unite religious and national commitments. To be a religious Jew, in Hess's account of tradition, is to be committed to a Jewish national identity. Religion, in reality, is heavenly politics.

I have employed the word *identity* to reflect particular aspects or characteristics of an underlying conception of self. A philosophy of the self maps out the features or attributes necessary for recognizing a self as a self. Identity is the particular expression of these formal attributes. In Hess's account of identity, Jews are the bearers of a religious history that instills special hopes and aspirations for a political homeland. Underlying this image of Jewish identity is a self constituted by a religious history and a political community. A self without religious or political ideals simply would not count as a self at all in Hess's schema. For a self to be recognized as such, it must be embedded in traditions that affirm religious and political values.

Underlying Hess's discussion of the Jewish national tradition is an account of Jewish identity and the requirements of self-constitution. In an essay published in the same year as *Rome and Jerusalem*, Hess argues that Judaism as a national tradition (*Kultus*) is a carrier of shared memories, texts, and commandments. The German Jewish Reformers abandon that tradition when they re-interpret the sources of Jewish identity. Following Mendelssohn, these Reformers call the Mosaic law *Zeremonialgesetz* (ceremonial laws). But "ceremonies" are not commandments from Sinai. Commandments are divine instructions, obligations transferred from God to Moses, and from Moses to Israel. Hess's point is not that a Jew must affirm the divine reception of the Mosaic law. Rather, his concern lies with how this new, "enlightened" interpretation will affect Jewish memory, text, and identity. "Our tradition," Hess emphasizes, is a "bond" that ties "the past and future together": it is "our flesh and bones."[97] The German Reformers weaken these bonds when they re-evaluate the sources of Jewish law. In altering Jewish memory, they also re-imagine Jewish tradition.

On one level, Hess's critique of Reform Jewry amounts to a basic disagreement over the authentic reading of Hebrew texts and tradition. The Reformers are surely not abandoning Jewish tradition; they only offer an alternative narrative history. In this light, Hess's demand for an authentic, national/religious tradition seems rather facile. An appeal to "our flesh and bones" would surely not convince a Reformer who, like the Hess of *Religion und Sittlichkeit*, distinguishes private religion from public politics. Moreover, how would one adjudicate differences between Hess's reconstructive narrative of Jewish tradition and the Reform account? Hess implies that his story is more authentic, but leaves his readers only with a claim without standards of assessment.

The significance of this debate, however, lies in what Hess assumes: traditions, and the memories they foster, shape Jewish identity. For Hess, a national/religious tradition, like "flesh and bones," is an inescapable feature of self-constitution. One cannot simply abandon a tradition, just as one cannot leap out of one's skin. The Reform Jewish tradition, with an alternative account of Jewish history, text, and memory, offers a rival narrative that informs Jewish identity. In both versions, however, Hess assumes that a self without a tradition would not count as a self at all.

Hess categorically refuses to entertain alternative narrative accounts of the Jewish tradition. The national/religious tradition provides the normative, authentic account for affirming Jewish identity in the modern world. The *Kulturjuden*, in Hess's story, abandon the very basis of their Jewish identity. In *Rome and Jerusalem*, they appear foolish, even tragic to Hess:

> No reform of the Jewish tradition is for the educated German Jew radical enough. Even conversion does not free him from the nightmare of German Jew-hatred. The Germans hate the Jewish religion less than their race, less their peculiar faith than their peculiar noses. Neither reform nor conversion, education nor emancipation opens completely for the German Jews the gates of social life.[98]

German Jews seek to rewrite the story of German political history in order to forge a place within it. Hess calls them "Jews of culture" (*Kulturjuden*) because they imagine that German culture can embrace a diversity of religious values. But toleration has its price, and the "educated German Jew" is willing to abandon Jewish national ties to gain political and social status. But German anti-Semitism is part of the very culture that these educated Jews adopt. They may deny their Jewish national heritage, but they cannot escape "their peculiar noses." The Jewish national tradition is an inescapable framework for Jewish identity because as "flesh and bones," it is inscribed on the faces of every German Jew.

For modern Jews with peculiar noses, Hess believes that only a national homeland will offer the framework within which Jews can affirm their national/religious identity.[99] Those fighting for a national rebirth find their justification, says Hess,

> first of all, in the Jewish tradition, in the national essence (*Wesen*) of Judaism; and then in the general historical development of humanity and its result: in the present international situation.[100]

An analysis of the Jewish tradition is what Hess calls an "inner justification," and the study of European nationalism provides an "external" rationale for a Jewish homeland. Hess claims that a European nation cannot deny the Jewish people the right to a national homeland without undermining the very basis of its own national ideology. But Hess is less concerned with the politics of modern nationalism than he is with "the national essence of Judaism." The modern nationalist movements only provide the fertile soil to plant the already national character of Judaism. One must defend a return to Palestine not on the grounds of modern nationalism, but in an account of Jewish identity rooted in tradition. In *Rome and Jerusalem*, Hess examines the national and religious features of the Jewish tradition. As the "inner justification" for the creation of a Jewish homeland in Palestine, *Rome and Jerusalem* also explores the structure of the self and Jewish identity. The web of interconnections among national commitments, historical memories, and religious hopes fosters an identity distinct from a "Jew of culture." The conception of self embedded in Hess's analysis of tradition provides the framework within which Jews can meaningfully affirm their religious and national identities.

Hess criticizes the "rationalistic and philanthropic illusions" of those who misunderstand "the national meaning of the Jewish tradition." But he also speaks out against those "dogmatic zealots" who,

> unable to develop our historical religion according to modern science [*Wissen-schaft*], escape out of despair into the womb of sweet ignorance and remain in conscious contradiction to the achievements of spirit and critique.[101]

Orthodox Jews, too, fail to articulate the religious and national features of the Jewish tradition in a modern, critical environment. Hess ridicules the nihilism of the Reformers, "who never learned anything," and detests the despairing reaction of the Orthodox, "who never forgot anything."[102] The middle path that avoids both extremes is rooted in the "new Jewish critique" of *Wissenschaft*. Rather than absorb a "foreign tradition" (Reform), or retreat into dogmatic absurdity (Orthodox), the new science promises to recover the "national-humanitarian historical tradition." Hess thus broadens his account of Jewish tradition to include what the Orthodox deny (historical development) and what the Reformers renounce (nationality) as well as covet (humanitarian ideals).

The new "Jewish science" is supported by two claims: 1) the national/religious tradition is our "flesh and bones," and 2) Jewish national identity is part of a broader historical trend that fosters national communities (the "external" justification). The former claim emerges out of Hess's essays from 1842/43, in which religion and politics were increasingly recognized as inseparable, and from Hess's scientific research in the 1850s, when race science informed socialist debates on community, state, and self.[103] Regarding the second claim, Hess learned from Mazzini's national movement in Italy (1859) that, "humanity comes in nationalities . . . that humanity is vindicated through the mediation of nations and nationalities."[104] Thus Hess could claim that, "when I work for the rebirth of my own people, I have not given up my humanistic efforts."[105] Hess understood history as nation building, and counted the Jewish people as one exemplary model of a national/religious community. But to demonstrate the inescapable features of national identity, Hess turned to racial descriptions of "flesh and bones" and "peculiar noses." If religion is a heavenly politics "inseparably united in the inalienable land of the fathers," then Jewish identity too is rooted in the authentic facial features of the Jewish nose. Religion, politics, and race all confirmed Hess's theory that Jewish identity is unavoidably embedded within the Jewish *Kultus*.

Yet Hess's discussion of human freedom and necessity sits uneasily with this view. In the tenth letter of *Rome and Jerusalem*, Hess observes the mysterious and open character of the self. There, he celebrates historical contingency for the infinite possibilities it affords to human creativity. But there are limits to human potential, and epistemological constraints are imposed on how to articulate the inner development of identity and history. A divine plan, concealed within history and nature, ensures meaningful progress in human development, though its telos remains obscure and unknown. Identity is weighed down by indecision, cryptic historical trajectories, and indeterminate future possibilities. The claim in the preface to *Rome and Jerusalem* that identity is inescapably rooted in a Jewish national/ religious tradition is at odds with this account. A reader of the tenth letter might ask, how can one make sense of inescapability, rootedness, and tradition when identity is so undetermined and exposed to new possibilities? Hess appears to be working with two narratives. The one tells the story of an unchanging and stable identity that is unavoidably embedded in a tradition and race that inform Jewish national and religious commitments. To be a Jew is to be identified with this tradition and race. The other narrative re-imagines the self within a constellation of competing commitments and opportunities in which the self oscillates between unexplored human potentials (freedom) and historical contingency and limits (necessity). In *Rome and Jerusalem*, there are two narratives, two selves, and two accounts of Jewish identity.

From his early works on holy history, through his socialist articles and scientific essays of the 1840s and '50s, Hess's narrative is singular. Identity is accessible to rational reconstruction, rooted in a recognizable history or racial lineage, and unified in its commitments and responsibilities. In *Rome and Jerusalem*, another narrative unfolds in which identity is mysterious, fragmented, and negotiated within a complex world of new possibilities and attachments. The tension between these two narratives of Jewish identity is a peculiar feature of *Rome and Jerusalem*, and is that which distinguishes this work from among Hess's vast literary achievements. Part of the complexity and difficulty of *Rome and Jerusalem* lies in Hess's transition from the one account to the other. He will open new doors of discovery and complexity, only to quickly shut them, fearful that indeterminate meanings would imperil the balance of religious and national commitments. Hess's construction of a national and religious Jewish identity at times rests on both narratives. It is this complex and ambiguous relation to openness and concealment, instability and security, and creativity and inescapability, that makes *Rome and Jerusalem* such an intriguing and insightful book for contemporary discussions on modern Jewish identity.

The next three chapters each focus on one or more of the issues raised in the previous discussion: narrative constructions of identity, inescapable frameworks, racial theory, self-affirmation, and the concept of tradition. *Rome and Jerusalem* and Hess's later essays are fruitful texts in which to entertain these issues because Hess vacillates between competing theories of the self that advance discordant images of community, identity, and history. Hess combines various impulses and commitments, sometimes affirming the one while denying the other, only to return to that repressed commitment at some later point. He manages and balances his principles and beliefs by pragmatically selecting the ideals and values that reinforce claims that he will later undermine by appealing to a different set of principles. *Rome and Jerusalem* is not a coherent work; it often betrays an author struggling to unite competing visions of the good. It is precisely for these reasons that *Rome and Jerusalem* is an important text for modern Jewish identity.

Hess's "Return" to Judaism and Narrative Identity

3

A general consensus exists among historians of Zionism that Moses Hess's *Rome and Jerusalem* marks a strong departure from his previous works on socialism and science. Only Shlomo Avineri contends that this visionary work—concerning Jewish nationalism, German anti-Semitism, and the illusions of Jewish emancipation—indicates Hess's continued struggle and concern with Jewish identity. Yet even Avineri recognizes that much of *Rome and Jerusalem* is new, and this because (as the majority of scholars insist) it establishes Hess's return to Judaism, the Jewish people, and to Jewish nationalism. In earlier works, Hess had vilified religion as a dehumanizing "heavenly politics," encouraged interreligious marriages to advance Jewish assimilation, and defended an ethical socialism that promoted universal equality and freedom. But by 1862 Hess had returned to the Judaism of his youth. He now recognized that European nationalism developed out of Jewish literary and prophetic sources, and that the Jewish love for family had nourished an incipient national movement that would one day blossom into a Jewish state in Palestine. Jewish nationalism would mean the return from incoherent wanderings to a more authentic, rooted home. It would mean a return to the Jewish liturgical year, and a renewed sense of pride for a people who had maintained a vibrant cultural, religious, and political heritage. In short, the Jewish return home would be Hess's own personal biography writ large.

This scholarly reading subsumes Hess's text under what I will call a narrative quest. A narrative quest is teleological in character. The ending imparts an interpretive lens to discern the meaning of past actions, literary pursuits, and intellectual ideals. Through the perspective obtained at the end, a person recognizes that she has become what she has been all along. Her life is now read as a coherent and meaningful quest toward a more expressive disclosure of identity. Hess's "return" to Judaism thus informs a new reading of his life as a quest toward national Jewish identity. *Rome and Jerusalem* provides that "sense of an ending"[1] in terms of which his past literary achievements are read and understood. The end imparts a new reading of the beginning, and, following Hegel's philosophy of history, the middle years of Hess's life are now recognized "as detour, as struggle toward the end" that "suggests a return, a new beginning: a rereading."[2] Hess has become what he, indeed, has repressed all along. His return represents a narrative quest toward an expressive Jewish national identity.

Taylor's discussion of narrative reveals how Hess's stories help to constitute his Jewish identity. As story-telling animals, human beings narrate the meaning and significance of their lives. Through epistemological gains achieved through more articulate narratives, one secures a more fitting account of identity informed by a limited number of concerns, questions, and ethical possibilities. Taylor argues that only within such a narrative can a person recognize herself as this *kind* of being, and thus affirm a particular identity. Through telling clearer and clearer stories about identity, an agent recognizes, in the end, that she has been this kind of being all along. This type of narrative is essentially a Hegelian one in which the ending is a return and repetition of the once inchoate meanings of the beginning, now fully expressive and recognized to be so.[3] It is also, as I have already suggested, the narrative of those who read Hess's *Rome and Jerusalem* as a quest toward Jewish national identity.

But reading *Rome and Jerusalem* as a narrative quest silences the conflicting stories in the text. Hess's narrative identity is neither uniform nor teleological. A reappraisal of the first and fifth letters in *Rome and Jerusalem,* within the context of the work as a whole, shows that Hess offers two conflicting readings of his "return" to Judaism. In the first letter, his emotional encounter with a woman in mourning forces Hess to reconsider his commitments to family, people, and nation. Hess recognizes that this return is fraught with conflicted commitments. Rather than concentrating on a recovery of wholeness, Hess appreciates the tensions inherent in modern Jewish identity. Here, reflective emotional response and chance encounters are cited to explain his "return." Yet in the fifth letter, Hess argues that his defense of Jewish nationalism, which he formalized in his writings in 1862, has always been central to his political and religious beliefs. He presents a coherent literary narrative that underscores his continual attachment to the Jewish state. This is not a return inspired by an opportune emotional encounter with family. Instead, Hess describes a consistent, intellectual pursuit of an ideal in which *Rome and Jerusalem* is but the latest and most public example.

In his pursuit of a national identity, Hess forces religious and political values within a narrowly defined, yet coherently formulated story. The reader detects Hess's openness to conversionary moments depicted in the first letter, only to witness those moments subsumed and finally enclosed within Hess's own account of a narrative quest. We see this in Hess's blatant misreading of his literary past, and in his appeal to a document that prefigures his *Rome and Jerusalem,* but one that he either never authored or substantially rewrote much later. Hess yearns for narrative unity, but discloses conflicting impulses and ideals in the very attempt to achieve it. The dynamic between moments of disruption, and the repression of those moments within a narrative quest, must be preserved if one is to recognize the conflicting accounts of Jewish identity in *Rome and Jerusalem.*

The very structure of narrative as quest tends to minimize and obscure important tensions in Hess's account of Jewish identity, and more generally in the identity of modern Jews. In the first letter of *Rome and Jerusalem,* chance encounter and epiphanic moments of concern initiate Hess's reappraisal of religious and political commitments. Yet it is precisely this kind of evaluation that Hess minimizes and constrains in his narrative account of Jewish identity in the fifth letter. The former is open to conversionary moments that may challenge well-grounded beliefs; the latter stifles such encounters within a more certain and decisive trajectory of resolution.

A life depicted as quest is a life always attempting to overcome conflicted commitments, abrupt reversals, and inconsistency. Hess's narrative quest is a journey that represses significant moments of conflict and discontinuity. But he is not alone. Many modern Jewish thinkers arduously construct narrative quests that minimize conflicting attachments and emotions. I will look at one powerful contemporary account by the Jewish philosopher Lenn Goodman that tells a uniform and harmonious story of Jewish religious identity that, much like Hess's, seeks to minimize conflicting narrative strains. The comparison to Goodman helps to show the motivating impulses behind Hess's quest for narrative unity. Like Goodman, Hess too easily suppresses conflicting patterns of thought as he works toward narrative wholeness. This motivated suppression reveals how stories as narrative quest work to resolve disruptive moments of shock and uncertainty, and cover over the conflicting narratives of modern Jewish identity.

Discontinuity and Resolution in Hess's "Return" to Judaism

Hess begins his first letter to an anonymous woman[4] in *Rome and Jerusalem* with a now famous account of his Jewish identity:

> Here I stand again, after some twenty years of estrangement [*Entfremdung*], in the midst of my people, to take part in my people's joyous and mourning festivals, in its memories and hopes, in its spiritual struggles within its own house and with the cultured societies. Yet, despite its two thousand year struggle to live together with its neighbors, my people [*meines Volk*] still cannot grow united and whole [*organisch*].[5]

What Hess calls his *Rückkehr nach Hause* is a return home in two senses: it represents Hess's own turn to Jewish life and reflection, but also signals a turning toward a more personal analysis of Jewish identity. Hess returns not to abstract philosophy, but to the Jewish liturgical year; not to dogma, but to the "memories and hopes" of the Jewish people. Yet this intimate turn does not recapture the earlier certitude and ease evoked in *The Holy History* and elsewhere concerning the self and identity. Here, Hess focuses on the persistent "spiritual struggles" both within the Jewish tradition and among European communities. He lives "in the midst" between an unknown beginning and a distant future. A Jewish "home," as Hess envisions it, is a contested arena within which "spiritual struggles" are recognized and explored. It is also the primary religious and social location from which a Jew engages the broader "cultured societies."

Hess's return is not a recovery of wholeness: his *Entfremdung* and return home do not obscure nor deny his conflicting commitments. Jewish ritual, memories and hopes, and spiritual struggles raise competing claims. Hess implicitly recognizes this when he admits that the Jewish community has not developed "united and whole." Jewish ritual observance often is at odds with the secular European

45

calendar, military conscription, cultural dietary habits, and economic exchange.[6] Hess's home is thus not secure, and certainly not uniform. To work for the spiritual struggles both "within its own house and with the cultured societies" often means making a choice. And perhaps the difficulty in adjudicating between conflicting commitments better accounts for why the Jewish community "cannot grow united and whole." Hess's coming home is a return to an identity in conflict.

Hess stands again with his people after some "twenty years of estrangement," a remark that defines the Damascus affair (1840) as the moment at which Hess first recognized the political, religious, and social force of his Jewish heritage. This event marks, for the Hess of *Rome and Jerusalem*, the "beginning" of his Jewish identity. The blood libel, in which Jews in Syria were accused of murdering an Italian monk and his servant, affected Hess in the way it angered most German Jews. He felt betrayed by the lack of public indignation from his German compatriots.[7] How could modern persons believe that Jews require Christian blood for their Passover observance? Such superstition betrayed not only a total ignorance of Jewish tradition, but also assaulted the ideals and commitments of Enlightenment rationality and toleration.

The Damascus affair, for Hess and other German Jews, exposed the dissonance between Enlightenment rhetoric and the irrational fear of Germans toward Jews and Judaism. Hess responded to this hypocrisy by exploring the relative weakness of Polish and Jewish persons in world politics, and their ability to again rebuild an independent nation free from foreign domination. In an unpublished document entitled *The Poles and the Jews* (1841),[8] Hess considered Jewish colonization in Palestine as a fitting response to "the Jewish question" in Europe. But ultimately Hess could not imagine how "the political rebirth of a people [could] be realized without its own free and powerful will—and that will is here totally absent."[9] Despondent over the future possibility of a self-emancipated Jewry, Hess intensified his efforts in the German workers movement. The Damascus affair provoked only a temporary commitment to Jewish solidarity. Twenty years later, Hess imagines his *Rome and Jerusalem* as a return to that initial moment of belonging with the Jewish people.

This sense of belonging is echoed in the language of Hess's confessional claim, for he characterizes his return home as a re-discovery of his Jewish national identity. Hess calls his "standing again" as a repressed thought: "A thought, which I believed to be forever buried in my chest, stands before me again full of life. It is the thought of my nationality."[10] The emotional depth attributed to a thought (*Gedanke*) "buried" deep within underscores its power. For a number of years, Hess later tells us, this thought "pounded in his closed chest," demanding outward expression. It was a thought discovered, resurrected, brought to life, but not a thought actively chosen. The *Gedanke* simply overwhelms him, and he yields to its pure force. The imagery of "return" does not fit the sheer passivity of Hess's national belonging. It is not so much a return home as a profound recognition that one *is* home. The return to "spiritual struggles" is a re-discovery, a conscious affirmation, and an acceptance.

The rediscovery of national identity also exposes long suppressed religious and political commitments. Hess's recovery of Jewish nationality is "inseparably tied to the inheritance of my fathers, the holy land and the eternal city—the birthplace of the faith in the divine unity of life and the future brotherhood of all humanity."[11] This is one of Hess's characteristic rhetorical flourishes in which he weaves complex arguments into sweeping and weighty claims. He is also undoubtedly sincere, for throughout *Rome and Jerusalem* Hess unites particular Jewish visions of the good life with universal paradigms of justice.[12] Jerusalem, as the eternal city of a Jewish state, marks the beginning of universal redemption: the particular Jewish state inaugurates the humanitarian movement toward a socialist utopia. But especially here, when Hess unites such expansive ideals of the good, the return to "spiritual struggles" becomes most apparent. Together with Hess's renewed sense of belonging to the Jewish people is a pressing need to unite his socialist vision with Jewish history and religion. But when Hess conflates universal (socialist) with particular (Jewish) commitments, he tends to suppress more unyielding tensions. If the Jewish tradition is the source of universal goods, how can Hess claim that his nationality is inseparably tied to "the heritage of his fathers"? One must belong to the Jewish nation in order to recognize the common good. But one cannot simply adopt a people (*Volk*) and a national inheritance (*Erbteil*), Hess concludes, because the "thought" of Jewish belonging means, in reality, an "infinite love for family," and such "unconditional love for family is capable only in a Jewish heart." The Jewish people, apparently, are uniquely capable of that universal love necessary for the socialist utopia. Even as Hess attempts to minimize "spiritual struggles," his attachment to both socialist and Jewish ideals only reinforces them.

One already senses in the first letter that Hess has too easily combined rival commitments. When Hess claims that "if I work for the regeneration of my people, I do not thereby give up my humanitarian efforts,"[13] it sounds more like rhetorical flourish than considered judgment. At the very least, Hess must explain how a particular Jewish ancestry is the unique source for universal human aspirations. Appealing to the Jewish love for family will not suffice. The tension between Hess's nationalism and socialism is one kind of "spiritual struggle" that he seems unwilling to resolve fully, despite his pleas to the contrary. Yet this conflict typifies a "return home" that is anything but harmonious and easy. It is not simply a return to his nationalist ideology in the wake of the Damascus affair, for Hess is firmly committed to socialist principles that he worked out only after 1840. Hess's claim to recapture the "spiritual struggles" as part of his Jewish belonging undermines his more naive rhetorical statements. For he must accept, as he so readily admits, the family inheritance, religious traditions, and political culture that are "inseparably" tied to a historical *Volk*. But it is no easy task to unite the demands of a religious and political tradition with a secular vision of socialist society. Hess's "return" to the Jewish people is a study in conflicting commitments and emotions.

The "spiritual struggles" characteristic of Hess's return home is most evident in his use of the term *Volk*. Hess links the return to his *Volk* with his national reawakening: standing again "in the midst of my people [*Volkes*]" arouses "the thought of my nationality [*Nationalität*]." By associating family heritage (*Volk*) with political identity (*Nationalität*), Hess draws from the rich significance attributed to the *Volk* in eighteenth- and nineteenth-century German philosophy. The influential concept of the *Volk* in German literature begins with Herder's analysis of communities or *Völker* that preserve separate and unique identities.[14] For Herder, the *Volk* is the most important collectivity, determined by climate, education, and relations with neighbors. Each *Volk* maintains its own identity through language, character, and environment. Yet Herder despises nation-states as nothing but despotic, harmful, and ultimately debilitating and unnatural growths of human society. His *Volk* builds from natural relations: "Father and mother, husband and wife, son and brother, friend and man, are natural relations, in which we may be happy: the state gives us nothing but instruments of art, and these, alas! may rob us of something far more essential, may rob us of ourselves."[15]

Herder's concept of the *Volk* dominated nineteenth-century German debates about political identity and kinship.[16] The majority of German philosophers and historians accepted Herder's view that a *Volk* was, in James Sheehan's phrase, "a distinctive historical collectivity upon whose foundation a national history might be erected." But for Herder, *Volk* and state belonged to "different realms, the one authentic, historic, humane, the other, mechanical, contrived, imposed upon men." German political philosophers, however, argued that this *Volk* could only flourish in and through the state. For them, "a national state is the most mature stage in the life of a *Volk*, the proper destination in its journey towards self-expression."[17] By the time Hess composed his *Rome and Jerusalem*, the concept of the state and nation (*Volk*) were theoretically inseparable.

The German philosophical tradition provided Hess with a vocabulary to describe the Jewish *Volk* as a nation distinguished by its religious activity, education, language, culture, and environment. He effectively adopted a view of *Volk* that, in his day, was applied to thwart Jewish integration into German culture.[18] But by usurping the vocabulary of conservative German politics, Hess could argue that the Jewish (and not the German) *Volk* structured Jewish national identity. Moreover, Hess—like Herder—identified the *Volk* in part by its geographical location and influence. He criticized other *Völker* for a "subjugating despotism" that harmed Jewish spiritual and national renewal. Hess's nationalism, to be sure, owed much to Herder's concept of *Volk*. But he, like the rest of his generation, politicized Herder's account. The Jews were also a political family with a just claim to a state of their own.

Hess secures the desire for a political base, for a nation unencumbered by external pressures and attack, in family love. In the second letter of *Rome and Jerusalem*, Hess depicts the Jewish *Volk* as a natural, organic development of the family:

> Judaism never distinguishes between the individual and the family, the family from the nation, the nation from humanity, humanity from the organic and cosmic creation, and creation from its creator.

Judaism, "rooted in the love for family," is an "active knowledge, and Jewish nationalism develops organically out of it."[19] The Jewish *Volk* is only a more comprehensive Jewish family. By collapsing distinctions between familial and national obligations, Hess broadens the intimacy of familial love. Indeed, national attachments, in Jewish liturgy and "memories and hopes," publicly express a more basic and fundamental familial love. The return home is a return to both the private family and the public national *Volk*.

But Hess also claims that the Jewish *Volk* is indistinguishable from humanity in general. He strives to defend a unique and insular Jewish national community that is grounded in familial love, even as that community is integrally related to humanity, creation, and creator. How can we make sense of this? What kind of *Volk* could be unique yet ubiquitous? Hess, as we see here, endeavors to defend his dubious claim that, "if I work for the regeneration of my people, I do not thereby give up my humanitarian efforts." But in doing so, he conflates important distinctions between private attachments to his people and public commitments to the welfare of humanity. These "spiritual struggles" cannot be so easily dismissed by rhetorical hyperbole.

Hess seeks to dissolve these "spiritual struggles" by embracing both religious and political commitments within the more inclusive term of *Volk*. Recall an earlier essay published in 1843, in which Hess labeled religion "heavenly politics," a mirror image of earthly political servitude:

> Religion and politics stand and fall with each other, for the inner enslavement of Spirit, heavenly politics, supports the outer, which again only sustains and nourishes the inner.[20]

In 1843, Hess could only see politics and religion as prisons for human bondage. By 1862, Hess still links religion to politics, but he now recognizes that religious and political communities are potential sources for human freedom. Religion is no longer, as Feuerbach and Marx implied, a projection of social and political reality, but a genuine human engagement and understanding of the world. As we have seen, unifying universal socialist commitments with Jewish tradition was a prominent feature of Hess's "spiritual struggles." By conflating religious and political attachments within the Jewish *Volk*, Hess dislodges the boundaries between private religion and public politics. The Jewish love for family is equally a love for national unity and humanitarian ideals. Political and religious identities are fused, however tenuously, in the Jewish *Volk*. But the spiritual struggles do not disappear.

This marriage between private and public life is as fragile as Hess's alliance between his socialist and national principles. Witness Hess's account of fitting religious reform in Germany:

> I myself, if I had a family, would, despite my dogmatic heterodoxy, not only join a traditional Jewish community, but also in my house celebrate all the Jewish holidays, in order to maintain in me and my children a lively sense of the Jewish tradition. . . . In short, I would support everything that would contribute to the

elevation and education of the community, without undermining our old tradition.[21]

An admirable statement, but Hess had no children, nor a Jewish wife to celebrate with him the venerated Jewish customs. He had no need to face, therefore, the normative implications of his critique of Jewish religious education. This is significant, because Hess was undoubtedly aware that the content and role of secular and religious education presented intractable problems for the Jewish and German communities. Simply to propose a synthesis between the "education of the community" and "our old tradition" was both politically and religiously naive. Hess could endorse such a program only because his private life was shielded from the public debate on education. Even as he collapsed the private/public distinction, he relied upon it to free himself from his own critique. Hess's appeal to *Volk* carries little weight, even in his own life. At the very moment when he integrates private and public commitments, the "spiritual struggles" become ever sharper.

Scholars portray these "spiritual struggles" as primarily intellectual battles. For example, Shulamit Volkov argues that Hess converts from one "faith" to another, beginning as a Spinozean pantheist, then a Christian disciple. But his Christian period would soon give way to a radical atheistic humanism and an equally revolutionary communism. In the end, he rekindles his ties to Judaism and Jewish nationalism: "Only after several years of indecision, confusion and vain attempts to reach yet another kind of emotional and intellectual harmony, does Hess return to Judaism." With *Rome and Jerusalem*, Hess's "intellectual problems are finally resolved."[22] Volkov's Hess converts to new "faiths" as one tries on new hats: he finds intellectual and emotional fulfillment in the most popular crop of political and social movements, only to be quickly and inevitably dissatisfied.

But in the first letter to *Rome and Jerusalem*, Hess defends his Jewish nationalist vision by appealing to a momentous encounter with a bereaved woman at the death of a relative. It is this event, and not the one-sided "intellectual problems" that Volkov stresses, that provokes Hess to reconsider the Jewish national ideal:

> Only when I saw you in your sorrow, my chest was opened, and the coffin that covered the slumbering thought of my people was easily lifted. I have discovered the source out of which your faith in the eternity of spirit originates. What moved me to resolutely decide to act for the national rebirth of my people was your infinite sorrow of soul over the death of a loved one.[23]

Recall that earlier in the letter Hess had described a "thought" of "nationality" which he believed to be forever stifled in his chest. Here, in this emotional encounter with a bereaved other, that thought suddenly "pounded in his closed chest," demanding an outward, expressive act; this, even as the resolute choice to work for the Jewish national struggle is rooted in an "infinite sorrow of soul." The distinctions between thought and emotion, as they are for private and public, socialist and Jewish, are beginning to break down. The committed love for the departed initiates Hess's account of familial love that resides only in the Jewish heart. The "eternity of spirit" dwells in Jewish familial love, and Hess correlates this private devotion with the public commitment to *Volk*. The "spiritual struggles" among private and public commitments, reason and emotion, universal and particular ideals, and socialist and Jewish attachments all begin here with his witnessing of the passionate suffering of the other. The moment of chance encounter is *the* intellectual problem, not finally resolved, but a "spiritual struggle" that returns Hess to the Jewish national movement.

Hess appears startled that a fleeting moment could transform so "easily" an entrenched socialism ever hostile to national commitments. He asks rhetorically if luck alone could explain how an unhappy woman moved him to defend and promote Jewish national identity.[24] Unable to absorb the full significance of his conversionary experience, Hess argues that luck could not fully account for the redemptive role women have played in his own life.[25] Not chance, but the "influence of women upon the development of Judaism" moves Hess toward a nationalist vision. He now envisions his chance encounter as part of a larger historical trajectory in which women continually inspire Jewish ideals. Immediately after citing the transformative meeting with a bereaved woman, Hess re-imagines his conversionary moment within a broader narrative. He now reads his conversion as only a moment within the narrative quest that he calls "the development of Judaism," a development, no less, stifled in his own chest for some twenty years. Hess minimizes his fortunate encounter, one that he readily admits evoked his feeling of national belonging, in order to situate his life within a consistent, established story of Jewish progress. He subverts the discontinuity of this transformative event by linking it to a meaningful (though until now repressed) quest toward Jewish development. This, as Volkov suggests, is really a "return" and recovery of an incipient national Jewish identity. Instead of "spiritual struggles" and abrupt reversals of commitments, we find appeals to a story of Jewish continuity and development. Hess continually suppresses conflict beneath an all-absorbing narrative of return to the Jewish *Volk*.

There are two tendencies in *Rome and Jerusalem*: the one reveals conflicted commitments, transformative moments, and unresolved tensions; the other hides these discontinuities in rhetorical claims that harmonize diverse human experiences. I have tried to recapture the former quality, in part because Hess continually undermines it by appealing to narrative quests. This is already clear in the first letter, where Hess conflates private/public and universal/particular distinctions within his conception of *Volk*, and quickly absorbs his epiphanic moment into a broader historical schema that links beginning and middle to a resolute end. But the peculiar feature of denying tensions, and absorbing transformative experiences within a meaningful narrative quest, is most evident in the fifth letter, where Hess reconstructs a coherent narrative of his own: a rereading of his philosophical and religious thought in the form of intellectual autobiography. Looking back to his works from 1837 on, Hess envisions a singular, coherent, and consistent direction in his intellectual pursuits.[26] In conformity with Avineri's reading, Hess argues that *Rome and Jerusalem* is nothing extraordinary, but merely another literary attempt to persuade his readers of thoughts held long ago. His literary career is reinterpreted to be a sustained argument for the national struggle of European Jewry, interrupted only by his few socialist and scientific works of the 1840s and 1850s. Hess's narrative, perhaps more than anything else, has persuaded scholars to view Hess the way Hess wished to be understood. But as the previous chapter suggests, Hess's rereading is a blatant misreading of his literary works, and presents a very different image of "return" than the account of "spiritual struggles" and conversionary moments in the first letter. Perhaps the first letter offers another retrospective view of his turn to Jewish nationalism, one equally distorting and misleading. But I am not concerned with the "real" or "literal" reading so much as with Hess's own desire to unify a life in narrative. Hess's misreading underscores one strong tendency in *Rome and Jerusalem:* the drive to overcome discontinuity in the search for a coherent narrative identity.

Acutely aware that his discussion on Jewish nationalism would surprise his readers, Hess devoted a section in his fifth letter to a review of his literary corpus. Certainly Abraham Geiger, in his review, considered this section, entitled "Retrospect," to be one last pathetic attempt for a readership from an old socialist revolutionary.[27] Hess defended his new departure by appealing to his first two books, *The Holy History* (1837) and *The European Triarchy* (1841), contending that there, too, he had discussed the Jewish return to Palestine. Taking responsibility for his past literary efforts, Hess considered "a few characteristic moments" of his literary career to prove his sustained and consistent approach to the Jewish national question. He recalled the Damascus affair of 1840 and noted how, though outraged, he had restrained his Jewish national passion to fight for the European socialist movement. Only after his racial scientific studies of the 1850s did Hess once again confront the Damascus episode. In 1859, during the Italian wars of liberation, Hess recognized correlations between his racial theories and European national movements. Here are his recollections:

> Since the beginning of the Italian wars, I discovered a real connection between my racial studies and modern national movements. . . . Above all it was my own people, the Jewish, which began to captivate me more and more. The ghosts of my unfortunate brethren, which hovered over me in my youth, appeared to me again, and the long suppressed feelings could no longer be denied. The pain, which at the time of the Damascus affair was only temporary, would now become a dominating and lasting part of my philosophical thought. No longer did I seek to suppress the voice of my Jewish conscience.[28]

In reviewing his earlier writings, Hess retrieved an old manuscript written, he claimed, in 1840. He copied this passage about Jewish nationalism, anti-Semitism, and "enlightened" Jewry, word for word, or so Hess tells us, into *Rome and Jerusalem.* Even Hess "was not a little surprised" to discover a passage that was an "anticipatory justification" for his present-day Jewish concerns.

If Hess was "not a little surprised," his biographers were shocked. There is no record of such an earlier document, nor was it ever published. The only evidence we have comes from Hess himself in *Rome and Jerusalem*. In the unpublished essay mentioned earlier, *The Poles and the Jews* (1841), Hess had discussed national questions.[29] But nothing in this document could prepare Hess's readers for the claim that in his "old manuscript" could be found the very ideas and argument of *Rome and Jerusalem*. Scholars have not been entirely convinced. Shlomo Na'aman believes that Hess's manuscript of 1840 was written from the perspective of 1862.[30] Svante Lundgren agrees with Na'aman that the manuscript is indeed a forgery, a deceptive attempt by Hess to cover over embarrassing past commitments.[31] Silberner, however, defends the manuscript's authenticity, contending that "Hess had obviously changed only the form, but not the content" of the essay. Yet even Silberner recognizes that Hess substantially altered the manuscript. He admits that more corrections and new expressions, supposedly devoted to the 1840 essay, are found in the original pages of *Rome and Jerusalem*, than in any other section.[32] Scholars have thus been divided: either Hess wrote a completely new document, or he had merely reworked an essay from 1840, changing its "form" but not its substance. What kind of story was Hess telling?

Let us review the evidence. Silberner is most concerned to protect Hess's integrity, and his defense relies on two claims: 1) only the form, or the use of "new expressions," had changed from the original, and 2) the numerous marks and corrections in the original manuscript of *Rome and Jerusalem* support the first claim, for they suggest that Hess merely "rounded off" the original 1840 document with formal alterations. Silberner, a careful scholar, is simply wrong about this issue. The pages devoted to the 1840 essay in the original manuscript of *Rome and Jerusalem* are extraordinary for their lack of corrections and marked changes![33] Indeed, these pages are striking in comparison when one notes the many corrections Hess made in other sections of the book.[34] Perhaps Hess first reworked the original 1840 manuscript, and then copied it perfectly into *Rome and Jerusalem*. Here too, Silberner is less than convincing: it is not "obvious" that only the form of the essay has been altered, for the supposedly "new expressions" radically transform the very content of the message. Hess employs the phrase *gebildete deutsche Juden* in the 1840 document to refer to assimilated Jewry. It is an expression that I have not found in any work published by Hess in the 1840s, and one that has a singular significance to Hess's critique of Reform Judaism in *Rome and Jerusalem*. Hess also claims in the manuscript that "the teutomaniac loves in his fatherland not the state, but the race dominance." Yet Hess himself confesses that he did not recognize the importance of race or racial domination until his scientific investigations of the 1850s. When speaking of France, Hess confides, "even the Jew is here a Frenchman," a peculiar remark by a man who first moved to France in 1842, and in *The European Triarchy* (1841) would speak admiringly of "We Germans." Hess concludes his 1840 essay with a familiar argument from his racial account in *Rome and Jerusalem*: it is impossible for Jews to deny their nationality. Yet in *The European Triarchy* (1841), Hess compares favorably the Christian "God of humanity" to the Jewish "national God," calling Jews "soulless mummies," suggesting that only mixed marriages would raise the Jews from their despicable condition.[35] These alterations are not merely formal changes to the 1840 document, but are radical departures from anything we know about Hess's philosophical and religious thought of the 1840s, including Hess's brief discussion of Jewish nationalism in *The Poles and the Jews*. In fact, all three of Hess's concerns mentioned here—cultured Jewry, race, and nation—are all central and unique to Hess's *Rome and Jerusalem*.

The first section of the 1840 document may indeed be original, for it concerns Hess's reaction to the Damascus affair, the Hep Hep riots in Germany (a series of anti-Jewish riots in 1819 and again in 1830; Hep Hep refers to a rallying cry against the Jews, but the origin of the slogan is still somewhat obscure), and his wounded pride after Nikolas Becker rejected his musical piece for a German national poem. These events were certainly fresh in Hess's mind in the early 1840s. But the text shifts quickly to commentary, a tone so familiar to the reader of *Rome and Jerusalem*. The change is marked by one word, *Heute*, and the question before the reader is, which "today" is Hess referring to, 1840 or 1862? All of the stylistic and substantial alterations that I mention above come after the *Heute*. The most charitable reading of Hess's 1840 document suggests that only the first section was original; after the *Heute*, we read commentary from Hess in 1862. Still, Hess misleads his readers by claiming that his 1840 essay is "characteristic" of his thoughts in the past. The "logical development" from his first book of 1837 to his present work on Jewish nationalism is a reading of beginnings determined by a sense of the end. It is a narrative plot, to adopt Peter Brooks's account of the great nineteenth-century novel, "of an attempted homecoming: of the effort to reach an assertion of origin through ending, to find the same in the different, the time before in the time after."[36] It is a story about a personal narrative quest.

Hess's rereading is his attempt to construct a coherent account of a life in narrative. Hess therefore recasts his earlier philosophical claims to align more congenially with his present national vision. He creates a story that makes sense of his present philosophical position by dismissing conflicting claims from the past. A "logic" develops clearly and comfortably to confirm his nationalist agenda as *the* agenda for his social, political, and religious values.

Harold Bloom's work on the anxiety of influence in poetry helps to explain the pressures upon Hess to cover over discontinuities in his thought.[37] According to Bloom, the strong poet's urge to misread a precursor's poem, to create a "revisionary swerve" in order to make room for the later poet's own creative influences, is the stuff of modern poetry. Bloom's interpretive cry—"know each poem by its *clinamen*" (revisionary swerve)—reveals that all strong reading is a misreading, a distortion and "willful revisionism without which modern poetry as such could not exist." The heroism of the strong poet is the model for the authentic self, a person who willfully, though tragically, attempts to overcome past influences. If Bloom is right that the strong poet fears "belatedness"—that all has been said and written before—then coherent narrative accounts may manifest a related concern: the fear of fragmentation and lost meaning. Bloom alerts us to the ways in which narratives rely on deceit, misreading, and revision in order to create sense or meaning. We should not understand narratives according to what they say, but according to how they intend to distort and rewrite. Coherency in narrative, with a Bloomian read-ing, disguises the human will to overcome past influences. It is the heroic but tragic attempt to dominate and subdue the past.

The later poet, the *ephebe*, wants us to reread the precursor poet through the lens of her misinterpretation. Access to the meaning of past influences is filtered through the strong poet's revisionary reading of that past:

> The [*ephebe's*] poem is now *held* open to the precursor, where once it *was* open, and the uncanny effect is that the new poem's achievement makes it seem to us, not as though the precursor were writing it, but as though the later poet himself had written the precursor's characteristic work.

> The mighty dead return, but they return in our colors, and speaking in our voices, at least in part, at least in moments, moments that testify to our persistence, and not to their own.[38]

The new work is now primary and thus authoritative, the ultimate rebellion and slaying of the father. The poet "is not so much a man speaking to men as a man rebelling against being spoken to by a dead man."[39] Critics, Bloom tells us, love continuities, "but he who lives with continuity alone cannot be a poet."[40]

Hess, it would seem, is not a strong poet who rebels against belatedness, but a strong critic who yearns for continuities. Yet Bloom reveals the mechanisms that might impel Hess to misread his literary corpus, and thus to become Bloom's strong poet. Hess's precursor is the Hess of *The Holy History* and *The European Triarchy*. Hess the *ephebe* and Jewish nationalist rereads his earlier works through the normative lens of *Rome and Jerusalem*. His "revisionary swerve" is a misinter-pretation of his past so that the past now speaks through the present. It is a fear that his dead, his past, might return to "darken the living."[41] To counter these forces, Hess narrates his past so that *Rome and Jerusalem* becomes "characteristic" of his thought; the beginning is now read through the interpretive lens of the end. It is for this reason that Hess deceives himself and his readers into believing that an "old manuscript" was originally conceived in 1840. *Rome and Jerusalem* now dominates the reading of the beginning, middle, and end of Hess's philosophical and religious narrative. I mentioned earlier that there are really two tendencies in *Rome and Jerusalem:* the one open to discontinuity, the other always seeking clo-sure. In his appeal to the 1840 document, Hess overcomes discontinuity by con-structing a linear, coherent narrative of a Jewish national quest.

Poetry is property, Bloom claims. If so, Hess, like all strong poets, owns his past. The tragedy of the strong poet, however, is that even as he rebels, the past remains more "outrageously alive than himself."[42] Even the strong poet is not se-cure from influences from the past. This is certainly true of Hess's re-reading of his narrative life. Even as he overcomes his "earlier" identity, that identity, exposed in the first letter in *Rome and Jerusalem*, will not leave him untouched. For there one reads Hess's account of a chance emotional encounter with a grieving relative and other spiritual struggles that expose his deep conflict. Hess links his "return" to Judaism with moments of inspiration, though he quickly turns to the narrative of Jewish development in order to situate transformative events within a broader scheme. The fifth letter only expands this tendency in Hess to describe a continuous, philosophical commitment to Jewish nationalism that underlies his literary works. In this narrative, Hess's racial studies of the 1850s replace his epiphanic encounter with a suffering other as the central turning event in his national politics. *Rome and Jerusalem* is thereby reinterpreted as one final installment in Hess's quest toward Jewish national identity. But the Hess of the first letter rebels. However much he later minimizes strong emotional attachments, conversionary moments of encounter, or spiritual struggles, the entangled narratives in the text challenge Hess's repression of discontinuity. If Hess plots a harmonious temporal movement toward Jewish national identity, then other spiritual struggles emerge to provide revisionary force to identity as narrative quest.

The Reading of Hess's "Return" as Resolution

There are indeed two tendencies or plots in *Rome and Jerusalem*, but only one of them has decisively influenced Hess's later interpreters. Following Hess, Zionist scholars have understood *Rome and Jerusalem* as a recovery of the most persuasive and powerful commitments of his youth. Like Hess's 1840 document, earlier material is cited as the source and context for Hess's national ideology. It becomes increasingly clear that even as Hess attempts to own his past, he is far more successful in limiting future readings of his text. The drive for a coherent narrative quest returns in the scholarly understanding of *Rome and Jerusalem*.

The most persuasive case for understanding *Rome and Jerusalem* as a return to Hess's earliest Jewish convictions has been made by Jonathan Frankel.[43] He is most interested in Hess's transition from radical politics in the 1840s to his new-found nationalism and proto-Zionism in the 1860s. In Frankel's reading (partially discussed in the second chapter), Hess's first book, *The Holy History* (1837), provides the blueprint for his historical interests and claims, a positive evaluation of Judaism, and a belief in a socialist utopia grounded in Jewish messianism. *Rome and Jerusalem* draws its inspiration from this earlier work, and should be understood as a "return" to its fundamental assumptions and convictions. But Frankel adds that "Hess is reaching back across twenty years of his life. Always open to new discoveries, his own past now comes to him as the latest, and perhaps the most startling, of them all." He surrenders to "an old idea rediscovered" and decides to "go back to the crossroads of 1840 and follow the path he had then rejected." By "reestablishing ties with his family, his youth, his early ideas," Hess returns to a line of thought "so long neglected."[44]

"The crossroads of 1840," and not merely Hess's first book, are the sources for Hess's "return." Frankel cites the lengthy passage in *Rome and Jerusalem* purportedly from the 1840 document, in which Hess strongly identifies with Jewish nationalism, denounces German anti-Semitism, and rejects Jewish social emancipation as a naive ideal. This unpublished 1840 paper, as I have argued, resonates with much that Hess affirms later in *Rome and Jerusalem*. It is this document, and Hess's emotional response to the Damascus affair, that represent the "crossroads" in Hess's intellectual career. *Rome and Jerusalem,* in Frankel's narrative, signifies Hess's "return" to "one brief moment, in 1840."[45]

Frankel assumes that Hess did, in fact, write an unpublished essay in 1840 on Jewish national sentiment and German anti-Semitism. But we have seen that there are strong indications in *Rome and Jerusalem* that suggest otherwise. Indeed, in a later study, Frankel is much more cautious.[46] He recognizes that Hess is less than honest with his readers in interpreting his past in the light of present national commitments. But for the Frankel of *Prophecy and Politics,* the image of "return" is so dominant that he fails to notice Hess's deception. With his decision "to go back to his earliest writings," Frankel argues that Hess "had liberated himself from the pressures to conform."[47] We can witness in Hess "the power of pride—pride in the Jewish 'nation' as he came to call it." Hess became, in Frankel's powerful and appropriate image, a "reluctant heretic." Unable to conform, Hess opts for Jewish nationalism, a return to his repressed convictions of 1840.

This image of "return" dominates the view of Hess as a "forerunner" to a Jewish national movement that would become a powerful force some thirty years later. In biographical accounts of seminal Zionist thinkers, the image of "return" is central to Zionist self-definition. According to Felix Weltsch, Hess's biography and "tschuva" (return) are typical of the "Zionist reaction."[48] This is transparent in Gershon Winer's interpretation:

> The record of the Hess conversion is not unique. The annals of Zionist history are studded with tales of repentant renegades, the zealous devotees of any number of current foreign fads, who suddenly were shocked into an awareness of their responsibilities to their own people.[49]

The Zionist enterprise as a whole is a return to a central place, a re-entry into world history and the fulfillment of religious yearnings. It is a recovery of Jewish power, politics, and authenticity.[50] Hess's biography is the story of Zionism itself, the existential movement of return to land, Judaism, and Jewish identity. Recall that for Shulamit Volkov, Hess reaches "emotional and intellectual harmony" in his recovery of Jewish nationalism. But this is so because the Zionist enterprise is only Hess's biography writ large in Jewish history. The image of return provides the hermeneutical key to understand Hess's *Rome and Jerusalem,* for the symbolic power of return underlies the existential commitments that are fundamental to the Zionist movement. Reading Hess is an act of self-appropriation, as much a justification for Zionism as it is a recovery of authentic Jewish identity. The Zionist narrative as quest guides the scholarly literature, as it did in Hess's own reading of *Rome and Jerusalem.*

Robert Wistrich's account of Hess's "return" clearly shows the hermeneutical gymnastics required to view Hess's life as a coherent narrative quest. Following Frankel and Volkov's reading of Hess's "return," Wistrich characterizes *Rome and Jerusalem* as "the culmination of a long and painful process of overcoming the estrangement he had initially felt towards the Jewish people and its traditions." Referring to the 1840 document, Wistrich argues that the Damascus affair, together with the rebuff from Nikolas Becker, first convinced Hess that European Jewry would forever be outsiders to European society. Significantly, Wistrich does not recognize the 1840 document as a potential forgery. Indeed, the unpublished paper supports Wistrich's claim that Hess harbored private, nationalist thoughts that he could ill afford to make public:

> As a cosmopolitan socialist, Hess felt obligated to keep these insights for himself,
> so that his *public* utterances on the Jewish problem in the 1840s were scarcely
> distinguishable from those of liberal and radical assimilationists.[51]

Those "public" thoughts were published in Hess's books of 1837 and 1841, but his private "insights" were concealed in the document of 1840. By distinguishing public from private utterances, Wistrich can explain why the 1840 paper was never published, yet still can confirm Hess's claim that his *Rome and Jerusalem* is but a reworking of those private convictions. Wistrich's account relies on the rather dubious claims that the 1840 document was indeed original, and that Hess had consciously edited his private commitments from his public statements. Neither claim can be supported by a close reading of the 1840 paper, and Hess himself collapsed private/public distinctions in essays written in the 1840s. To defend a narrative quest as a return to original (private) convictions, Wistrich must blindly follow Hess's own deceptive narrative in *Rome and Jerusalem,* in which origins (the 1840 document) are informed by a sense of an ending.

Historians of German socialism such as Wistrich are recognizably uncomfortable when they confront *Rome and Jerusalem.* Wistrich links Hess's Jewish nationalism to his earlier socialist works through an appeal to a private and unpublished document. He even hears echoes of private attachments "to the Jewish messianic idea" in Hess's socialist works. There are, however, other versions of Hess's "return" that challenge Wistrich's decidedly Zionist reading. As I noted in chapter 2, alternative historical accounts center on Hess's socialist works in the 1840s, often comparing (unfavorably) Hess's "ethical" socialism to Marx's material dialectic.

But for all, the trope of "return" dominates the reception of Hess's *Rome and Jerusalem,* whether it is Frankel's "crossroads of 1840," Lademacher's "*Gedankenwelt*" of Hess's socialist works, or Avineri's account of unity in Hess's return to Jewish thought. For each of these critics, Hess returns to the dominant intellectual or emotional strands of an earlier period. The first letter in *Rome and Jerusalem* opens with the confession that, "Here I stand again, after some twenty years of estrangement, in the midst of my people." The imagery is striking, and it strongly encourages those who want to see in Hess the embodiment of the Zionist vision, or the durability of socialist ideology. Hess appears to truly own his past. But one biographer, Shlomo Na'aman, warns that we should not blindly accept all of Hess's "confessional" claims. Na'aman cites Hess's defiance in wishing his name were "Itzig" so that his detractors could easily identify his Jewish heritage. Yet this bravado seems hardly convincing, for Hess consistently signs his essays, correspondences, and books as Moritz or M. Hess. Nor does Na'aman trust Hess's claim to return "suddenly" to Judaism and the Jewish people. Instead, Na'aman contends (like Volkov) that this moment of return "is a thoroughly intellectual process" that solves critical problems left unresolved from Hess's previous works.[52] We need not agree with all of Na'aman's claims to recognize his point that the Zionist image of return is more nostalgia than reliable biography, a product of inspired memory rather than sensible history.

The redemptive role of chance encounter, uncovered in the first letter of *Rome and Jerusalem,* hardly fits Zionist readings of Hess's intellectual career, or socialist ones that stress Hess's consistent approach to social justice. The tensions in Hess's attempted alliance between universal and particular claims, and private and public life, unravel narrative accounts that order Hess's life into "crossroads," distinctive periods, or abiding philosophical interests. Hess's account of "return" is a far more difficult and negotiated path of mixed emotions, unresolved anxieties, and sweeping visions that conflate important distinctions. The narrative quest of "return" to nascent socialist or national ideals, so central in the plot of Zionist and socialist readings, obscures these issues. The conversionary encounter with a bereaved other, and the "spiritual struggles" it raises, are subsumed under a more exalted narrative.

Narrative Identity

The trope of "return" generates normative claims about the meaning of conversionary experiences. It suggests that Hess recovers something lost, or re-establishes ties to a forgotten past. It means, as Hegel argued, to take back what was, in the beginning, authentically one's own, and to repossess it with vigor, passion, and commitment. More subtly, a return indicates a response to unsolved problems, lingering doubts, and lost wanderings. The image of return has been indispensable to Zionist biographical and historical works that retrieve from the past a defense and an apology for the future. Hess's "return" is a conversion narrative, but one that, like so many others, establishes its authenticity in being rooted in an authoritative past. Paula Fredriksen has, in another context, discussed the meaning of conversion narratives in Western Christianity. Her account of Paul and Augustine's reconstructed narratives fits Hess's own rereading:

> That moment [of conversion] exists only retrospectively, when the convert, examining his life, attempts to interpret his present in light of his past ('How did I get here?'). But he comes to his past only through his present, and it is from his vantage point in the present that the convert constructs a narrative that renders past and present continuous, intelligible, and coherent ('This is how I got here').[53]

In sections of the first letter in *Rome and Jerusalem,* and certainly in the entire fifth letter, Hess is what Fredriksen calls a "retrospective self" who defines his past through his present concerns. Yet when Hess owns up to the conversionary experience in the first letter, he affirms that reflective emotional response to chance encounter plays an important role in his turn to Jewish nationalism. Conversion narratives are not, as Fredriksen suggests, all of a piece. Hess reveals, however unwittingly, that intelligible narratives can be undermined by other subtle and discontinuous narratives in the text. The retrospective self cannot, like Bloom's *ephebe*, wholly own the past. At least Hess cannot do so, because he is deeply conflicted about the very meaning of past experiences and their influence upon the present.

Yet we must tell some story of our past, and that story, as Taylor argues, shapes a meaningful and coherent identity. To make sense of a life, Taylor believes we require an orientation to the good, but "this sense of the good has to be woven into my understanding of my life as an unfolding story." This means to "grasp our lives in a *narrative*" as an unveiling of who we are, "how we have become, and of where we are going." A narrative is an "unfolding" as it traces the "coherent" trajectory of "my sense of how I have come here."[54] Narrative understanding is a taking stock of a life retrospectively, and a vision of how an orientation to the good unfolds in a unified life. This sense of meaningful direction is what Taylor calls a quest, a term of art he appropriates from Alasdair MacIntyre's account of narrative unity. MacIntyre examines the "concept of a self whose unity resides in the unity of a narrative which links birth to life to death as narrative beginning to middle to end." Thinking of the self in "narrative mode" is "natural," for we are essentially story-telling animals. For MacIntyre, we are all on "narrative quests" in which we seek to discover the meaning and content of our lives.[55] Our search resembles stories in which there is an intelligible beginning that leads to struggles and deliberations, and finally to an end to which we strive. Taylor accepts this account of narrative, but goes further than MacIntyre in insisting that the "narrative mode" is more than "natural." Narrative understanding is, instead, constitutive and a "basic condition" for "making sense of one's life." Taylor insists that recognizing our lives in narrative is one of the "inescapable structural requirements of human agency."[56]

A narrative quest is an "unfolding story" of a person who acts, deliberates, and strives from beginning, to middle, to end. As an individual reviews a life, she determines the meaning of her life by "the story of how she got there." This story is read retrospectively, and each successive narrative account achieves greater clarity into one's "orientation to the good." The adjective "unfolding" is therefore crucial for appreciating Taylor's theory of narrative quests. A new story is more articulate if it expresses an authentic account of how one orders a life in relation to the good. One can show how that ordering was inchoate or inarticulate in previous narrative tellings, and relate the good to a life now more fully expressive in the new narrative reading. Moreover, persons can clarify how the orientation to the good "unfolds" in a life always dedicated to that good, but only retrospectively perceived to be so. The notion of "unfolding" gives a "sense of an ending" that is now recognized to be an inchoate beginning struggling for a more expressive articulation. A narrative quest, in Taylor's account, is an updated Hegelian reading in which Spirit becomes what it has always been, now consciously, resolutely, and identifiably so.

Taylor's theory shows us how Hess's retrospective gloss on his life history is really a constructed story of identity. To shape a coherent narrative, Hess describes a life dedicated to one powerful good: the Jewish national struggle. Indeed, we could call Jewish nationalism, in Taylor's vocabulary, a "moral source" that commands Hess's respect and thereby empowers him to live better by that ultimate good.[57] The struggle for a national Jewish identity shapes the meaning and value of Hess's other projects and concerns, and provides the controlling moral source to mold a coherent narrative quest. Hess's identity now "unfolds" before him ("Here I stand—") as a consistent and continuing pursuit of an ideal.

Yet this pursuit blinds Hess to other narrative strains. He was "not a little surprised" to discover the 1840 document on Jewish nationalism because it so forcefully confirmed his "sense of the ending." But, as I have argued, Hess did not find that essay; rather, he put it there. It was the narrative of Jewish national belonging that produced such a document. Hess could not imagine other, conflicting stories of personal struggle. There were no wrong turns, moments of regret, or deep anguish in Hess's narrative quest. His was a true unfolding of latent meanings yearning for articulation. The narrative quest truly shaped Hess's sense of self, but it also repressed other forms of self-expression.

Narrative strains, as well as pre-emptive narrative closures, are clearly felt in *Rome and Jerusalem*. Hess reports conversionary moments of encounter, and affirms emotional complexity and conflicted commitments, yet he quickly subsumes these stories within a more confined and coherent account of quest toward national Jewish identity. This new "sense of an ending" determines the possible candidates for fitting beginnings, and ultimately stifles the revisionary pressures informed by competing narratives. In this chapter, we have located two conflicting readings of Hess's turn to Jewish national identity, but only one emerges as the master narrative, and this because it offers a more coherent and meaningful account of a life as quest. Hess constructs his narrative quest by re-reading his past to fit present national commitments. So too his scholarly readers, who like Hess embrace conversionary moments of chance encounter within a patterned historical scheme. This "sense of an ending," I have suggested, is rooted in what Taylor calls a quest, in which a whole life is now recognized to be that which it has always already been, but unconsciously so. Subversive narratives that deconstruct the linear and coherent trajectory of a quest are tangential; they also jeopardize the need for closure and moral meaning. Yet the story of Hess's exposure to conversionary moments that are then concealed and suppressed within a personal quest is one narrative that neither Hess nor his scholarly readers recognize as a meaningful narrative of its own.

Hess and his interpretive readers are not alone in believing that conflicting narrative accounts undermine rather than inform personal identity. Modern persons, as Taylor persuasively argues, are immersed in competing claims to identity and moral goods that require complex negotiations among contrasting visions of identity, morality, and society. But Taylor, like Hess, constructs modern identity to keep these dislocating forces at bay. This is true also for many modern Jewish thinkers who have become enthralled by the process of modernity and its effects on Jewish tradition. This is one of the more powerful claims in Arnold Eisen's recent study of modern Judaism.[58] Eisen traces the various protective strategies of Jewish ritual identity in such figures as S. R. Hirsch, Abraham Geiger, Martin

Buber, and Franz Rosenzweig. They all appeal, in various and distinctive ways, to integrative moral sources that unify Jewish identity within the myriad and complex relations of modern life. In this brief conclusion, I want to look at a more contemporary thinker who appeals to many of the protective strategies outlined by Eisen. Lenn Goodman, an influential Jewish theologian who has recently published a philosophical defense of Jewish monotheism, offers a coherent, integrative theory of the good.[59] Goodman's account of Jewish identity and his critique of tragedy highlight features that resonate with Hess's desire for a narrative quest. Through a reading of Goodman's text, we will be in a better position to assess Hess's significance for modern Jewish thought.

Goodman defines the divine as the extraordinary, a value concept in which "the One becomes the Good, the highest god, because it is the source of every value—truth, stability, unity, constancy, integrity, sameness, intelligibility, and beauty."[60] This list of "every value" is selective, and reveals more about what Goodman prizes than about what value may consist in. But more than this, Goodman claims that the one God integrates every human value into a coherent, ordered concept of the good, for "integration is demanded by the values themselves." Socratic philosophy, at least the version Goodman follows, reveals that "conflict was more a devise of theater [tragedy] than a fact of nature. It proposed a goodness that was not achieved at the expense of any other. Surely the cosmos had some principle of integration."[61]

But it is the biblical Abraham at Mount Moriah who affirms that all human values are integrated and unified within God's goodness such that faith becomes the "conscious and increasingly confident loyalty to the inner logic of God." Goodman reads Genesis 22 as Abraham's struggle between two competing voices: God's request to sacrifice his only son Isaac, and the angel who intervenes. Abraham's decision, with knife in hand, relies upon an earlier moment (in Genesis 18) when he demanded God's justice for Sodom and Gomorra. Abraham's moral insight that God's justice is absolute wins for him the divine blessing. The trial in Genesis 22, in Goodman's reading, tests Abraham's understanding of God's nature. Surely he had already affirmed that God is alien to evil in Genesis 18, but "he had not seen fully what this meant when he set out for Mount Moriah." Only in Genesis 22 will Abraham gain philosophical clarity by "refining, strengthening, giving substance to his nascent conviction of God's goodness."[62] Goodman does not explain how such "refining" is possible when Abraham's decision not to offer Isaac was "impulsive" (a point that Goodman quickly concedes); indeed, Abraham traveled three full days in which to reflect upon God's request, apparently concluding that the sacrifice was a just demand. Nor does Goodman seriously consider what David Hartman regards as the scandal of Abraham's sacrifice of his son Isaac: "the feeling that in God we encounter a furious irrational Force Whose unpredictability makes it impossible for us to rely on His commitments to us." For Hartman, Genesis 22 tragically signals "the basic unintelligibility and mystery of God's actions."[63] But like Socrates, Goodman's Abraham overcomes tragedy and conflict by showing how the nature of God's goodness integrates all "affirmative values." "Refining, strengthening, [and] giving substance" means to unify all value into one integrative Good (the God of Abraham).

Integrating all "affirmative values" as a paradigm for the universal Good is a contested value. Goodman stubbornly admits that "Martha Nussbaum sees a deeper truth in the denial of its possibility [the possibility of a good that integrates all affirmative values] that reaches its epitome in Greek tragedy." She argues that pursuit of the good life inevitably awakens irresolvable conflicts. But Goodman can barely hide his contempt for this view: Nussbaum "rejects and seems to resent conciliation—the avenue so often pointed to by the tragedians themselves," and "the very idea of a hierarchy of values for her smacks of insincerity or inauthenticity." Nussbaum's message that persons are vulnerable to events beyond their control, such that irreconcilable conflict is a permanent feature of a human life, "seems profoundly wrong." Hers is but a "homely, social moral," a "bad faith" that results from not confronting the seriousness of moral decisions.[64] Simply, Nussbaum lacks the philosophical nerve to seek coherence and integration of the virtues. While much of his polemic misses the subtlety of Nussbaum's position, the significance of Goodman's critique lies in what he fears: moral coherence and integration would disappear in the tragic world described by Nussbaum. If conflict is really ineradicable, then "moral coherence would be lost and, with it, the very possibility of an idea of God."[65] But this is special pleading: only Goodman's conception of goodness as an integrative value is really at issue here. The stakes are clear and ultimate for Goodman: either coherence or conflict, integration or disintegration, a standard of morality or "passively floundering."[66] This becomes clear in his defense of "critical theology": "The pitting of value against value (which tact forbids in most social contexts) demands a higher integration and ultimate synthesis, achieved through the purgation of the negative."[67] The "negative" points to the dubious values of openness, contingency, conflict, and fragility. Modern Jewish identity, to the extent that it is "critical" and "affirmative," will subvert these vices in order to secure a coherent, unified, and integral vision of the good as the guiding source of the self.

Goodman's narrative quest toward an integrative and moral Jewish identity is Hess's as well. For Goodman, God's all-encompassing and unifying goodness makes possible a coherent narrative identity, one that, in the image of God, unifies all the positive virtues. But replace Jewish national struggle for Goodman's unifying goodness in the sentence above, and we have Hess's construction of modern Jewish identity. Hess is indeed a retrospective self who constructs a coherent story of Jewish national identity that, like Goodman's story, secures an integral vision of the good as the guiding source of the self. But Hess's text harbors resources that point to discontinuous narratives, conflicting commitments, and epiphanic moments of encounter. Goodman represses all that, and offers instead a clean, coherent, and integrative narrative of Jewish identity.

I submit that Hess's significance for modern Jewish thought lies precisely in the competing visions of self in *Rome and Jerusalem* that challenge this unified narrative quest. Hess's account of "return" in the first and fifth letters defies "greater lucidity" and resolution, and instead suggests ambiguous relations, dubious claims, and chance encounters. Narrative as quest conceals these discontinuities and wrong turns, for it frames a life and text too partial and negotiated to fit neatly within the borders of a coherent narrative journey. Hess's text shows us why the protective strategies developed by modern Jewish thinkers constrict the robust complexity and challenges of modern Jewish practice.

Rome and Jerusalem also reveals why integrative theories of narrative identity minimize and obscure important tensions in modern Jewish identity. Reconstructing personal narratives as quests will conceal possible avenues of personal disclosure that can significantly change the identity of persons. Roads not taken, or possibilities left unresolved, disturb the harmony of life as quest. Hess alerts us to eruptions of discontinuity in the first letter, for there luck, emotional sensitivity, and epiphanic moments play a decisive role in reassessing political and religious commitments. But Hess deflates these radical pressures in his reconstruction of Jewish identity as quest for national belonging. In his retelling, there were never missteps, unresolved tensions, or competing attachments in his narrative life. There is, in the end, nothing to regret. Narrative as quest, in *Rome and Jerusalem* and other accounts of "return," undermines another, more incoherent narrative: an open and responsive encounter with moments of shock and uncertainty that inspire re-evaluations of personal identity.

When Hess subsumes his conversionary moment of encounter within a narrative rooted in the "stability" of Jewish national identity, he stifles a notable feature of moral insight. For story-telling animals, we express important moral virtues that expose the self to conversionary moments of encounter. *Rome and Jerusalem* is indeed an ambivalent work that is continuously open to those transformative experiences, even as it confines them within a more secure and stable "sense of an ending." It is this very dynamic of openness and concealment that offers a revisionary challenge to narrative quests.

Hess's reconstructed narrative of "return" should be construed as a narrative of ambivalence. He is torn between a comprehensive vision of the good life and the unique Jewish love for family and nation. His private life is shielded from his own political critique, even as he softens distinctions between private and public values. Hess acknowledges that a moment of chance encounter has converted him to Jewish nationalism, though he soon denies blind fate a role in his personal fortune. In *Rome and Jerusalem,* Hess is a modern Jew struggling to accommodate various impulses and concerns as he "returns" to his people. He continually negotiates among strong oppositions and struggles to unite competing visions of identity.

I have argued that *Rome and Jerusalem* can help us to see why modern identity cannot be fully expressive within a story as narrative quest. The force of this claim relies upon the human capacity to imagine Hess's predicament as one's own. I take the central question to be phenomenological: has *Rome and Jerusalem* opened one aspect of human experience that is recognizable to some human beings? Or to put the question more personally, can I imagine the complexity of emotions and commitments that confront Hess, and the strategies he employs to unify often diverse values, as a possible experience for me? Is this, as William James would ask, a live option for me or for another recognizable human being? If we answer affirmatively, then we should ask whether there are accounts of identity that obscure this aspect of human experience. Are there ways in which we talk about human experience that obscure or deny a central place for epiphanic moments of conversion and new values, or that transform a live possibility into a dead option? I have suggested that narratives constructed as quests tend to hide complex experiences behind more coherent and "logical" stories. We need to find other stories that uncover and preserve chance encounters and indecision as counterpressures to narratives as quest. Recovering the tensions in *Rome and Jerusalem* is but one aspect of this project. Moral conflicts, as Taylor suggests, do indeed rage within modern persons. But so too does the urge to "greater lucidity" that reconciles these tensions. Narratives that allow moral conflicts to stand unresolved can be as revelatory for persons like Hess, as they should be for other modern Jews.

Inescapable Frameworks: Emotions, Race, and the Rhetoric of Jewish Identity

4

Most Hess scholars contend that Hess's appeal to emotional attachments in *Rome and Jerusalem* is more befitting to a personal confession than to a sophisticated philosophical argument.[1] Indeed, these scholars apologize for his "unsystematic" thinking or philosophical immaturity. They cite Hess's apparent random ordering of topics, the curious division of *Rome and Jerusalem* into letters, notes, and epilogue, and the constant barrage of personal stories and emotional appeals. Isaiah Berlin's appraisal is typical: "The language of *Rome and Jerusalem,* after a hundred years, seems antiquated. The style is by turns sentimental, rhetorical and at times merely flat; there are a good many digressions and references to issues now totally forgotten. And yet it is a masterpiece."[2] In Berlin's account, *Rome and Jerusalem* is extraordinary *despite* its sentimental and often rhetorical style. Most scholars would agree with Edmund Silberner's description that "Hess did not have the gift to explain his thoughts in a clear and organized fashion, and none of his works is as little systematically laid out as this one."[3]

I want to argue that Hess's unsystematic philosophical wandering instead reveals a sophisticated rhetorical strategy that recognizes emotional responses as clues to Jewish religious and national commitments. Not system, but evocative emotional language draws the reader into the text so that one reads Jewish identity out of the text. We have already witnessed this rhetorical play in the previous chapter, where Hess cites an emotional encounter that exposes strong attachments to Jewish nationalism. Hess believes that evocative language uncovers veiled commitments that in part define who we are and where we stand. He awakens in the reader, by means of his own personal "confessions," strong emotions that bring equally "natural" commitments to the fore. The form or style of story-telling is therefore integral to Hess's philosophical project.[4] Rediscovering passionate attachments to Jewish history and tradition can help to reinvigorate and reinforce Jewish identity. Through Hess's emotional style, the reader discovers that Jewish identity is expressed through strong commitments informed by emotions.

The expressive language in *Rome and Jerusalem* evokes one particular Jewish commitment: racial belonging. In Hess's racial theory, emotions uncover the reliable, enduring attachment to the Jewish *Volk*. Jewish identity is rooted in a racial narrative that remains impervious to reflective critique and historical progress. Hess argues that racial belonging is a "natural feeling," and the Jew who denies this racial bond is a "traitor to his people, his race, and to his family." Jews maintain specific intellectual, physical, and emotional characteristics that neither they nor other races can deny. Hess's emotional language evokes in the Jewish reader an undeniable commitment to the Jewish people.

Race informs values and commitments. It is what Taylor would call an inescapable framework.[5] A framework is that in virtue of which one recognizes important moral and religious goods that in part constitute identity. It is the background an agent draws upon to make sense of her life. Conceptions of self, ideals of autonomy and dignity, nationality, and gender are all frameworks within which modern persons deliberate about ethical goods and religious values. There are often intractable disagreements in ethics and religion because persons reason within competing frameworks. So a framework is deemed "inescapable" if without it one could not recognize oneself, or reflect about what is most valuable in a life. Inescapable frameworks are transcendental conditions for human agency, for one could not act, feel, or deliberate without them. Hess argues that race is one such inescapable framework that fashions Jewish identity. As a distinctive and original type with unchanging and uniform bodily features, the Jewish race expresses an ethical and religious commitment to social progress. These features are those in virtue of which modern Jews recognize important ethical, political, and religious goods that inescapably determine identity.

My concern with Hess's racial theory is not to dismiss race as one inescapable framework (although there are good reasons to do so). Instead, I want to explore how Hess constructs Jewish identity when one aspect of human experience (race) becomes an inescapable framework for constructing identity. Taylor claims that identity would be integrally damaged without a framework within which to deliberate about the good life. Hess is concerned about the integrity and coherency of personal identity, and so appeals to race as an inescapable framework to impede the disintegrating forces of modernity. His evocative language is a rhetorical strategy designed to soften the fragmented culture of modern life, and to fashion a more secure and stable Jewish identity.

Evocative Language in *Rome and Jerusalem*

Hess appeals to personal commitments, motivations, and family ties throughout the twelve letters in *Rome and Jerusalem*. His language is provocative, impulsive, rarely precise but always expressive. The structure of a personal correspondence fits well Hess's literary style, for it allows him to integrate engaging form with passionate content. Edmund Silberner has argued that Hess drafts each letter to Josephine Hirsch, whose sister Emilie married Hess's brother Samuel. But the reader would not recognize this from the text. Each letter directly addresses a question or issue that Hess imagines Hirsch, at that moment, to be pondering, but the question moves beyond her to address the public reader as well. Hess shows remarkable consistency in this regard. Following his own confessional response in the first letter, Hess begins his second letter with yet another disclosure: "Pain, like joy, is infectious [*ansteckend*]. You, my friend, have infected me [*angesteckt*] with your thoughts on death and immortality." The third letter again addresses the reader, "You wonder why the Old Testament teaches nothing about the modern belief in immortality." In the fourth letter, Hess introduces his racial theory and boasts:

"You see, my esteemed friend, that it does not help Jews to deny their heritage through baptism or marriage to the Indo-Germanic or Mongolian races. The Jewish type cannot be eradicated. It is, indeed, unmistakable." Note the tone in the fifth letter: "You ask whether I seriously believe in the redemption from exile?" The style and evocative prose continues throughout, culminating in the twelfth and last letter: "The French pamphlet from which I quoted some excerpts[6] appears to have awakened in you new thoughts."[7] Each letter draws the reader, and not only Hirsch, into Hess's own personal analysis of Jewish identity, and opens a dialogue between the reader's expectations and Hess's response.[8]

Rome and Jerusalem is an intimate personal dialogue between Hess and his readers. Hess repeatedly questions, invokes, and responds to the "you" in discourse, and one need not be Josephine Hirsch to recognize his appeal. If, as Yosef Yerushalmi and Arnold Eisen rightly argue, those alienated from the past require evocation as well as explanation,[9] then Hess's text can be read as an evocative challenge to German Jews estranged from the Jewish national tradition. Each letter is crafted to appeal to sensitive and persistent German-Jewish dilemmas, which include community and tradition (first letter), historical research (seventh), personal autonomy (tenth), and Jewish ritual (eleventh). Hess's lengthy discussions on such general topics as Greek and Israelite society, Christ and Spinoza, and racial conflict are all consigned to the Epilogue at the end of the work. Yet even these more obscure discussions help to clarify controversial claims in the text (as we shall see in Hess's defense of Spinoza). The structure of *Rome and Jerusalem* suggests a constructive technique of persuasion: begin with evocative language in dialogue to move the reader into more sustained conceptual discourse that informs those expressive claims. Only after appealing to his and the reader's own sense of familial obligation, for example, will Hess then turn to racial theory to support the "natural feeling" of racial belonging. Expressive dialogue moves the reader to assent to the conceptual framework (race) that makes sense of familial attachments.

Hess's confession of childhood loss provides a model for the reader's responsive self-reflection. He quotes an extended passage from Pierre Mercier's introduction to Ludwig Wihl's *Westöstliche Schwalben*.[10] Mercier extols the virtue of maternal rather than sexual love. It is maternal love, says Mercier, "which in the Jewish novels is the basis of family life in its passion and mystery."[11] Hess immediately turns away from Mercier and challenges his readers to recall their personal encounter with maternal love: "When you read these words of Mercier, you will certainly think of your own mother." As if to offer an example, Hess revisits a painful experience of loss (his mother's death) and the one vivid memory of his youth:

> I lost her as a youth at the age of fourteen, but until most recently she appeared to me almost every night in my dreams. As if it were yesterday, I recall the words she spoke to me from her soul when she visited me in Bonn. I was just seven years old. We lay there in bed, and I had just finished the evening prayer, when in a stirring voice she said: "Listen, my child, you must study diligently. . . . It is said that wherever grandfather and grandson study Torah, the teaching of God will never leave the generations."[12]

Hess's most intense memory of maternal love spawns a wealth of associations: religious observance, Jewish continuity, family life, Torah study, and obligations to both past and future generations. Appearing before him "as if it were yesterday," this memory locates Hess within a constellation of values, commitments, emotions, and history. He associates Torah study with the love for his dead mother, the religious observance of his youth, and the obligations he feels toward his children and grandchildren. Although these are certainly nostalgic recollections and desires (Hess, for example, had no children), the emotional attachments expose deep personal bonds that express value and commitment. And so too for the reader, who is moved to reflect on childhood memories and family continuity. Hess's memory is not his alone, but a feature of dialogue in which his memory (it is hoped) resonates with the reader's personal reflections. The confessional prose is effective only if the reader responds to the emotional cadence. Hess's autobiographical piece is a model for turning toward the other in dialogue that represents also, at the same moment, a turning toward one's self.[13] This model for communicative reflection suggests that emotional responses reveal hidden commitments that cultivate identity.

Spinoza as Model for Passionate Philosophy

If emotions uncover strong attachments, then suppressed commitments are integrally related to the passions. Hess wants to argue that conceptual thinking is informed by emotional response. This is the point of his defense of Spinoza and his philosophy. Spinoza's intellectual love of God is not an abstract, other-worldly philosophy, but a deeply moving, engaging activity. His philosophy offers contemporary German Jews a model for how the emotions foster and are informed by conceptual thinking. Spinoza as passionate, engaged philosopher helps to illustrate the methodological point that evocative emotions reveal the ethical and religious frameworks that in turn make sense of emotional response.

Hess is a "Spinozist" because he sees in Spinoza a model for his own life and thought.[14] The subtitle to Hess's first work, *The Holy History*, is revealing: "*Von einem jünger Spinozas*" (by a disciple of Spinoza). Shlomo Avineri argues that "the reference to Spinoza is a symbolic challenge: at a time when radical German philosophers are beginning to call themselves 'Young Hegelians,' Hess' heralding of Spinoza becomes a clue to much of the message of his book." It is also a clue, says Avineri, to Hess's ambivalent relationship to Judaism and Christianity. Hess finds in Spinoza "his intellectual inspiration—a thinker who, while rejected by his own people, did not convert to Christianity."[15] Other scholars have noted that Hess consistently appeals to Spinoza's philosophy as a guide for his socialist politics.[16] From his earliest work in 1837 on through his *Rome and Jerusalem* in 1862, Hess appropriates Spinoza's philosophy, and recognizes in Spinoza another Jew struggling with the meaning of modern Jewish identity.

Spinoza should also be a model, according to Hess, for other modern European Jews. But the model itself changes with Hess's shifting account of Spinoza. In *The Holy History*, Hess divides world history into three periods: God the father, God the son, and the reign of the Holy Spirit. Adam was the prototype of the first period, Jesus of the second, and Spinoza of the third and final period. We should all become "pure human beings" [*reine Menschen*], in the image of Spinoza.[17] This Spinoza, however, is not the Spinoza of *Rome and Jerusalem*. Here, the "*reine Mensch*" becomes a passionate philosopher infused with the intellectual love of God.

To be sure, Hess's reading of Spinoza in *Rome and Jerusalem* is seriously flawed.[18] Indeed, we might wonder how Hess would interpret Spinoza's comparison of active, resourceful reason to passive, debilitating emotions:

> If men lived according to the guidance of reason, everyone would enjoy this right [to preserve what he loves and destroy what he hates] without injuring anyone else. But because men are subject to emotions which far surpass human power or virtue, they are often drawn in different directions, and are contrary to one another.

True virtue, argues Spinoza, "consists in living according to the guidance of reason alone."[19] But Hess need not defend Spinoza's interpretation of the emotions to underscore the emotional resources that philosophers must draw upon to engage actively in critical thinking. Spinoza—even if he fails to recognize the philosophical significance of emotions—still epitomizes passionate intellectual activity. This point is crucial if Hess is to reclaim emotions as meaningful indicators of strong attachments. If even the most disengaged, "rational" thinkers like Spinoza are motivated by passion, then the emotions might reveal passionate sources and the commitments they engender. Not Spinoza's philosophical account of the emotions, but his passionate engagement in philosophical thinking is the model for modern German Jews.

In a section of the Epilogue to *Rome and Jerusalem*, entitled "The Genetic View of the World," Hess criticizes the judgment of Italian Jewish scholar Samuel David Luzzatto (1800–1865) that Spinoza's work is emotionless (*Gemütlosigkeit*).[20] For Hess, analytical reason by itself fails to account for the creativity, imagination, and courage in Spinoza's philosophy. Only a "creative being of spirit" could discover philosophical truths, while "analytical reason" alone cannot reach such heights ("der analysierende Verstand für sich allein unfähig ist"). Luzzatto's criticism, for Hess, represents a serious misreading of Spinoza's philosophy, for he disregards the emotional and creative activity in Spinoza's critical thinking. Hess's dispute with Luzzatto does not concern Spinoza's evaluation of the emotions. It involves solely the character of Spinoza's philosophical enterprise. For Hess, Spinoza's philosophy "presupposes an *inspiration*" that infuses all of his "rational" philosophy.[21]

Luzzatto's criticism echoed a long tradition of German commentary on Spinoza, and so too Hess's defense. The publication of Jacobi's conversations with Lessing in *Über die Lehre Spinozas in Briefen an den Herrn Moses Mendelssohn* (1785) sparked a revival in both critical appraisal and condemnation of Spinoza's philosophy.[22] Friedrich Jacobi (1743–1819) poses a relentless pietistic critique of Enlightenment philosophy, directed especially at the Berlin *Aufklärung* and its

leader Mendelssohn. For Jacobi, Spinoza had provided the most rational philosophical system. If Spinozism led to atheism or pantheism, then it also revealed
the atheistic tendency in the systematic philosophy of the Enlightenment.[23] As
David Bell has argued, "Jacobi's interpretation of Spinoza must therefore ultimately be seen as part of his own philosophy of faith, implacably opposed to the
Aufklärung."[24] Spinozism and atheism became synonymous in the wake of Jacobi's
attack, and Luzzatto's criticism in part reflects this inherited critical stance.

But if Jacobi's attack on Spinoza reveals his own "philosophy of faith," then
Hess's defense of Spinoza similarly discloses Hess's assumptions about emotional
attachments. To better understand Hess's dispute with Luzzatto, we need to appreciate the context of Spinoza's reception in Germany, both in terms of Jacobi's *Pan-
theismusstreit* with Mendelssohn, and its effect on later philosophical and religious
discourse.[25]

Moses Mendelssohn (1729–1786) attempted to shore up Spinoza's reputation
in the wake of Christian Wolff's influential critique of Spinozism as atheism.
Wolff (1679–1754), Mendelssohn's teacher of philosophy and a noted Christian
theologian, had argued persuasively that Spinozism dismissed religion altogether.
Spinoza found God not through religious worship or conviction but through universal causal laws. His system banished freedom of will and Providence altogether
from serious philosophical thinking. In Wolff's critique, Spinozism and atheism
amount to the same thing.[26] Jacobi's critical account of Spinoza's closed philosophical system has its roots in Wolff's critique. Mendelssohn thus faced an entrenched
philosophical disdain for Spinoza when he defended him in his *Philosophical Dia-
logues* (1755). He argued that Spinoza's philosophy would be more acceptable "if
applied to the world as it existed solely in God's mind prior to its becoming real by
his decree." Mendelssohn reminded his readers of Leibnitz's claim that the world
had a two-fold existence: the first in the divine intellect as one possible world
among others, and, then, as the best real world. In Spinoza's picture of the universe,
God never created the real world, and all things remain only in God's mind. Mendelssohn calls this "purified Spinozism," and believes it freed Spinoza from the
Schimpfwort (a term of abuse) of atheism. According to Alexander Altmann, Mendelssohn had discovered in Spinoza a Jewish philosopher, like himself, raised "in
the tradition of medieval Jewish philosophy."[27] Moses Hess, too, found in Spinoza
a Jewish philosopher sorely misunderstood by the German philosophical tradition.
He would follow Mendelssohn by reclaiming not only Spinoza's philosophical sophistication, but also his Jewish heritage.

Others found in Spinoza a champion for the German Enlightenment critique
against superstition. Spinoza was seen as a great fighter for freedom of thought and
feeling over blind belief in authority, and a forerunner for those combating scholas-
ticism and orthodoxy.[28] For both Herder and Goethe, Spinoza was more than an
enlightened critic of religious orthodoxy. He was also a deeply spiritual philosopher who infused nature with divinity and power.[29] The members of the *Sturm und
Drang* movement discussed Spinoza's philosophy often, and in a letter to Jacobi on
January 12, 1785, Goethe sided with Herder's panentheist interpretation of Spi-

noza that God is not only in the world, but the world is also in God.[30] Goethe's Spinoza divinized nature, making it holy and alive. This panentheistic account would have an increasingly powerful affect on early nineteenth-century German philosophy.

This was also true of Hegel's understanding of Spinoza's divine Substance as a rigid, ahistorical, and abstract concept.[31] By the time Hegel composed his *Phenomenology*, his appreciation and critique of Spinoza's philosophy had crystallized:

> Everything turns on grasping and expressing the True, not only as *Substance*, but equally as *Subject*. . . . Further, the living Substance is being which is in truth *Subject*, or, what is the same, is in truth actual [*wirklich*] only in so far as it is the movement of positing itself, or is the mediation of its self-othering with itself.[32]

Spinoza's concept of substance lacked the movement, the conflict, the self-positing and self-othering of Spirit, or what Hegel called "the seriousness, the suffering, the patience, and the labor of the negative."[33] It was an abstract theoretical entity that never achieved full articulation or reality because it remained external to historical progress. Spinoza failed to understand the Christian Trinitarian position that substance is "only one moment in the determination of God as spirit."[34] Yet Spinoza's philosophy, as Hegel understood it, was a necessary precursor to Hegel's own more *wirklich* conception of Spirit as a historical, differentiated, and finally unified Subject.

We can now see how Luzzatto's criticism against Spinoza's "rationalism" falls within a well-articulated and lengthy debate. Luzzatto, like Jacobi before him, believes that passionate sources underlie all religious encounters with God. An emotionless (*Gemütlosigkeit*) philosophy, without the sensual and historical reality that Hegel and Feuerbach demand, can too easily slide into an abstract and atheistic account of nature and human religious activity. Luzzatto would therefore be sympathetic to Wolff and Jacobi's censure of Spinozism as atheism. He does not believe that Spinoza is the "God-intoxicated man" that Novalis and Hess take him to be.

Hess's quarrel with Luzzatto draws much from Herder and Goethe's panentheism that infuses nature and human activity with divine passion. Clearly, Hess's "Spinozism" is an inherited one with rich historical significance. But Hess's inquiry into the emotional basis for spiritual insight moves one step further. He claims that God's law, which is not in heaven nor in far distant places but instead "in our spirit and heart," is central to Jewish tradition, and "a similar expression occurs in the Talmud: the *Shekinah* has never descended to earth, nor has Moses ever ascended to heaven."[35] Like Herder and Goethe's notion of divinity, God's revelation is found *in* the world as a dynamic power, as an immanent, ever-present reality, and God's immediacy sustains religious worship and reflection:

> A distant God [*ein jenseitiger Gott*], who does not act as an immediate ever present creator and revealer, is neither the God of the Jews nor the Christian or Muslim God. . . . An external Godhead [*eine außerweltliche Gottheit*], of whom we can know nothing, is like a godless world, a fruit of reflective reason without influence on our social and ethical-spiritual life.[36]

Spinoza's God is not Jacobi's transcendent being without reality, nor Hegel's Substance without actuality. It is not the God of the philosophers, who conceive a removed, abstract, and empty Godhead. Luzzatto simply places Spinoza in the wrong philosophical tradition. Spinoza's God infuses the world, envelops it, and is at one with it: God is ever-present, and is the one who creates, reveals, and enlivens social and spiritual activity. Reflective reason alone would create, indeed worship, an empty Godhead. But Spinoza appeals to deeper sources. In Hess's account, Spinoza is motivated by a profound spiritual inspiration that searches for an immanent, accessible, and recognizable God.

Hess's defense of Spinoza is central to his more general claim that we are all moved by emotional sources that inspire. To call Spinoza a rational philosopher without emotional warmth is simply to misunderstand the nature of serious intellectual engagement. Intellectual pursuits are either infused with emotional depth, or, like an external Godhead, are the fruit of reflective reason without influence. Hess's Spinoza combines intellectual rigor with passionate struggle. Spinoza's seemingly analytic rational analysis is moved by strong emotional commitments that inspire his philosophical work.

Much like Mendelssohn before him, Hess reclaims Spinoza as a "Jewish philosopher" who unites philosophical integrity with a passionate commitment to Jewish nationalism:

> Spinoza conceives Judaism as nationalism and thinks (see the conclusion to the third chapter of his theological Tractatus) the restoration of the Jewish kingdom depends only on the courage of the Jewish people. Just as Christian dualism has been overcome theoretically by Spinoza, so too in life the ancient Jewish people work practically against the disease of dualism through its healthy, ideal family life.[37]

Hess's first two books, *The Holy History of Mankind* (1837) and *The European Triarchy* (1841), are riddled with quotes from Spinoza's *Ethics*. But Hess turns here to the *Tractatus* to link Spinoza's philosophy with Jewish nationalism.[38] To be sure, Hess misunderstands Spinoza's critique of Judaism. He mistakenly believes that the *Tractatus* expresses Spinoza's love for the Jewish people rather than, as most scholars contend, barely veiled disgust with Jewish particularity and religious observance. Despite Hess's questionable reading, in *Rome and Jerusalem* Spinoza is the model national Jew who, despite his solitary existence, is inspired by his love for family. Hess's account of Spinoza in the Epilogue reinforces the image of maternal love and Hess's own memories of childhood in the letters. With Spinoza as their model, modern European Jews can courageously face their emotional ties to family, and the national commitments they help to foster.

In the end, both Luzzatto and Hess can agree that emotions inspire religious and intellectual pursuits. They disagree, however, on whether Spinoza is an appropriate model for modern Jews. Hess defends both the passionate sources of Spinoza's philosophy, showing how his God-language draws from deep emotional attachments, and Spinoza himself, who inspires through creativity and passion.

Spinoza thus mirrors Hess's model for the German Jew whose rational assent to Jewish nationalism is informed by emotional familial ties. Though Hess distorts both Spinoza's philosophy of emotions in the *Ethics* and the critique of Judaism in the *Tractatus,* he certainly imagines Spinoza as a Jewish intellectual with emotional warmth. With Hess's Spinoza as their authority, European Jews can affirm their own passionate commitments without fear of intellectual shabbiness. In Spinoza, modern Jews can find a Jew committed, in Hess's language, to "spiritual struggles within its own [Jewish] house and with the cultured societies."

As Luzzatto is blinded to Spinoza's deeper inspirational gift, so too modern German Jews recoil from emotional response, and thus further conceal the sources of Jewish identity. We have seen that for Hess, familial love and its rich associations —historical continuity, education, religious worship, and genealogy—empower, ground, and inspire intellectual endeavors. His evocative prose stimulates reflective meditations on Jewish identity and tradition. Insensitivity to emotions and their expressions of value, however, conceal features of modern Jewish identity. Indifference to the sources of identity is a philosophical problem for Hess because it covers over the emotional triggers that disclose religious and national commitments. Apathy can too easily lead to the worship of an "external Godhead," an over-valuation of analytic reasoning, and inattentiveness to inspiration and spiritual insight. A godless world, to Hess, leads to a shallow conception of Jewish identity. One not only loses an immanent God, but also sacrifices important emotional attachments. Indifference to emotions, then, leads to a loss of authentic identity.

The use of passionate prose in *Rome and Jerusalem* is a sophisticated rhetorical strategy through which Hess moves and inspires his readers. Hess's deeply personal account is intimately tied to the underlying philosophical point: emotions are clues to deep commitments that express value. The reader recognizes this claim throughout the work. In the second letter, Hess movingly describes his visit to his parents' grave site. This impassioned story leads to a meditation on the meaning of death and the influences from the past, and leads Hess to reflect upon continuity and discontinuity in modern Jewish life. In the fourth letter, Hess weaves together his critique of German education (*Bildung*) with yet another family story of his grandfather. Here, Hess portrays a significant though problematic contrast between Jewish tradition and the goods of European culture. In these and other texts already discussed, style and emotive language express what is most valuable to Hess. Through his emotional and confessional style, Hess encourages and invites his readers to follow his example. As Spinoza is a model for Hess, so too Hess becomes a model for his readers. Hess challenges his readers to respond in reflective dialogue.

> The question you put to me, and, I confess, a question that is one of the greatest and most difficult problems for nineteenth-century Judaism, shows me that you are becoming interested in Judaism.[39]

Those questions, and Hess's responses, constitute a mutual dialogue that, Hess hopes, moves the reader into sustained interest in Jewish tradition.

Hess's challenge is direct and personal, and expresses, in the very form of letter writing, the many values and commitments of modern Jewry. In *Rome and Jerusalem,* form and style are not neutral. Style, argues Martha Nussbaum,

> itself makes claims, expresses its own sense of what matters. Literary form is not separable from philosophical content, but is, itself, a part of content—an integral part, then, of the search for and the statement of truth.[40]

Hess's sentimental prose expresses multiple commitments to family, tradition, text, and nation.[41] The very style of emotional story telling is intimately connected to the content of his message. Good philosophy, according to some scholars, requires a detached survey of value and truth. But such philosophy, Hess would argue, denies ethical and religious value to emotive responses. For Hess weaves together insightful analysis of Jewish identity with personal reflection, drawing philosophy back into the realm of particulars to discover his own "spiritual struggles," and perhaps the reader's as well. Hess's style and structure of argument reveal an account of Jewish identity attuned to the axiological character of emotions and the role they play in forming intellectual pursuits. The emotions, however, reveal one value that binds family and nation ever tighter: the value of racial belonging.

Hess's Racial Theory

We have seen how Hess's personal reflections underscore the philosophical point that emotions carry meaning. Here as elsewhere, form and content work together in Hess's philosophical analysis. But the memories of family commitment, and the national attachments they foster, serve an important rhetorical function: they encourage a reappraisal of modern Jewish identity as racial belonging. Hess's emotional prose moves his readers to concede that race unavoidably structures and informs modern commitments. Hess's racial theory, based on his scientific research of the 1850s, is an attempt to offer scientific justification for Jewish national solidarity. Part of this argument is a defense of the Jewish love for family. If, as science tells us, the Jewish "type" is indestructible, then emotional love for the Jewish *Volk* is but a "natural feeling" in response to an established scientific fact: Jews are a separate and distinctive race that maintains ineradicable physical, psychological, intellectual, and emotional traits. In Hess's racial theory, emotional ties reflect the primal, irreducible connection to race. Identity, in this picture, is rooted in the emotional attachment to racial belonging.

Hess justifies familial love with racial, scientific evidence.[42] Yet scholars, as they did emotions, too easily dismiss Hess's analysis of race. Hess is most often blamed for confounding "race" with "nation," interchanging one term for the other and thereby creating unnecessary confusion. Assuming the word *nation* is far less problematic, these scholars replace *nation* for all cases of *race*, thus diffusing the racial issue.[43] Felix Weltsch worries that Hess's use of the term *race* would be misconstrued in the post-Nazi era. He prefers the term *calling* as a more adequate rendering of race.[44] The English, French, Germans, Americans, and Jews all have a specific and special "calling" that affords a "natural foundation for specific cultural manifestations." One scholar jettisons Hess's racial theory altogether:

> The limited knowledge of anthropology of his day led Hess to believe in the existence of a pure Jewish race; but these errors are more than balanced by his remarkable insight into the nature of religion, particularly Jewish religion.[45]

Even Jonathan Frankel dismisses Hess's "ethnographical research" concerning Jewish "unmixed blood" as merely "unconvincing."[46] But Hess describes Jewish patriotism, the love of the Jewish people, as a "true, natural feeling," and locates racial integrity in the original and fundamental simplicity (*Einfachheit*) of the emotions.[47] Yet not one of these scholars recognizes the importance of Hess's racial theory for his account of modern Jewish identity.

Hess's defense of the polygenetic view of race is central to his racial theory of identity.[48] First advanced by Paracelsus in 1520, polygenists insisted that originally there were a plurality of races. While the number and type of races differed among various scientific theories, the polygenists all maintained a distinctly non-orthodox creationist picture. The orthodox position defended the biblical account of one original race (monogenesis), and held that all racial divisions were mere variations of this original type. While acknowledging the diversity of various peoples, monogenists accounted for this diversity in terms of climate, nutrition, and prevailing ways of life. Race for the monogenists was a "degenerative" modification of a migrating species, a "modification that was accidental and reversible under the influence of more favorable geographical or human surroundings."[49] Polygenists, many of them reacting to the religious orthodoxy underpinning the monogenetic theory, argued that environment alone could not account for such diversity, and offered an alternative, more pluralistic account of human development.

Hess adopts this pluralistic account to argue that Jews maintained specific hereditary features from one original race. There were, in the beginning, distinct racial "types," and modern *Völker*, of which the Jews were one of the more conspicuous, inherited cultural and racial traits:

> Social life is, first of all, a product of specific races [*Menschenrassen*] as original and distinctive tribal races [*Volksstämme*], which adapt to life in their own particular fashion.

> History confirms what we already know through anthropology, that there are original and distinctive races [*Menschenrassen*] and tribal races [*Volksstämme*].[50]

Under the subheading *Race and Folk Types*, Hess integrates his polygenetic racial view within his theory of nature:

> As nature does not produce flowers and fruits, nor animals or plants in general, but rather types of plants and animals, so too the creator produces only folk types [*Volkstypen*] in history.[51]

The monogenetic ideal of a "fusion of traditions," which assumed an original race that fractured but would someday be re-united, was bad history and bad science.

For Hess, the social/human life sphere began as a primal deviation among folk types that were soon absorbed into one unified race. But in the end, each folk type would live one for the other in solidarity without sacrificing particularity. Hess seeks to preserve the special qualities of *Volkstypen* (expressed in culture, language, and history) without dissolving their uniqueness. Jews as a modern *Volk* should not seek uniformity, but should instead develop their natural peculiarities, even as they work toward the flourishing of different ethnic communities as "noble rivals and true allies."[52]

Hess contrasts four primal races and their corresponding geographical locations: Egyptian (Northern Africa), Negro (Africa), Indo-Germanic (Europe), and Semitic (Europe and Western Asia). Of these four original races, Hess discusses only the Indo-Germanic and the Semitic people, "out of which our civilization emerged." The Hellenes are the classical expression of the Indo-Germanic race, just as the Israelites are the purest example of the Semites. Hess apparently believes that all European culture and ethnic variety can be traced to one of these two original racial types. But he offers no account of this progression, nor does he explain how only these original races (and not modern ethnic groups) can reproduce with "integrity."[53] His primary concern is to establish the Israelites as an original and distinctive *Menschenrasse* in marked contrast to the other original type, the Indo-Germanic race.[54]

Of the two most significant original races, only the Israelites, with their grounded historical consciousness and ethical-religious spirit, recognize the divine plan that guides human activity toward a more perfected messianic age. The Israelites are thus contrasted favorably to the other primal type, the Hellenes, who lack their historical sensitivity and "genius." In his *Dynamische Stofflehre* (1875), Hess maps out the distinguishing characteristics of Jewish and Hellenistic society: the Israelites possess a "subjective, practical interest," while Greek concerns are "objective," passionless, and "theoretical"; the Jewish God rules and judges the social human sphere that continually develops, but Jupiter and Olympus govern the already perfected cosmic and organic life spheres; the God of the Hebrew Bible works for "das Rechte der Menschen und Völker," but the Greek gods are concerned with power and beauty; the Israelites make the world holy and ethical, while the Greeks explain and beautify.[55] Where Greek culture is a world of "being," a society complete in its harmonious perfection, the Israelite society is always "becoming," tainted by social inequality and imperfection. Not convinced that beauty and perfection are complete, the Israelites demand renewed worldly engagement that still awaits, even as it prepares for the messianic age. Modern Jews, the descendants of the ancient Israelite race, are identified by their passionate struggle for social equality and worldly redemption.[56]

Hess shares much with Heine, who compared Greek and Jewish society in his poetic masterpiece, *Atta Troll: Ein Sommernachtstraum* (1843).[57] The midsummer's night dream (an obvious reference to Shakespeare) is the story of a dancing bear (Atta Troll), an old German fable not of Heine's invention.[58] At the heart of this dream is the "Wild Hunt," which one Heine biographer claims "is an allegorized vision of the sources of Heine's imagination."[59] The dream explores the appeal of three characters and the traditions they represent: Abunde (Romanticism), Diana (Greek classicism), and Herodias (Judaism). Heine describes Diana's features as "white as marble, and as marble cold." She appears rigid and pale, almost numb. Herodias, in contrast, is a succulent beauty, ravishing to the eyes with soft lips like pomegranates. Yet Herodias lies dead and buried in Jerusalem, sleeping in a *Marmorsarge* (a marble coffin). Even in death, the poet loves Herodias more than Diana—"Lieb' ich dich, du todte Jüdinn!"[60] (I love you, you dead Jewess). For Heine, the Greeks represent the "marble coffin" of a cold and abstract self. Yet Heine's Herodias is buried in marble stone, crushed by the onslaught, it seems, of Greek civilization. As a *todte Jüdinn*, Herodias is superseded, however cruelly, by a numb Greek goddess. Herodias's erotic appeals, her expressive gaze and moist lips, are shackled and repressed by the Greek *Marmorsarge*. Even Hess in his *Triarchy*, written perhaps at the same time as Heine's *Atta Troll*,[61] describes the Jews as soulless mummies who wander the world like ghosts "who cannot die, yet cannot be resurrected."[62]

But in *Rome and Jerusalem*, Hess reverses the fortunes of Jewish and Greek culture. No longer stagnated and overcome by Greek conceptions of beauty and self-perfection, Judaism flourishes in its practical, this-worldly appeal, and in its messianic gaze to a perfected future. Hess appropriates Heine's depiction of Greek society, but challenges his critique of a dead, superseded Judaism. Greek society is dispassionate, cold, and perfect in its stoic composure, but Hebrew society suffers toward perfection, dedicated to "genuine human beings." Herodias's erotic appeal has become, in Hess's redescription, ethical and religious commitment rooted in the passions. Where Heine accepts the Christian critique of a superseded Judaism, Hess instead describes a historical, alive, and flourishing Judaism. This critical reversal is therefore part of Hess's wider critique of Christian supercessionism.[63]

It is also a crucial part of his racial account of Jewish identity. Hess's comparison between Greeks and Israelites highlights those features most characteristic of the Jewish race: messianic hope, passionate ethical/religious commitment to social reform, and historical sensitivity. Jews recognize themselves as Jews by discerning these special attributes as part of their own, racial heritage. The distinctive Jewish characteristics are abiding features, immune to historical and cultural change. So Jewish identity can be at home in the modern world only when that world bends to Jewish aspirations. Indeed, Hess argues that with the awakening of nationalist movements, the modern world itself is becoming more Jewish.

Against the backdrop of German reflection upon ancient Greece, Hess's comparative analysis of Greek and Jewish culture acquires an even greater depth. The story of eighteenth- and nineteenth-century German views of Greek society begins with the art historian Johann Joachim Winckelmann (1717–1768).[64] Winckelmann considers *Laocoon*, the statue of a father and two sons entangled by serpents just before their death, to be the ideal of Greek beauty: "noble serenity and serene greatness in the pose as well as in the expression," and the "greatness and composure of soul in the throes of whatever passion."[65] Greek beauty represents simplicity, serenity and greatness, and Germans would do well to imitate this aesthetic ideal of composure in the face of death.

Almost immediately, his *Imitation of Greek Works* sparked renewed interest in Greek art. Only a year after its publication, Moses Mendelssohn introduced Lessing (1729–1781) to Winckelmann's essay. In 1766, Lessing published *Laocoon, or the Boundaries between Painting and Poetry*, as a direct response to Winckelmann's study. Though Lessing never visited the Vatican which housed the model of Laocoon that Winckelmann admired,[66] he is less concerned with the work itself, and more interested in the limits of artistic expression. He accepts Winckelmann's rendering of Greek painting and sculpture as a sign of "noble simplicity and quiet grandeur, both of attitude and expression." But Laocoon has not attained "the true pathos of suffering" that we would expect of a Greek hero.[67] Lessing distinguishes this sterile, almost stoic depiction from Homer's poetic style:

> High as Homer exalts his heroes in other respects above human nature, they yet remain true to it in their sensitiveness to pain and injuries and in the expression of their feelings by cries or tears or revilings. Judged by their deeds they are creatures of a higher order; in their feelings they are genuine human beings.[68]

Lessing contrasts Homer's emotional characters who "expressed their pain and their grief," to those modern Germans who have lost this sense of the heroic. The poet, rather than the artist, can depict a more expressive and complex nobility. The sculptor dedicates his art to beauty, but passion often disfigures, and "throws the whole body into such unnatural positions as to destroy all the beautiful lines that mark it when in a state of greater repose." Pain, passion, and movement are not compatible with beauty:

> The painter could give the chin the most graceful curve and the prettiest dimple . . . he could give the neck the softest pink, but that is all. The motion of that beautiful neck, the play of the muscles, now deepening and now half concealing the dimple, the essential charm exceeded his powers.[69]

Complexity of character and emotion is left to the poet. Only a Homer can reveal the cries of passion that truly express the noble Greek character.

For both Winckelmann and Lessing, the Greeks represented their most cherished ideals: stability, composure, and security for Winckelmann; and passion, expression, and emotional complexity for Lessing. These distinctions were still prevalent in the nineteenth century.[70] Heine compares Goethe's works to the cold, marble statues of Greek art that Lessing found so wanting of emotional warmth:

> Strange to say these ancient statues reminded me of Goethe's works, which are just as perfect, just as glorious, just as serene, and which also appear to feel with sadness that their rigidity and coldness separate them from our present warm and stirring life, that they cannot suffer and rejoice with us, that they are not human beings, but unhappy hybrids of godhead and stone.[71]

To critics of culture and literature, Germany faired poorly in relation to Greek society.[72] Winckelmann and Lessing had set the terms of the debate: cold, dispassionate self-sufficiency, or warm, emotional resonance.

If Winckelmann and Lessing appeal to their Greek ideal, Hess thinks modern Jews should look no farther than their own *Volk,* who reflect the physical, emotional, and intellectual traits of a vibrant, Israelite cultural tradition. Hess counters the dominant German critique of a cold, barren and superseded Judaism through his racial theory. Not Jews, but Greeks express those qualities that Lessing finds so spiritually shallow. And Hess can do this because Winckelmann and Lessing have already done his work for him. He simply appropriates their critical language in order to defend the vitality of the Jewish race in the modern world.

The polygenetic theory, and the favorable comparison of Israelites to Greeks, serve Hess's Jewish national agenda well. Races are distinctive historical groups with singular physical, emotional, and intellectual properties. Hess believes he discovers a "divine plan" at work underlying the pure development of racial types:

> Race remains the root of the social life sphere just as cosmic bodies are the root of the organic life sphere. All races and folk types which we know through either historical monuments or, for those still living today, through their original homeland or foreign country, despite all climatic and cultural influences, have reproduced themselves in their integrity [*Integrität*], such that the expert can distinguish, at a glance, their physiological and psychological characteristics.[73]

Race refers to the building blocks, the cosmic bodies that underlie social and cultural distinctions. As a "type" (a distinctive racial group), it is not equated with these features, but rather accounts for and sustains their "integrity." Adam and Eve are not the parents of all racial types, but only the progenitors of the Jewish race. Biblical history is therefore Jewish history, and the special "physiological and psychological characteristics" of biblical personalities are now securely adopted by modern Jews. By effectively blocking Christian supercessionism through the polygenetic theory, Hess can usurp the biblical tradition as his own, racial heritage. He can also justify his program for Jewish national renewal by asserting that the Jews, among other races, are an "original distinctive folk group." With their own tradition, history, culture, and intellectual dispositions, Jews should develop "their own direction of life," while other racial types, as "faithful allies," should offer their support.

Within the scientific community, there was strong agreement that the Jews were a special and distinctive race. Christian theologians and politicians (Bruno Bauer was undoubtedly the most famous)[74] advanced arguments similar to Hess's. Although disagreements surfaced concerning the singular characteristics of the Jewish race, Hess could still draw upon the scientific consensus that Jews remained a separate and peculiar people.[75] The French military physician Julien-Joseph Virey (1775–1846) who, despite his monogenetic account, was widely read by polygenists, claimed in 1824 that while "races were no more than fluctuating modifications of a single primordial species" (his words reflect the monogenetic thesis), the Jews "maintained their physiognomy all over the world."[76] For William Edwards (1776/77–1842), the father of French ethnology, the supposed historical "integrity" of the Jews supported his thesis that races "unfailingly retained their fundamental characteristics and behaviors." The Jewish "national countenance" prevailed in all climates, and one can see in Da Vinci's *The Last Supper* that Jews were painted "feature for feature." Edwards believed that Jews pictured in an Egyptian tomb exhibited in London showed a "striking" resemblance to the Jews living in London in his day (1829).[77] Johann Friedrich Blumenbach (1752–1840), the founder of modern German anthropology, argued that, "the nation of the Jews, who, under every climate, remain the same as far as the fundamental configuration of face goes, were remarkable for a racial character almost universal." Karl Asmund Rudolphi (1771–1832), an anthropologist from Berlin, claimed that climate altered every race except gypsies and Jews.[78] And Richard Andree, in his *Zur Volkskunde der Juden* (1881), summed up his scientific account of the Jewish race in this way:

> No other racial type displays such a constancy of form, withstanding the influences of time and environment as does this one. They have overcome proportionately strong admixtures of foreign blood, and . . . no new type, no new amalgamation has taken place.[79]

With this scientific consensus behind him, Hess utilized the fruits of scientific studies to argue that the Jews are one of only a few primary races with *Integrität*. Zlocisti, Hess's first biographer, claims that Hess's racial theory remained central to his Zionist program. His *Judenheit* and Zionism developed out of an analysis of history, race, and nationality.[80] For Hess, race science offers a pragmatic and authoritative (because scientific) defense for progressive Jewish politics.

Hess's scientific writings in the 1850s, and his racial theory in *Rome and Jerusalem*, should be understood as part of the radical reaction to the failure of liberal politics in the 1840s.[81] Kurt Bayertz, in his article on the reception of natural sciences within the German socialist movement, argues that Hess was not alone in his turn to the natural sciences. The synthesis of natural scientific theory with socialist economic praxis produced a compelling ideology for the socialist labor movement. Socialists like Hess regarded the natural sciences as an essential "motive power of social development." Already the early socialists in France (especially the Saint-Simonians) claimed that changes in political and social life were linked directly to science and technology.[82] The German socialists, as well, easily manipulated the scientific critique of religion and metaphysics to further their own radical agenda. The scientific method thus became an "ideological weapon for the penetration of the political and social goals into the labor movement." If, as Bayertz contends, the social movement required an ideology, then the natural sciences provided one for Hess, Marx, Engels, and Kautsky. In the hands of the social revolutionaries, natural sciences authorized and legitimated political radicalism in nineteenth-century Germany.[83]

Similarly, natural sciences assumed a distinctive conception of self. The German scientist Hermann von Helmholtz's lectures on science in the 1850s and '60s provide an instructive example. In his paper, "The Relation of Natural Science to Science in General" (1862),[84] Helmholtz distinguishes between natural and "moral sciences" (he uses the term *Geisteswissenschaften*—a general field that includes ethics, theology, philology, history, and jurisprudence). While natural sciences (*Naturwissenschaften*) rest on "sharply-defined general rules and principles [*Regeln und Gesetzen*]," moral sciences "have to do with conclusions arrived at by psychological instinct." Moral sciences rely on "aesthetic" judgments, while natural sciences seek "logical induction" for principled conclusions that are "valid under all circumstances."[85] Natural sciences overcome deficiencies in moral sciences that lack scientific rigor and factual data:

> Nature does not allow us for a moment to doubt that we have to do with a rigid chain of cause and effect [*Causalnexus*], admitting of no exceptions. Therefore to us, as her students, goes forth the mandate to labor on till we have discovered unvarying laws; till then we dare not rest satisfied, for then only can our knowledge grapple victoriously with time and space and the forces of the universe. . . . [Natural Science is] undisturbed alike by collateral ideas on the one hand, and by wishes and hopes on the other.

> Knowledge is power. Our age, more than any other, is in a position to demonstrate the truth of this maxim. We have taught the forces of inanimate nature to minister to the wants of human life and the designs of the human intellect.[86]

Helmholtz's clear preference for the natural sciences betrays an underlying conception of self that mirrors the clear, logical forces of "inanimate nature." Only a secure and rational self could be unmoved by "wishes and hopes." Such a self, dominated by a logical human intellect, subjugates nature to "minister to the wants of human life." Helmholtz hopes to find in nature universal laws (*Gesetze*) that, like the axioms of mathematics, "stand at the head of the reasoning" of human agents.[87] Not psychological instincts, but universal rules, not judgments of beauty, but factual data reflect the superiority of mind and matter over "wishes and hopes." To find such laws in nature is to reveal the logical power of the self.

We have seen Hess make this same argument in his 1855 essay, *Zur Entwicklungsgeschichte von Natur und Gesellschaft*. Hess's scientific research, in this essay and others in the 1850s, seeks to discover objective and universal laws in nature. In these works, the secrets of human development are open to the researcher's gaze, and Hess discovers a natural, logical self. Persons are fully exposed to rational articulation, and stripped of tension and conflict.

Hess's racial theory in *Rome and Jerusalem* also assumes a logical and accessible self. Recall that race defines the "building blocks," the "cosmic bodies" that remain unchanged through historical transformations. Race as "type" underlies cultural diversity while sustaining a people's "integrity." And race is a carrier of intellectual, psychological, and physical characteristics that, despite climatic and cultural variation, remain always unchanged. Persons who belong to a "primal type" are complete and uniform, for they express permanent and pure qualities shared by their ancestors and future generations. Their selves are ubiquitous, stable, and accessible to logical, scientific investigation. A racial theory that purports to be scientific requires a logical self that mirrors the law-like structure of nature.

Emotions as expressions of value can easily "disturb" the calm, calculating power of scientific inquiry. They might destabilize, and bring commitments to the fore that, as Helmholtz suggests, are often in tension with other valued, "scientific" attachments. For emotions to have any scientific value at all, they must reflect the enduring and logical self in scientific theory. To Hess, emotions mirror *Gesetze* and factual data. Their value lies in reflecting the law-like structure of race and nature. Racial familial love reveals only that one is, in fact, a member of one's *Volk*.

The emotions are an "immediate product of race," which typically forms its social institutions according to natural pre-dispositions and inclinations. These inclinations generate specific forms of life. Each race produces a corresponding number of unique modes of human expression. *Leben* produces a view of life (*Lebensanschauung*), which in turn "modifies" but never radically re-creates the original *Typus*. Race is thus an *ursprüngliche Typus* that generates race-specific inclinations. As such, race is an abstraction without content. Distinguishable from *Leben* (life), *Lebensanschauung* (view of life), and *Anlagen* (natural inclinations), race becomes a "type" that underlies difference and uniqueness, while remaining impervious to change and corruption.[88] In this schema, emotions, those "true natural feelings," are *Anlagen*—natural pre-dispositions and inclinations. They are instinctive expressions of a racial "type." Emotions reveal a stable and uniform *ursprüngliche Typus* that "can be neither demonstrated nor demonstrated to the contrary."

The racial "type" is recognized most clearly, Hess believes, in the cases of intermarriage. Hess's "scientific" analysis is worth quoting in full:

> Concerning the indestructibility of the Jewish race in intermarriage with the Indo-Germanic people, I can cite for you an example taken from my own study. It is known that in the crossbreeding between the Indo-Germanic and Mongolian races, the Mongolian type predominates; the Russian nobles, who have only taken in a little Mongolian blood, carry the Mongolian type today. Among my friends there is a Russian nobleman who, like all true Russian boyars, betrays his Mongolian descent through his features, and his Indo-Germanic descent through his fine spirit. This friend married a Polish Jew and with her had many sons, all of whom have the Jewish type to a noticeable degree. You see, my esteemed friend, that it does not help Jews to deny their heritage through baptism or marriage to the Indo-Germanic or Mongolian races. The Jewish type cannot be eradicated. It is, indeed, unmistakable. In its most noble representatives, where it is hardly distinguishable from the ancient Greek type, it even surpasses the Greek type with its soul expression. The Jewish type remains for the expert a clear mirror upon which the coat of arms of the most ancient nobles of the world-historical people has been stamped. Thus I was not surprised when, traveling through Antwerp, I showed an artist the beautiful picture known to you which would have honored the work of a Phidias. The artist could not admire it enough and finally, as if the light had suddenly shined on him, exclaimed: I wager that this is a picture of a Jewess.[89]

If the "Jewish type" cannot be eradicated, then Jewish love of *Volk* is but a natural recognition of one's "unmistakable" Jewish essence. This becomes clear when Hess defends the "Jewish patriot." The "newly fashionable Jew [*der neumodische Jude*]"[90] remains in the starry heavens of rational abstraction. But the Jewish patriot relies on emotional attachments that are impervious to rational critique:

> The Jewish patriot is not a German abstraction which dissolves itself in being and appearance, realism and idealism; it [Jewish patriotism] is instead a true, natural feeling [*ein naturwahres Gefühl*], which in its originality [*Ursprünglichkeit*] and its fundamental simplicity [*Einfachheit*] can be neither demonstrated nor demonstrated to the contrary.[91]

An immediate, undeniable and "primal" emotion justifies Hess's nationalism turned patriotism. Beyond rational articulation, and as a "true and natural feeling," the primacy of emotion resists both critique and judgment. The "new" Jew who denies his nationality is now not only an "apostate," but a "traitor to his people, his race, and to his family."[92] He denies what is undeniable: the true natural feeling of Jewish patriotism. This is racial belonging: an inescapable framework for Jewish identity.

Inescapable Frameworks

I have adopted the term "inescapable framework" from Taylor's account of the self. For Taylor, a framework "is that in virtue of which we make sense of our lives spiritually." We all exist in a space of questions, moral intuitions, and qualitative distinctions that form the background to our lives. Without this moral orientation, we would not even know how to ask an appropriate question, nor be capable of defending our most valued ethical concerns. Frameworks thus provide the horizon, explicitly or implicitly, within which we consider moral judgments and reactions. Taylor's theory is self-consciously transcendental in *Sources of the Self*, for he wants to "spell out what it is that we presuppose" when we evaluate one form of life as more worthy or valuable than another. As an account of the "transcendental conditions" that explore "the limits of the conceivable in human life," frameworks are not optional extras, but constitutive features of human agency.[93]

Persons cannot live outside a framework that informs moral judgments. We all rely upon them to answer the question, Who am I? Indeed, in *Sources of the Self*, Taylor argues that frameworks are inescapable because they make human identity possible:

> My identity is defined by the commitments and identifications which provide the frame or horizon within which I can try to determine from case to case what is good, or valuable, or what ought to be done, or what I endorse or oppose. In other words, it is the horizon within which I am capable of taking a stand.[94]

Persons who lose this identification "would be at sea," suffering "an acute form of disorientation." But it is important to see here that frameworks are more than transcendental conditions for human personhood. They are also necessary to forge a coherent identity. Put another way, frameworks are not merely formal requirements for human agency; they also establish substantive claims about the nature of that agency. A framework in Taylor's taxonomy does not only enable moral reflection, but it also provides a moral orientation. Frameworks are "ontologically basic" for answering questions about the good, such that they provide "the horizon within which we know where we stand, and what meanings things have for us." In Taylor's account, frameworks are not something we either invent nor merely require for identity, but are answers to questions "which inescapably pre-exist for us, independent of our answer or inability to answer."[95] Frameworks demand something from us, and we either unreflectively float "at sea" or find our bearings, and thus our identity, within the space of moral questions and answers that frameworks impose.

To illustrate this point, Taylor cites a "famous Sartrian example" in which a young man is torn between two conflicting commitments: staying with his ailing mother or joining the French resistance.[96] Sartre's point is that the man confronts a radical choice in which he cannot adjudicate between these two moral claims. He simply chooses the one instead of the other. But on Taylor's reading, the conflict of the young man's predicament cannot be understood in terms of radical choice. In Sartre's description of the case, there really is no impasse, for the young man simply chooses without recourse to any moral claim or concern. He lives outside frameworks that inform moral deliberations. Yet for the young man to recognize the conflict as a moral one, says Taylor, he must draw upon background theories of justice, care, family obligations, and the like. He must take seriously these considerations if he is to recognize, defend, and act according to his ethical commitments. One simply cannot make sense of moral concerns without drawing upon reflective commitments of worth. In Sartre's hypothetical case, the young man "has no language in which the superiority of one alternative over the other can be articulated . . . he just throws himself one way."[97] Only a theory of moral evaluation can make sense of a choice between conflicting claims; a theory that explains how Sartre's young man draws upon frameworks of worth to make ethical decisions. Moreover, the young man must rely upon moral frameworks that foster a coherent and articulate identity. Throwing himself one way means to lose his way, to be incapable of taking a stand on significant moral concerns. Frameworks orient persons within a space of ethical choices that sustain a coherent identity.

Sartre is unaware, in Taylor's reading, of the frameworks that underlie ethical choice. For this reason, articulacy—the capacity to outline and recognize frameworks of meaning—provides moral orientation for modern persons. The search for a meaningful identity requires adequate and appropriate description. Failure in this regard leads to a loss of identity: "To lose this orientation, or not to have found it, is not to know who one is. And this orientation, once attained, defines where you answer from, hence your identity."[98]

By articulating the background that makes sense of ethical responses, Taylor believes he can draw a "moral map" that shapes human experience.[99] This moral grid, or "map of our moral world," offers guidance, stability, and meaningful answers to basic concerns. Though "full of gaps, erasures, and blurrings," a map of moral frameworks can therapeutically help recover orientation, meaning, and secure identities in the modern world.[100]

Hess's racial theory functions as an inescapable framework in precisely this sense: it recovers meaning and orientation for Jews confronted with the destabilizing forces of modernity. Like other Jewish thinkers interested in racial theory, Hess appropriates nineteenth-century scientific discourse to make normative claims about Jewish identity.[101] His expressive language enabled his readers to articulate the racial underpinnings of their familial attachments. By adopting racial scientific method and language to affirm Jewish love for family, Hess could defend a patriotism based on racial "type." Racial belonging was, for Hess, an inescapable framework within which modern Jews deliberated about value. It provided that basic orientation and "moral map" necessary for good ethical reflection. But Hess's racial theory was one kind of inescapable framework that evaded reflective judgment. According to Hess, the pure "Jewish type" manifested superior physical, ethical, and religious traits that could be "neither demonstrated nor demonstrated to the contrary." Race as framework was closed to critique and judgment, yet it provided the authoritative ground for Jewish ethical and political reflection about the good.

There are good reasons to simply dismiss Hess's racial theory as a corrupt and debilitating framework of nineteenth-century race science, an orientation that, gratefully, we have moved far beyond. Even if racial theory is still with us today, we should claim other frameworks (class, gender, community, language) as far more expressive of modern identity. But Hess's racial theory is an important source for understanding the function of identity politics in his religious thought. In his appeal to race science, Hess seeks to overcome the dislocating factors of modern life. He fears that without some basic orientation like racial belonging, modern Jews will remain "at sea" in the wake of European Enlightenment and emancipation:

> Even baptism does not free him [the German Jew] from the nightmare of German anti-Semitism. The Germans hate less the religion of the Jews than their race, less their peculiar beliefs than their noses. Neither reform nor baptism, neither education [*Bildung*] nor emancipation, completely opens the gates of social life to the German Jews. They therefore desire to deny their racial descent. . . . [But] Jewish noses cannot be reformed, and the black, frizzy Jewish hair cannot through conversion be turned into blond, nor by means of a comb become smooth. The Jewish race is one of the original races which, despite climatic influences, has reproduced itself with integrity. The Jewish type throughout the centuries has remained the same.[102]

Clearly, if Jews are a pure race, they should not mingle with inferior races. But even when they do, Jewish integrity and purity remain undamaged. The integrity of Jewish blood prevails, despite the allure of European culture, politics, society, and education. Identity is secure in race; it is sheltered and protected from hostile political and cultural forces. Thus modernity loses its sting in Hess's racial theory. When Hess turns to race science, his religious politics become a politics of racial belonging. Hess's politics of identity are rooted in race science.

Yet modernity encourages, even protects multiple cultural expressions that too often fragment and dislodge singular identities.[103] Proponents of multiculturalism applaud this decentering because no one culture, people, or value can become normative and potentially oppressive.[104] But for Hess, a multicultural world threatens the stability and security of racial belonging. The modern world is hostile to Jewish identity in its denial and continual challenge to Jewish uniformity. Hess's essentialism thus transcends historical and cultural forces, and is thereby immune to modern threats that dislodge the self.[105] Race science works as a "protective strategy"[106] designed to ward off this cultural fragmentation. It is at base a reaction to modernity, a pre-emptive closing of "the gates of social life" for modern Jews. Race is a framework designed to be inescapable.

Frameworks and narratives are problematic only when we recognize that something is wrong with them. There is a felt inconsistency or incongruity between the "answers" they provide and the questions we pursue. But how would an agent pursue questions that move beyond the frameworks that inform identity? What would motivate a person to recognize the poverty of their background justifications? Hess's racial theory, I have argued throughout, is an inescapable framework that he is unwilling to challenge. Indeed, he regards Jews who dispute his scientific findings as traitors to their people, race, and family. His is a closed argument that defends racial belonging by appealing to racial belonging, but its very circularity strengthens it against attacks and reflective scrutiny. Even if others recognize the inadequacy of Hess's racial account, the framework offers a coherency and stability unmatched by other modern theories. It provides a bastion for those "at sea," and a secure defense against a crisis of identity. There is no need to move beyond race science, because critical questions would never arise. Hess's racial theory is a powerful account for modern Jewish identity because it promises security and stability without loss of meaning. The desire for a coherent identity, rooted in a racial narrative, can truly make a framework inescapable.

Recognizing other frameworks as imaginative possibilities restricts one's own, and makes it less inescapable. But this Hess cannot do. It is not that Hess fails to recognize the existence of other frameworks of meaning (he does). Instead, Hess cannot imagine other frameworks that could plausibly secure a coherent Jewish identity. This is why I have emphasized that "inescapable" functions in two ways for Taylor: the sense in which a self must live within a framework (the formal criterion), and the sense in which *this kind of* framework prevents pathology and crisis in identity (the substantive concern). Hess adopts both meanings because he wants more than a transcendental account of the modern predicament. He requires a substantive theory that is secure and stable enough to withstand the onslaught of modern discontinuity.

Hess's racial theory is one strategy he utilizes to deny features of modernity a role in fashioning Jewish identity, even if, ironically, race science is a peculiarly modern project. Race science overcomes the destabilizing forces of historical contingency and religious pluralism. For Hess, racial heritage is the only available narrative that can, despite competing modern options, still distinguish Jews from other peoples. Hess may be assimilated into German high culture, disconnected from Jewish religious history and ritual, even married to a Christian woman, but he is a Jew by race nonetheless. Jewish racial identity is thus immune to competing frameworks of meaning. It is one boundary that cannot be negotiated nor crossed.

Martha Nussbaum's discussion of Creon's defense of civic duty helps us to understand why Hess should be attentive to the multiple, and perhaps conflicting frameworks that inform individual identities. In Sophocles's *Antigone*, Creon is faced with a choice: to bury Polynices's corpse as familial obligations require, or, as the city's representative, not to honor Polynices with burial at all. However, he fails to see the choice as a choice: Creon rearranges values so that they "all connect to the well-being of the city, the single intrinsic good, and Creon acknowledges no separate goods." This revisionist stance, says Nussbaum, has a cost:

> Insoluble conflicts cannot arise, because there is only a single supreme good, and all other values are functions of that good. . . . If I say to Creon, "Here is a conflict: on the one side, the demands of piety and love; on the other, the requirements of civic justice," he will reply that I have misdescribed the case.[107]

Creon faces two obligations, but in the end dismisses one as not worthy, as less valuable, or simply not good. Instead, as Nussbaum argues, Creon should recognize his inability to do what is required of him; he should regret any action taken and acknowledge the other commitment as a standing one for him. Conflicting commitments, in this picture, are insoluble. But Creon overcomes opposition by essentially denying it. He, like Hess, recognizes only one framework of meaning that controls questions of value. Civic duty is *the* inescapable framework that informs Creon's sense of value, and not because other frameworks do not exist. To recognize "separate goods" would require a more conflicted picture of political identity, and this both Creon and Hess refuse to entertain as a serious option.

In Hess's racial account, conflict is deceptive. It may cause one to misidentify one's race, to become an "apostate"—a "traitor to his people, his race, and to his family." Emotions do not raise troubling choices, but instead confirm racial identity. It is a choice that, in the end, is no choice at all. Here, struggle leads only to apostasy. Hess relies on contrastive language to discriminate baser (Greek) from nobler (Jewish) commitments, and, like Creon, he dismisses one in order to save the "simplicity" and "originality" of the other. The qualitative comparison between Greeks and Jews in particular, and his racial theory in general, undermine the complexity and ambiguous character of modern Jewish identity.

Even as Hess affirms that many modern persons live within multiple frameworks of meaning, he orders values and commitments to secure identity in a fragmented world. Insoluble conflicts in a life reflect a pathological state, a confused and disoriented identity crisis. Racial integrity functions in *Rome and Jerusalem* as a foundational and secure base that Jews can always "return" to when faced with intractable modern dilemmas. Indeed, Hess can once again stand with his people, his *Volk*, because with science as his authority, he has never really left. Hess's racial theory is but one example of how narratives and frameworks combine to fashion a coherent, strong, and secure modern identity.

Yet even as Hess defends Jewish identity through race science, he becomes notably inarticulate when describing what racial integrity actually means. Recall that Hess defines race as an "original type" that produces race-specific inclinations. Race as "type" underlies difference and uniqueness, and is immune to change and corruption. It is that substratum or being that makes possible all becoming, and yet, as a natural feeling, "can be neither demonstrated nor demonstrated to the contrary." The paradox is obvious: Hess employs expressive language to evoke a commitment to race that is resistant to expressive discourse. He must dismiss his emotional and confessional style and adopt a scientific idiom to defend an inescapable framework that can only be blandly asserted, but not evocatively expressed. So even as emotive language moves the reader to accept racial belonging as the framework that informs identity, that language is ultimately undermined by the indeterminate content, status, and meaning of racial integrity.

But this should not surprise us. The frameworks that fashion identity are far more cryptic and vague than Hess takes them to be. If one asks Hess's patriotic Jew why he should value the Jewish race, he can only appeal to a "true, natural feeling" that cannot be demonstrated. Expressive language, for Hess, can only go so far. He avoids modern dissonance by appealing to pre-existing frameworks, narrative continuity, and expressive language of disclosure. Yet Hess's racial theory reveals how the modern need for reconciliation often dismisses, rather than confronts, insoluble conflicts. There are no "spiritual struggles" here. It is for this reason that Hess becomes strangely inarticulate. To be expressive about modern Jewish identity, finally, means to negotiate among conflicting commitments that cannot be summarily resolved by a substantive account of race, inescapable or otherwise. Identity politics should articulate and inform, rather than dismiss and undermine, the inescapable fragments of modern Jewish identity.

Traditions and Scars: Hess's Critique of Reform and Orthodox Judaism

5

Throughout *Rome and Jerusalem,* as well as in his later essays, Hess argues that modern Reform Jews abandon their attachments to the Jewish national tradition and pursue the illusory goal of civic and political emancipation in Germany. They sacrifice their national heritage without replacing it with a tangible and sustainable community. According to Avineri, Hess treated Reform Judaism as a Jewish assimilationist strategy modeled on Protestant Christianity that "ignores the fact that the Jews are a nation and saw Judaism in religious terms only."[1] This critique was made before by Hess's contemporaries and later German historians. If this were all Hess could offer, we would do well to look elsewhere. But Hess's critique is a significant and unique study of how conceptions of tradition inform notions of identity. The problem is not only which political tradition the Reformers adopt as their own. The more troubling issue is how they recognize and explore Jewish attachments within that community. Hess argues that the German community, premised on the ideal of *Bildung,* renders the Jew incapable of acknowledging features of Jewish identity. Although Hess directs his polemic at the Reformers, he faults Orthodox Jews as well for restrictive adherence to a rabbinic tradition that renounces legitimate modern commitments. They too are blinded to constitutive features of modern Jewish identity. Hess seeks to find a middle way, between what he calls "the nihilism of the Reformers, who never learned anything," and "the desperate reactionaries, who never forgot anything."[2] In Hess's account, Jewish identity is fashioned by modern national and humanitarian movements, yet is rooted in Jewish culture, religion, character, and race; Hess seeks to learn from the present without forgetting the past.

Yet Hess offers two divergent accounts of Jewish tradition in his critique of Reform and Orthodox Judaism. In his discussion of Jewish Orthodoxy, Hess appeals to hermeneutical creativity that overturns Orthodox rigidity and claims to religious authority. But in his analysis of Jewish Reform, Hess returns to the rhetoric of *Kultus* discussed in the second chapter. Jewish tradition exposes the enduring differences that firmly root Jews in a distinctive racial history. But Hess criticizes the Reform tradition for much that we have come to associate with his racial theory—abstract continuity and undifferentiated unity. It is as if Hess transfers the assumptions underlying his racial theory onto Reform Judaism, finds those claims wanting, yet still relies upon his racial theory to upend the Reform movement. He will not abandon his racial account even though it relies upon the very ideals of simple unity and integrity that he rejects in Reform Judaism. So two versions of tradition co-exist in unresolved tension in *Rome and Jerusalem:* the one attune to creativity and historical contingency, the other grounded in the ideals of unity and continuity. Hess pragmatically selects from the one or the other to reinforce his critique of Orthodoxy and Reform.

Appealing to both accounts, Hess renounces Reform Judaism in favor of a more contextual and embodied tradition and the strong distinctions that inform it. He insists that Reform Jews cannot adequately evaluate the Jewish tradition because they cannot recognize difference. The Reformers search for a new identity and community in the secular, liberal German state that promises civic and legal equality. This is the promise of German *Bildung:* the universal moral community of the liberal, self-educated, unique individual. But the *Bildung* community requires the denial of difference and particularity. Reform Jews cannot uncover features of the Jewish tradition because particular differences are suppressed within the *Bildung* community. The Orthodox, by contrast, characteristically reject the rhetoric of German *Bildung*. But their wholesale denial leads to an unhealthy retreat into a more stable and insular Jewish community. The Orthodox too easily deny modern social and intellectual movements that inevitably complicate attachments to the Jewish tradition. They, too, suppress difference in order to maintain a firm continuity with the authoritative rabbinic past. For both the Orthodox and Reform, an understanding of tradition is limited by a failure to assess different and historically contingent values and goods.

Hess, too, is deeply ambivalent about how to justify the different values that shape traditions, and the identities informed by them. Taylor's account of strong and weak evaluation can help us see why this is the case. A strong evaluator thinks in terms of better and worse, noble and base, such that certain goods acquire a higher status because they are recognized as "essential to our identity."[3] Such evaluation requires a comparative approach that qualitatively ranks values and commitments, and thus implicitly relies upon important differences between those values. Weak evaluators, by contrast, fail on two counts: they do not qualitatively contrast different values, and thus fail to offer a hierarchical ranking of those differences. To be sure, Hess is a strong evaluator. He qualitatively contrasts various racial traits, and argues that the Jewish tradition is more noble than that of the Greeks.

Hess also claims that Jewish emotional attachment to race "can be neither demonstrated nor demonstrated to the contrary." In this latter evaluation, Jewish racial attachment is better, more noble than other commitments, but it is also an unsupported claim. Hess will therefore provide a hierarchical ranking of different values, even as he cannot reasonably justify that ranking. I conclude, drawing from the insights of Stuart Hampshire, that Hess's confusion is a common situation in ethics where no fundamental justifications or knockdown arguments are readily available. Ambivalence is a peculiar feature of modern persons who, like Hess, recognize that conflicts of interpretation often evade adjudication and resolution. Hess's critique of and response to Reform and Orthodox traditions expose how conflict, ambiguity, and insufficient reasons for strong evaluations are significant features of persons informed by Jewish tradition.

Identity and Difference: Hess's Critique of *Bildung* and Jewish Reform

Hess argues that Reform German Jews could not abandon their Jewish national identity, if for no other reason than that the non-Jewish German society simply would not allow it. Jews were not equal citizens in Germany because German polity was not neutral, even as it claimed to be universal.[4] Though the *Bildung* culture valued universal citizenship, it simultaneously denied Jewish access to the goods of social and political life. German *Bildung*, despite the rhetoric, was closed and restricted—and not only to Jews, but to anybody attached to distinct and local communities. All for the better, Hess claimed, for the German image of *Bildung*, as an expression of human character, was rooted in an abstract conception of self. *Bildung* would thus render Jews incapable of deliberating about the particular differences that mark Jews as distinctive persons. Reform Jews, just one group of many that desired access into the modern German community, sought what no human being could achieve: an abstract, dehumanized and disembodied self. The German demand for *Bildung*, from Hess's standpoint, was haunted by the same abstract ghosts that plagued the Reformer's quest for universal citizenship.[5] The logic of *Bildung* required the destruction of difference.

One difference that marks Jews as distinctive is their national heritage. Hess secures his national ideology in the narrative of racial belonging. Indeed, Hess defines the Reform Jew as a typical "traitor to his race." Betrayal of the Jewish people runs deep, however, even as far back as the biblical Moses. Hess believes that Moses' silence about his Hebrew origins before Jethro's daughters offers an illustrative example and precedent for the modern Reform Jew who denies national commitments. He cites the midrash in which Moses asks God why the bones of Joseph are allowed to enter the Holy Land, but he, the leader of the Jewish people, is refused entry. Should not the just God act justly? God responds:

> He who praises his land is buried there, and he who does not praise his land is not buried there. Joseph acknowledged his land when the wife of Potiphar said, "[H]e [Potiphar] has brought to us a Hebrew man [*ish ivri*]." Joseph did not deny this, for he said, "I was stolen from the land of the Hebrews." Therefore, Joseph is buried in his own land. You [Moses] did not acknowledge your land, and therefore will not be buried in it. For when the daughters of Jethro said, "an Egyptian man [*ish mizri*] saved us from the hands of the shepherds," you [Moses] heard it and were silent, and therefore you will not be buried in your land.[6] (Dvarim Rabbah 2:8)

The midrashist asks us to read Joseph's response to Potiphar's wife as an explicit recognition of Hebrew identity and homeland. But Moses is not from the land of the Hebrews. God banishes Moses from the land of the Hebrews, Hess repeats, "because he allowed himself to be introduced as an Egyptian before Jethro, and not as a Hebrew." Recognition of who he is and where he belongs determines Moses' fate. By accepting the name *ish mizri*, he expresses far different commitments than Joseph, the *ish ivri*.

Moses' failings are also those of Reform Jews in Germany. These *gebildete Juden*, according to Hess, conceal their attachments to the Jewish nation. In the original manuscript of *Rome and Jerusalem*, the midrash on Moses and Joseph relates to the following indictment of German Jews:[7]

> The beautiful phrases about humanity and enlightenment which he [the enlightened, Reform Jew] employs as a gloss over his treason, his fear of being identified with his unfortunate brethren, will ultimately not protect him from the judgment of public opinion. In vain does the modern Jew offer his geographical and philosophical alibi. Take on a thousand masks, change your name, religion and values, travel throughout the world incognito, so that people may not recognize you as a Jew; yet every insult to the Jewish name will strike you, even more than the pious man, who admits his solidarity with his family and stands up for its honor.[8]

Naming reveals identity: Joseph accepts the name with which he is identified (*ish ivri*). Moses does not identify with this naming, and, according to Hess, neither do the enlightened (*gebildete*) Jews in Germany. They fear being "identified" with other Jews, and yet "public opinion" haunts them ("The Germans hate less the religion of the Jews than their race"). Every insult against the Jewish people strikes these modern Jews to the core, because at the core they maintain strong attachments to the Jewish family. The pious Jew only "admits" what the enlightened Jew tries, in vain, to cover up.

So too, it seems, with Moses of the midrash. Moses accepts the name *ish mizri*, fearing to be identified with his Jewish brethren. While the enlightened Jew cannot hide from public opinion, Moses must face God's judgment. And Moses too offers a geographical and philosophical alibi: he fails to recognize the connection between community and land, between *ish ivri* and the land of the Hebrews. Like his European Jewish successors will do symbolically, Moses hopes that Jethro's daughters will not recognize his Jewish identity. But ultimately Moses, no longer the "pious man" in Hess's eyes, calls forth God's punishment. So Hess cites rabbinic midrash to justify his critique of Reform Jewish identity. Egypt is not ancient history but present possibility: Moses, the tragic figure of the past, is re-inscribed as the modern, enlightened Jew. Recognizing one's name and family, and the national commitments they foster, is a struggle each must face, both the Moses of the past and the Jew of the modern world.

It is precisely this struggle for identity that the Reform German Jews fail to undertake. They are thus rendered incapable of recognizing constitutive aspects that inform national and religious commitments. Hess's label for enlightened or Reform Jews, *gebildete Juden*, underscores his point. The critique of German *Bildung*, then, is simultaneously a criticism of Reform (*gebildete*) Jews in Germany. By exposing the meaningless abstractions in German *Bildung* (to be discussed below), Hess contends that Reform Jews assimilate a diseased culture. Reform Jews who adopt the German conception of *Bildung* as their own also embrace a faulty conception of self.

The ideal of *Bildung* in nineteenth-century Germany,[9] according to German historian George Mosse, "combined the meaning carried by the English word 'education' with notions of character formation and moral education."[10] This ideal of self-education was "decisive" for German Jewry's quest for political and social emancipation:

> The centrality of the ideal of *Bildung* in German-Jewish consciousness must be understood from the very beginning—it was basic to Jewish engagement with liberalism and socialism, fundamental to the search for a new Jewish identity after emancipation.[11]

Bildung became for many Jews the content of their Jewishness. The German-Jewish author Berthold Auerbach,[12] a close friend of Moses Hess, wrote that, "formerly the religious spirit proceeded from revelation, the present starts with *Bildung*." He called for religion to become *Bildung*.[13] According to David Sorkin, *Bildung* represented a new secular form of individual salvation. "Personality formation now replaced pedigree,"[14] Sorkin claimed, and "the *gebildeter Mensch* was held to have achieved individual perfection through self-cultivation and refinement that was tantamount to virtue if not salvation itself."[15] Surely, argued Mosse, "here was an ideal ready-made for Jewish assimilation, because it transcended all differences of nationality and religion through the unfolding of the individual personality."[16]

Developments within the Jewish community in the eighteenth and nineteenth centuries made this ideal a real and attractive possibility for Jews. The Jewish community (*kehilla*) of the medieval and early modern period, with the rabbi as its leader, lost its autonomous authority both within the newly established centralized state, and from Jews now disgusted with rabbinic controversies. Displacing the rabbi as the communal source of authority, the German Jewish intellectual (*maskil*) was a student of German culture and philosophy. He prized secular knowledge and foreign languages, and envisioned Jewish history within a broader, European context. The rise of the *maskil* as a new Jewish leader and authority was thus a potent sign of the *kehilla's* demise. More to the point, the *maskil* valued the social, political, and philosophical goals of German *Bildung*.[17] The new, enlightened Jew would participate in secular reading groups and social gatherings that were part of what Jacob Katz has coined the "neutral society"—a universal, rational, and enlightened association.[18] During this period, when many Jews sought fuller economic, social and political freedom in Germany, *Israelite* and *Mosaist* were substituted for the term *Jew*. This suggested that only in religion, by now a private, personal affair, would the Jew be distinguished from the enlightened Christian.[19] In public life, the Jew could disappear altogether into liberal society to be a productive citizen. German *Bildung* required a new name, and with it a community detached from the religious and educational institutions of the *kehilla*.

To Hess, *Bildung* would damage communal patterns of Jewish observance. Social and political rights should be granted as a legal right, Hess argued, but they need not be earned nor bargained for.[20] Hess praised Gabriel Riesser (1806–1863), an eager fighter for Jewish emancipation in Germany, noting that Riesser "never fell into the error of modern German Jews, and other Germans, who considered the emancipation of the Jews incompatible with the tradition of Jewish nationalism." Indeed, the very title of Riesser's journal, *Der Jude*, was a stubborn protest against modern German Jews "of the Mosaic faith."[21] Hess accused "other" Reformers of "sucking the last marrow out of Judaism," leaving nothing left "but the shadow of a skeleton."[22] We find similar statements in Hess's articles written after the publication of *Rome and Jerusalem*. In *My Messianic Faith* (1862), Hess restated his past critique as an effort to counter the social integration demanded by the Reform movement: "You can find in my book why I consider every modern Reform religion a reflection of the social process of disintegration."[23] In Hess's French essay, *Lettres sur la Mission d'Israël dans l'Histoire de l'Humanité* (1864), religious reforms were seen as politically expedient changes, introduced only to win social emancipation.[24] As Jews left the *kehilla* to become productive citizens, Hess feared that they would lose the communal structures that maintained a distinctive Jewish community.[25]

In early essays and books, however, Hess was far kinder to the German conception of *Bildung*, and he discovered important similarities between the Jewish and German characters. In *Rome and Jerusalem*, we still find traces of Hess's ambivalent stance toward Germans and Jews: "In the whole organism of humanity there are no two people who attract and repel each other more than the German and Jewish people."[26] Hess is both an insider and outsider to both communities. He continually struggles to situate his own identity within the Jewish community, even as he, and those around him,[27] find this relationship tenuous at best.[28] This conflict occurs because the ideal of German *Bildung* attracts Hess as well. His repetitive distinctions between German abstract philosophy and Jewish national religious life belie Hess's own personal struggle to deny important influences on his own thinking. Hess adopts his Hebrew name "Moses" for *Rome and Jerusalem* (the only work in which Hess does so) and only regrets his name is not "Itzig."[29] But even as he criticizes the biblical Moses and those Reformers who call themselves "Mosaists," Hess too is a Moses figure caught between two cultures. The biblical enticements of Egyptian civilization find their analog in the modern German *Bildung* community.

We can see more clearly the influence of German *Bildung* on Hess's own thinking in his earlier works. In his *European Triarchy* (1841), Hess describes the German tendency to "spiritualize life," calling the German an "idealist" who represents social and spiritual freedom. The Germans are also the most universal, European of people (Hess at one point refers to *Wir Europäer*).[30] Silberner notes that before Hess wrote his *Triarchy*, Hess had called the Germans "das auserwählte [chosen] Volk der Neuzeit!"[31] Hess at that point fully identified with the new chosen people: the progressive, spiritual, and fully European (read "universal") Germans. In unpublished essays of the early 1840s,[32] Hess discovers significant parallels between Germans and Jews. In *Reflections on Jews in Germany* (1841–1842?),[33] he describes the Germans as "serious, thorough, faithful, and reasonable." The German is, "in a word, religious."[34] In *The Poles and the Jews* (1841),[35] he claims that the Poles were given a political mission in world history (much like the French), but that the Jews, like the Germans, were concerned with "spiritual rebirth." Hess even claims that "the mission [*Beruf*] for both nations [Germans and Jews] is fundamentally the same."[36] In the terminology that he would employ later, Hess calls this mission a "fusion of the historical traditions," one that levels distinctions and variations between Jewish and German culture.

Hess's discussion of German *Bildung*, while explicit in *Rome and Jerusalem*, thus underlies much of Hess's earlier thought. Germans and Jews, either as two nations united by the same "calling" or divided by competing visions, are mutually defined by the other. For Hess, to talk about German *Bildung* means to engage in "the Jewish problem." Silberner argues that *Rome and Jerusalem* is, among other things, a critique of Hess's earlier infatuation with German culture and *Bildung*, and that his hatred of Jewish Reform is really a denial of his *Vorleben* (former life). In Silberner's psychological reading, Hess's self-hatred of his own earlier rejection of the Jewish national tradition is suppressed and redirected against Reform Judaism.[37] By 1862, in the wake of the perceived disintegration of the Jewish community, Hess would see a need to undermine altogether the Jewish-German relationship. Silberner's comments support the thesis proposed in this book that *Rome and Jerusalem* marks an important change in Hess's understanding of Jewish identity, and is not simply a "return" to prior commitments.

Hess, to be sure, does not fully appreciate how conceptions of *Bildung* are materially rooted in cultural, social, and political structures in eighteenth- and nineteenth-century Germany.[38] Though his critique of *Bildung* is overdrawn, his analysis of Reform Jewry is sensitive to how identity is constituted by difference. In the fourth letter of *Rome and Jerusalem*, Hess states his case directly: "German *Bildung* appears to be incompatible with Jewish national aspirations." If he had not lived in France, Hess adds, he would not have concerned himself with the revival of Jewish nationality, for "our viewpoints and strivings are determined by the communities within which we live."[39] Hess fears that German Jews, so distorted by German education (*Bildung*), no longer recognize the depth of their own (Jewish) alienation. Hess himself can reflect upon the implications of *Bildung* only after his flight from Germany. He is an outsider looking in, a former *gebildeter Mensch* who can now comparatively evaluate his own struggle for identity. However, Jews living in a German community, saturated with German *Bildung*, cannot detect their own estrangement from Jewish national and religious commitments.

Hess characterizes German *Bildung* as an abstract, universal, and disembodied culture. It is thus hostile to particular national movements. Otto Wigand, Hess's former publisher, wrote that Hess's argument for Jewish nationalism is opposed to "my pure human nature." But this only shows Hess how much Wigand is conditioned by German *Bildung*. Wigand refuses to accept, according to Hess, that his "pure human nature" only typifies the pure German race.[40] The German "pure nature" reflects, instead, a very particular, indeed parochial conception of personhood. But this person is imagined only as a "pure" subject, and not as an agent involved in social historical movements. Wigand believes he operates beyond particular communities and worldly pursuits, and thus is dedicated all the more to universal aspirations.[41] But this, to Hess, is pure fantasy, fueled by the demands of *Bildung* itself.

Following his review of *Rome and Jerusalem* in a personal letter to Hess, Berthold Auerbach discusses his own identity as a German Jew:

> I am, and I admit it happily (even though you must find it ridiculous and disgraceful), a German Jew, a real German [*ein germanischer Jude, ein Deutscher*], as good, I believe, as anyone that exists.[42]

It is a slippery slope from a "German Jew" to a "real German." But in Hess's account, a "real German" can only exist in the abstract theory of *Bildung*. The *gebildete* Jews, in Hess's reading, profoundly misconceive the nature of both German and Jewish identity. Like social and political emancipation, the German conception of personhood is illusory.

This point is made clear in Hess's claim that German anti-Semitism is a distinctive consequence of *Bildung*. German *Bildung* might appear as a bulwark against anti-Semitism, for the notion of a universal and pure human nature could provide strong warrants for social and political toleration and acceptance. Yet Hess argues (and here his socialist critique is central) that political claims always repress differences; even as it searches for universals, political philosophy inevitably appeals to particular and local claims to truth. Witness how Hess describes the Jews who must divest themselves of all particular traits to achieve social and political emancipation:

> The Jew, who has been naturalized and residing in Germany for centuries, must first deny his race, his descent, his historical memories, his type, temperament, and his character, not to prove himself worthy to the state, but to a people who will never develop a modern political life, so long as it does not overcome its natural race prejudices.[43]

Clearly, to Hess, the price for political and social emancipation in Germany is too high. Despite the political rhetoric of *Bildung,* the Germans themselves are not prepared for Jewish emancipation. The state may seek an emancipated citizenry, but the German people harbor "natural race prejudices" that thwart Jewish integration. German political philosophy is really German racial policy. The Reformers not only divorce themselves from their Jewish heritage, but also embrace a culture that teaches racial superiority. While demanding uniformity, Germans distinguish between Jew and the "blond German." The emancipation that Jews seek, therefore, can never be fully realized:

> What help is emancipation to the Jew? What does it matter if here and there a Jew becomes a councilman or a representative, or even minister, so long as a stain is attached to the name "Jew," which every snooty fellow [*hochnäsige Bursche*], every obscure journalist, every dumb young kid, can exploit with sure success?[44]

An emancipation premised on the abandonment of Jewish community is really not emancipation at all, because the German will never allow Jews to divest themselves fully from their Jewish heritage. In the previous chapter, we noticed how Hess marshaled his own "scientific" evidence to make the same point. Here Germans only accept what the Reform Jews deny: the politics of race. So paradoxically, while *Bildung* as state ideology stifles Jewish racial and religious identity, German prejudices encourage the rhetoric of Jewish racial belonging. *Bildung* as political philosophy claims to be universal and available to all, even as it appeals to the local politics of race.

Hess claims that German racial prejudices filter into the political ideal of *Bildung* as the model for German citizenry.[45] When theory (*Bildung*) and practice (racial prejudice) conjoin, the German race becomes the "pure" and universal citizen required by German *Bildung:* "[H]e [the German] views his natural and spiritual endeavors not as German but as humanitarian tendencies."[46] The liberal citizen of the *Bildung* community affirms German racial superiority while professing universal values. "Humanistic tendencies" exist only in the theory of *Bildung,* whereas racial views prevail in "Praxis." In theory, Germans conceive themselves as "pure" human beings (cultivated in *Bildung*), yet in practice (Praxis) think and act as particular human beings with "natural sympathies." To conform to the ideal of *Bildung,* Germans repress racial prejudices only to re-inscribe them onto the cultivated ideal of liberal citizenry: the particular German value becomes the liberal human value. German anti-Semitism, then, results from this political commitment to a universal citizenry that masks the particular value of the German race. But that value is never in full view to assess or evaluate. Differences are concealed in order to protect the universal value of German *Bildung.* In theory, all share and ascribe to this value. But in practice, Germans are its sole owners: "The German hates the Jewish religion less than their race; less their peculiar beliefs than their peculiar noses."[47] What Germans really object to is the particular expressions of otherness that conflict with their "pure human nature." The Jewish race and nose confront Germans as pure otherness, but they cannot accept alterity as such. Differences must be subsumed under the more exalted value of a pure and universal human nature. German *Bildung* conditions Germans to detach themselves from their emotions and racial antipathies. We are all abstract selves, *Bildung* teaches, severed from our immediate surroundings, emotions, and bodies. But Hess replies that Germans and Jews are also embodied selves, with peculiar beliefs, traditions, and noses. The German rebels against this embodiment because it contradicts a deeper commitment to *Bildung,* for the *Bildung* community is one in which valued differences no longer make sense. The liberal commitment to a universal citizenry leads to the denial of difference.[48]

There are good reasons to believe, as I have suggested, that Hess's critique of *Bildung* is off the mark. But one need not subscribe to his theory of German anti-Semitism or *Bildung* to appreciate his claim that a commitment to purity must repress difference. It is significant that Hess could not recognize this in his own racial theory, where the Jews are perhaps the only race with "integrity." He is notably inarticulate when specifying the content of Jewish patriotism, and stakes a claim to purity that in principle can neither be demonstrated nor demonstrated to the contrary. Yet his critique of Reform Jews is no less powerful for his failure to recognize his own commitment to purity. Indeed, Reform Jewry appropriates the very faults in Hess's racial theory. Hess insists that German Reformers, to win citizenship, must substitute uniformity for difference, abstract selves for embodied persons, and a "neutral" society for particular and distinctive communities. Jews can no longer recognize singular attachments and values because the ideology of *Bildung* restrains difference. Commitments to abstract purity—whether in the idiom of race or *Bildung*—whitewash important differences, or even more, must eliminate them altogether.

Communities and languages are divisive, and often nourish goods that are foreign, perhaps even hostile to other communities. It is precisely this recognition of difference that the *gebildete* Jews deny. One kind of divisive good, according to Hess, is a Jewish homeland that will enable, even cultivate a rich Jewish life. The Jewish state is not an end, but a means to facilitate a more reflective Jewish existence. Only within the framework of national freedom, Hess argues, can Jews begin to recognize the depth and meaning of their identities.

To be sure, we should recognize how much Hess shares with his Reform colleagues. Both are attracted to abstract ideals: race for Hess and *Bildung* for the Reformers. For all that, or really in spite of it, *Rome and Jerusalem* calls for a national, reflective awakening as an alternative vision to Reform ideology. It is a call, to the Moses of the midrash as much as to his friend Berthold Auerbach, to return home, to recognize the distinctive commitments that sustain Jewish identity.

The failure of Reform ideology to recognize important differences that inform Jewish identity is most acute, Hess believes, in the writings of Reform rabbi Samuel Hirsch (1815–1889).[49] Hess offered only a biting reproach, rhetorical to the extreme, of Hirsch's book, *Die Humanität als Religion* (1854)[50]—a collection of lectures given by Hirsch to his fellow freemasons at the Luxembourg Masonic Lodge. In the preface, Hirsch summarizes his book as a challenge to the Prussian Masonic lodges that denied Jewish membership.[51] Hirsch's lodge in Luxembourg was open to both Christians and Jews, which in part explains the numerous quotations in his book from both the Hebrew Bible and New Testament. Jacob Katz argued that Hess "described it [Hirsch's text] correctly as an attempt to overcome the differences between the opposing religions on the basis of Masonic ideology."[52] In Hess's words,

> More topical [to our discussion] are the attempts of those fusionists, who, like my friend Hirsch from Luxembourg,[53] would like to make use of freemasonry in order to fuse the various historical traditions. The Luxembourg Rabbi, the antipode of his namesake, the Frankfurter Hirsch [Samson Raphael], has developed the idea of fusion so thoroughly in the excellent lectures given at the Luxembourg lodge and published under the title, *Humanity as Religion*, that with his work this

direction of argument can be considered closed. The Jewish rabbis have now nothing better to do than to close their Reform temples and lead their Jewish parish-
ioners into the temple of freemasonry.[54]

To Hess, Hirsch's book exemplifies the core of Reform ideology and the ideal of
German *Bildung*. With *Bildung* as their ideal, Jewish rationalists like Hirsch have
no reason at all to remain within Judaism. The fusion of historical traditions will
lead to the religion of universal humanity.

Though Hess does not explicitly offer a direct critique of Hirsch, it is clear
why Hess takes this work to be a paradigmatic statement for Reform Jewry. First,
Hirsch adopts an abstract philosophical concept (he labels it *Arbeit*) to understand
religious traditions, thus minimizing historical particularity and differences. But
the history of religious traditions does not concern Hirsch, for he focuses only upon
the eternal truths symbolized in religious practice, and not upon the practice itself. Hirsch must therefore curb religious and national particularity, and suppress
distinctions that impede full social and political acceptance within the German
polity.

In Hirsch's religious taxonomy, *Arbeit* is the essence of religion and "the concept of man." It is a kind of directed activity in which "others" become "fellow-
beings" (*Mitmenschen*) who express human freedom in their capacity to dominate
nature. This builds unifying relationships of love, represented in the universal
brotherhood of freemasonry:

> In the Masonic lodge true freedom prevails. We want only free beings, that is, be-
> ings who understand that freedom is gained in and through their activity [*Arbeit*].
> . . . In the end, the Masonic lodge is an image of honorable brotherly love. . . . We
> accomplish in life what the Masonic Lodge symbolically teaches us.[55]

The "religion of the future," in which toleration and love transform human interaction, begins with *Arbeit*, and ends in the freemason community.

Hirsch's theory of religious symbol develops out of his general discussion of
human creative activity. Symbols are helpful when *Arbeit* proves difficult or confusing, for they mediate and make clear "the idea of religious activity." Through
art—painting, sculpture, poetry, and music—symbols express the eternal, universal, and true ideas through tangible things and activities. The *Cultus*, Hirsch
claims, is "the art of religion," mediating eternal truths through tangible human
activity: it is the "symbolic expression of the idea of life" and "necessarily comprises
all of human life, as much secular life as one's inner being."[56] Historical cults, in
Hirsch's theory, express in their symbolic activity the same eternal truths, so that
only the truth proclaimed is of religious significance.[57] This is most pronounced in
Hirsch's analysis of the Hebrew Bible:

> For us, only the thoughts that were put into the mouth of Abraham and Moses
> are important. These thoughts exist. If Abraham and Moses had not spoken them,
> then some person living at a later time must have put these words into Abraham
> and Moses' mouth. This later person [and not Moses and Abraham] had these

thoughts, but these thoughts remain no less grand or true in his mouth, than in the mouth of an Abraham.[58]

Moses and Abraham are merely passive vessels for the true idea. But their character or historical context have no philosophical import. The passive construction—the words *were put* into their mouths—testifies to the philosophical power of the words, and not to the significance of the figures who reveal them.

Since cults are mere vessels for eternal truths, Hirsch minimizes, indeed obscures the differences between Judaism and Christianity. The birth of Israel is remembered in the Jewish Passover. But, Hirsch continues, the Christian Christmas refers to the same universal truths: the victory and eternity of truth over error, right over wrong, virtue over vice, the good life and justice over misery and evil. The Jews, though loyal to Jewish holidays, are still good Christians with respect to eternal truths:

> To the Jews Jesus could bring no new teachings—for their old writings contained the same teachings, the same axioms, the same principles as Jesus had taught and proclaimed. To merely call oneself Christian, to merely confess to the truth of Christianity as was taught by Jesus: this the Jews who lived at the time of Jesus did as passionately as Christians do today.[59]

Christianity is but Judaism in another name: the content is the same; only the form has changed. This is not a call for Jews to join Masonic lodges, as Hess would have it. Instead, these lodges, and Christianity itself, must become more Jewish. The "religion of the future" may be Judaism in the form of freemasonry, but it is Jewish nonetheless.

Hirsch's analysis of religion is a political and social defense of Jewish emancipation and the German liberal ideal of *Bildung*. Religious symbolism, if properly understood, promotes the toleration required for Jewish access to the political and social goods of European society. Understanding religious expression as symbolic activity supports religious toleration based on universal truths: every religious tradition maintains specific patterns of worship, yet each is committed to the same eternal ideas. But Hirsch is concerned only with the Christian and Jewish traditions. He sharply condemns Buddhism as "the true religion of atheism" that abandons this-worldly engagement.[60] Hindu, Egyptian, Roman and Greek religions fare no better.[61] Apparently, only Jews and Christians aspire to German *Bildung*. Jewish membership in Masonic lodges is thus but one entry into the wider *German* public arena of social and political associations.

It should be clear why Hess would reject Hirsch's conception of religion as symbolic directed activity. Hirsch expands the religious realm into a universal, human quality. *Arbeit* is not distinguished by its historical context, cultural expression, language, or ritual. The historical Abraham and Moses are forsaken for the pure, rational "word": only the pure, rational idea, and not the personal or cultic form it takes, is of philosophical and religious value. In *Du dernier Article de M. Hirsch* (1865), Hess refers to *Rome and Jerusalem*, claiming that there he criticized Reform rabbis who eliminated the historical character from "our ancient tradition" and imitated the "purely negative work of the Christian rationalists" in order "to procure emancipation."[62] In a later essay, Hess objects to Christian rationalists who "abstract from facticity and history" and sacrifice the real, historical Christ for the "rational, pure Christ." The Reformers, following the Christian theologians, conceive Judaism as a rational, ideal faith, rather than as a historical tradition.[63] Witness Hess's account of the Reform movement in his *Lettres sur la Mission d'Israël dans l'Histoire de l'Humanité* (1864):

> If the Israelite Reformers in Germany have changed the character of our tradition, it was not done in order to harmonize it with morality and modern precepts, but rather in the futile hope, which is contrary to the spirit of Judaism, to attract a Christian bystander into their temple.[64]

The Christian will feel comfortable in a Reform temple, for the "ideas of Protestant Christianity," Hess later tells us, can be found there too.[65] This is what Hess calls "the fusion of the various historical traditions." It is a "leveling tendency" in which historical and religious distinctions vanish, and universal articles of faith become the essence of a new, single, and uniform religious community.[66] In Hirsch's *Religion*, Judaism and Christianity dissolve into the symbolic activity of freemasonry. As shared human activity, Masonic religion unites diverse practices, and so fits well with the ideal of *Bildung*. Reform Jews would be more honest, Hess asserts, to work for the dissolution (*Auflösung*) of Judaism, rather than strive to defend it.[67] The Reform rabbis should close their temples rather than invite Christians in, and with only eternal truths to declare, send their community to Samuel Hirsch's Luxembourg Masonic lodge. Here, in the universal community of brotherly love, German *Bildung* can find its home.

Hess argues that a "fusion of cults" tears Jews away from their political, social, and religious ties to the Jewish community. Identity, in Hirsch's *Religion*, is premised on the notion that these historical ties are of little value: particular activities, rituals, and traditions symbolize universal truths that all humans share. The universal community (the Masonic lodge) is the *gebildete* religion of the future. This is exactly what Hess fears. In Hirsch's model, emancipation in Germany means only a freedom *from*, and not *to*, stronger Jewish attachments.[68] True religion must offer a thicker account of historical traditions:

> This "religion of the future,"[69] of which a few of the eighteenth-century philosophers and their present day blind adherents had dreamed . . . will not be a shadowy reflection of the neo-Christian and neo-Jewish skeleton, the possibility of which still haunts the minds of our religious Reformers like a ghost. Every nation must have its own historical tradition; every people must become, like the Jewish people, a people of God.[70]

Notice the imagery: Reformers are "blind," plagued by ghosts, shadows and skeletons. Built on the bones of a "neo-Christian and neo-Jewish skeleton," their "religion of the future" dissolves difference, thus destroying human identity. Like ghosts, the Reform conception of Jewish identity hovers in obscurity beyond reality. The Reformers renounce the "people of God," haunted as they are by the shadowy abstractions of German *Bildung*. Hess's religion of the future, by contrast, recognizes the distinctions of those who develop their own historical traditions. He even suggests that the category of difference marks a nation as a "people of God." Religious life is situated in separate and distinctive national-historical communities, and not in the skeletal framework of a deracinated, and ultimately unreal citizenship in the universal *Bildung* community.

How fair is Hess's critique of Hirsch's *Religion*? In his critical response to *Rome and Jerusalem*, Hirsch defends his view of religion and Judaism:

> I have already demonstrated in lectures held in the Lodge that Masonry amounts to nothing if it does not appropriate the basic principles of Judaism. Even the Freemasons require Jewish principles. No! [According to Hess] I am supposed to have demanded that the Jews become Masons.[71]

Hirsch insists that Jews need not become Freemasons, as Hess unjustly infers, but rather Freemasons must be more Jewish! The principles of Judaism form the basis of Masonic ideology. Thus freemasonry is only a public front for the true religion of the future: Judaism as the "religion of love and tolerance." Indeed, the ideal of German *Bildung* is, according to Hirsch, the basis of Judaism itself. By exposing the Jewish principles of freemasonry, Hirsch reveals the Jewish ideals that underlie German *Bildung*. The religion of the future, as Auerbach had claimed, is *Bildung*. But this is but a universal Judaism under a different name.

Hess seems oblivious to this point. This is striking, because Hess argues for much the same in his discussion of modern nationalism. According to Hess, European nationalist movements are rooted in the Jewish tradition. Jews need not adjust to a new modern development, but merely recognize their own Jewish nationalism as the source of European nation building.[72] Nationalism does not destroy Jewish particularity, but realizes instead its full flourishing. Hess's argument for Jewish nationalism is formally similar to Hirsch's claim that the ideal of *Bildung* develops out of Judaism. Yet Hess is seemingly unmoved by Hirsch's appeal for toleration and the concept of religion that justifies it. Their political commitments remain too far apart for any hope of consensus on religious issues. But more than this, their understanding of Jewish identity is radically dissimilar. Hess is surely right to argue that Hirsch's conception of symbolic activity will ultimately minimize distinctions between Christians and Jews. With *Bildung* as an ideal, universal truths become the content of religious identity, and not national history, racial belonging, or family ties. But it is unfair for Hess to simply dismiss Hirsch's conception of Judaism as a "fusion of cults" that no longer maintains ties to the Jewish community.

Even more striking is Hess's claim that Hirsch's *Religion* represents the programmatic statement of German Reform ideology. This is certainly not the case. The Reform movement was far more varied, and less unified than Hess suggests. He highlights an extreme case in order to denounce Reform as a whole. Witness Gotthold Salomon, the Reform rabbi of the Hamburg Temple, and his critique of symbolic interpretation:

> If we are permitted a symbolic explanation, if we see in the serpent of Satan, or in the tree of knowledge, something that cannot be perceived, then with what right can we reject the many and ridiculous absurdities with which one or another church, with this or ten other interpretations, has put forth, or even further (because the realm of the irrational is borderless) will put forth.[73]

Salomon, unlike Hirsch, discredits symbolic readings because he fears that such "irrational" accounts will undermine distinctive Jewish interpretations of those texts. Salomon's reform is not a "fusion of cults."

But Hess's critique of Hirsch's *Religion* is not merely rhetorical. There are substantive issues at stake, not the least of which is Hess's claim that embodied features are necessary if we are to distinguish and recognize identity. When *Bildung* becomes the sole content of religious and national traditions, identity ceases to be worthy of reflective reasoning because it is no longer problematic. Hirsch dissolves the complexity of Jewish identity because, in the end, identity masks a deeper concern for religious toleration. Freemasonry represents for Hirsch a home where Jews and Christians recognize their common humanity. Religious ritual and family history are now formal differences that conceal a more basic, because more common, identity. Freemasonry is not only a shared community, but a community of common persons. If Jewish principles underlie this conception of personhood, as Hirsch insists they do, then Jews are rendered incapable of evaluating differences that mark Jews as Jews, because there is no longer a Jewish identity to think about. Hess's critique of Hirsch's "fusion of cults" is particularly insightful on this point. To unite the various historical religions, Hirsch must locate common concerns and ideals, and he does this by means of symbolic interpretation. But his "fusion" also obscures important differences in religious identity. These differences must remain in view, Hess maintains, in order to recover the embodied richness of Jewish identity.

Recall Ludwig Philippson's complaint that Hess, who did not observe Jewish laws or customs, still urges strict Jewish ritual observance. To Philippson, this is the newest form of hypocrisy. Hess responds that Philippson badly misunderstands his book. In a letter to Philippson, Hess offers this rejoinder:

> One need not be Orthodox, nor a Jew in general, in order to come out in principle for the ancient Jewish tradition [*Kultus*] and against Reform Judaism, which I in my book convincingly demonstrate, without making the charge of hypocrisy.[74]

In 1873, some eleven years after its publication, Hess reminds his readers that in *Rome and Jerusalem* he argued that Jewish biblical religion should be understood as an "essentially social tradition [*Kultus*]."[75]

This social tradition is an embodied one that shapes particular Jewish identities. But the Reform Jews, Hess responds, appeal to a flawed conception of tradition in their "religion of the future." The Reform tradition is rooted in what Hess calls "modern individualism": the "religious need to secure unlimited well-being for the individual."[76] Hess's racial theory has already made clear that Jews cannot escape their religious tradition through enlightenment or conversion: "every Jew is, whether he wishes it or not, solidly united with the entire nation [*Nation*]."[77] The

Jewish community cannot be deserted for an alternative, secular culture premised on the sanctity of the individual. And this for two reasons: 1) Jewish race and tradition (as Hess understands them) define the contours of Jewish identity, and 2) modern Germany is not a "neutral society," but one that dissolves Jewish particularity altogether. Individual, secular culture is hostile, Hess claims, to Jewish communal aspirations. It is therefore also hostile to identities informed by religious traditions.

Grounded in a racial heritage with ties to the Jewish tradition, the enlightened Jew is a tragic figure, unable to become what the Reform ideology demands. Hess has only disgust, however, for the Reformer's "meaningless nihilism" and "unrestrained anarchy" that destroy "Jewish sensibilities."[78] This unconstrained contempt belies Hess's own entrenched commitments. He defends a strong communal solidarity in the face of modern individualism, and affirms an embodied identity that resists aspirations to German *Bildung*. In Hess's view, the ideal of self-cultivation can lead to significant misunderstandings. *Gebildete* Jews, believing themselves to be the creators of their own Jewish identities, fail to recognize the constraints of Jewish tradition and race upon their own self-formation. *Bildung* as *true* character formation (what Hess labels *Fortbildung*) is an embodied ideal shaped by a historical tradition. But the *gebildete* Jews are neither the citizens of the liberal polity, nor Jews attached to the broader Jewish community. They cannot find their selves because their selves are nowhere to be found.

Traditions: Race and Scars

Features of Hess's account of tradition are anchored in his racial theory. In *Lettres sur la Mission d'Israël dans l'Histoire de l'Humanité* (1864), Hess describes *notre culte* as a "bond" that ties "the past and future together": it is "our flesh and bones, the expression of the holy spirit." Jews cannot renounce the Jewish tradition, for it is their "flesh and bones," and Jews can only define themselves in terms of it. Hess never acknowledges that his racial theory shares much with his portrayal of Reform tradition, for both adopt (according to Hess) the ideal of universal purity that defies local differences and complexity. While he insists that Reformers will never become universal citizens in a neutral society, he still believes that race is the universal essence that secures Jewish purity and integrity. Hess relies on the authority of race science and base emotional ties for his national philosophy. The Reformers cannot recognize these deeper attachments, Hess thinks, because they are too wedded to their strong misreading of Mendelssohn's philosophy of Judaism:

> The tradition of Israel is a national tradition, just as every primitive tradition is at first. This Mendelssohn had already understood, but without mentioning its true cause. But the supernatural cause [of the tradition], upon which his thesis rests, is in plain contradiction to his rational philosophy. His students have adopted his rational philosophy, but abandoned the tradition which is based on a supernatural faith.[79]

The supernatural faith of Mendelssohn in the eighteenth century has become Hess's racial dogma in the nineteenth. Indeed, Hess contends that he, and not the Reformers, is Mendelssohn's true disciple. But Mendelssohn also affirms a natural philosophy that translates divine commandments into "ceremonial law." The "enlightened" Jews, following the "philosopher of Berlin" (Kant), adopt Mendelssohn's philosophical construction only.[80] In so doing, the Reformers naturalize a religious tradition that, for Hess, remains forever supernatural.

Judaism is a national tradition, a nexus of memories, rituals, texts, and race, but not, claims Hess, a repository of philosophical truths. This idea is, of course, in part faithful to Mendelssohn's claim that Judaism possesses a "divine legislation" without "universal propositions of reason."[81] But Mendelssohn's Reform disciples divide the "divine legislation" into rational and historical truths, translating Judaism into articles of faith. Hess's critique echoes much of Mendelssohn's *Jerusalem*:

> The Jew is not commanded to believe, but rather to search after the knowledge of God. Belief is a matter of conscience, for which we are accountable to ourselves only, and not even capable of being accountable to anyone else.[82] It is certainly as easy for shallow rationalism as it is for blind faith to proclaim its creed. But knowledge of God, which grows out of the innermost life of the spirit and sensibility, develops with the individual and humanity; it cannot become established once and for all through articles of faith [*Glaubensartikel*].

Tracings of Hess's racial theory persist just below the surface in such phrases as "the innermost life of the spirit and sensibility." Great thinkers of the past (the list includes Saadia, Maimonides, Spinoza, and Mendelssohn), understood the "lesson of Jewish historical religion," and never conceived of "reforming the historical basis of our tradition."[83] That basis, it appears, is Jewish racial belonging.

But if race provides one inescapable framework for the "historical basis" of Jewish tradition, then another, more complex account emerges in Hess's other texts. The "innermost life of the spirit," rather than signifying racial belonging, instead harbors conflicting attachments. These attachments inevitably complicate Hess's critique of Reform, and suggest a more nuanced view of how traditions fashion identity. This revisionary account of tradition is most evident in Hess's discussion of the sacrificial ritual.

Before turning to that account, I want to outline two sophisticated models for a tradition in order to better assess Hess's own. We have already charted much of Charles Taylor's account of a tradition as a "moral map." As a "map of our moral world," a tradition offers guidance, stability, and meaningful answers to basic concerns. A tradition is, Taylor claims, "an attempt to give shape to our experience."[84] Traditions provide the frameworks within which ethical and religious questions are meaningfully answered. Much of Taylor's theory draws from Alasdair MacIntyre's work on narrative and tradition. In an early essay, MacIntyre argues that when paralyzed by an epistemological crisis, a person searches for a new dramatic narrative that "enables the agent to understand *both* how he or she could intelligibly have held his or her original beliefs *and* how he or she could have been so drastically misled by them."[85] Traditions are littered by conflicting narrative accounts, such that every tradition could potentially fall into incoherence. When such epistemological crises occur, a new story is reconstituted that makes better sense of the old one, and offers a more plausible interpretation of that tradition. "Revolutionary reconstruction" is necessary and productive because, in Taylor's language, it gives better shape to the agent's experience. Strong evaluation, inescapable frameworks, and narrative identity are all important features of a tradition in good working order. A tradition, for both Taylor and MacIntyre, is a continual process of epistemological gain in which an agent constructs increasingly better dramatic narratives that give shape and meaning to a person's life.

Edward Shils's account of religious traditions is an influential second model.[86] Like Taylor, Shils calls a tradition a "guiding pattern" in which one learns techniques of conduct, virtuous behavior, ethical norms, and the ends of human fulfillment. Traditions are inescapable because persons are born into a range of traditional cognitive and emotional concerns that form the background to actions and thoughts. Yet traditions are "very seldom entirely adequate": "We could say that traditions change because they are never good enough for some of those who have received them. New possibilities previously hidden are perceivable when a tradition enters into a new state." Shils's account of how traditions change is instructive:

> They [human societies] accept what is given to them by the past but they do so gracelessly for the most part. The acquisition from the past furnishes their home but it is very seldom a home in which they are entirely at ease. They try to bend it to their own desires; they sometimes discard or replace some of the inherited furniture.[87]

Some elements of the tradition become more prominent, others less so, due to an agent's shift in focus and interest. When persons confront a crisis in meaning (when they are not "entirely at ease"), they select the most appealing aspects of a tradition in order to construct a workable and meaningful account. The image of "inherited furniture" suggests that one can easily replace, rework, or rearrange one's traditional home. Traditions are thus malleable enough to comply with contemporary needs and desires. What is achieved is not so much an epistemological gain as a reordering of the traditional furniture to acquire a more comfortable home. It is, in Shils's Weberian reading, the routinization of the charismatic message.[88]

Hess's ambivalent treatment of the Jewish sacrificial worship provides a significant contrast to both Shils's and Taylor's understanding of tradition. The sacrificial institution was a significant and fervent issue for nineteenth-century Jewry. Some Orthodox rabbis, notably Zvi Kalisher (1795–1874), supported the Jewish return to Palestine in order to rebuild the ancient Temple and restore sacrificial worship. This—even as the Reformers were erasing all mention of Palestine and sacrifice from their prayerbooks.[89] If, as Hess thought, the Jewish tradition harbored various commitments, memories, and messianic visions, then it would apparently include the animal sacrifices so prominent before the destruction of the Temple in 70 CE. Although the sacrifices were eventually abandoned, they still maintained a central place in daily religious prayers, and therefore bridged the historical space between the past and present in religious memory. The ancient sacrificial worship was part of the historical furniture, as Shils would have it, if not in practice, then in the memories and hopes of many religious Jews.

Leopold Löw, the Hungarian Reform rabbi and editor of *Ben Chananja,* challenged Hess's account of the Jewish tradition on exactly this issue.[90] Löw requested the details for implementing religious worship in Palestine. Would it include, he asked, the old *Opferkultus* (sacrificial worship)? If Hess could abandon the sacrifices of the past, Löw argued he must also give up the other ancient religious institutions. For Löw, either one accepts the old furniture or replaces it wholesale. Hess replied that his idea of tradition was far broader than Löw's more limited *Opferkultus,* for a historical tradition included "institutions" other than sacrificial worship. Hess argued against restoring the *Opferkultus* in the future Jewish state.[91] Yet Hess is far from certain, indeed very much ambivalent, about the place and value of sacrificial worship in Judaism. In *Rome and Jerusalem,* Hess presents two different accounts of the sacrifices and their place in the future Jewish state. Together, his views reveal how strong ambivalence may be a typical condition for persons dedicated to and informed by a vibrant tradition.

Hess claims that the sacrificial worship, as only a minor feature of Jewish tradition, is both dispensable to and unworthy of Jewish religious practice. He marshals an impressive array of medieval and modern biblical scholars to defend his position (a list that includes Maimonides, Avravanel, and Samuel David Luzzatto). But a second, equally powerful argument is found toward the end of *Rome and Jerusalem.* Despite his "individual conviction," Hess refuses to "anticipate history":

> There are questions, which a priori, that is, before the actual working out of them in praxis, are irresolvable, but find their solution in the course of historical development. To these questions belong the idea of the tradition in general, and especially the development of specific forms and norms of divine worship out of the ethical-religious spirit of a people, who in every epoch of its development was its own creator of its religion.[92]

The future Jewish tradition will not resemble its present form, just as the present tradition has changed from the ancient sacrificial institutions. The "ethical-religious spirit of a people" develops and changes, and so too do the religious rituals that embody it. Each generation develops its own tradition that fittingly expresses its deeper religious and ethical commitments. And since history can, for Hess, be only dynamic, creative, and open, so too tradition and Jewish identity: "The Jewish tradition which we will celebrate in the new Jerusalem," Hess concludes, "can and must remain an open question."[93]

On the one hand, Hess opposes restoring sacrificial worship. He cites authoritative commentators who question the value and viability of sacrifices even within a rebuilt temple. On the other hand, Hess recognizes that in the future such practices might be re-established. He is torn between a deep repugnance for the practice and a commitment to the indeterminacy of history and tradition. He cannot deny the practice even as he wishes to abolish it. This leads Hess to reconsider the very nature of sacrificial worship. Referring to the problem of sacrifice in ancient Judaism, Hess attempts to reconcile his conflicting emotions and commitments:

> True love, the love that dominates spirit and mind, is in actuality *blind.* Blind because it does not desire, philosophically or aesthetically, the perfection of the beloved being, but rather loves it just as it is with all its excellences and faults. . . . The scar on the face of my beloved does not harm my love, but rather makes it even the more precious—who knows?—perhaps more precious than her beautiful eyes, which can be found in other beautiful women, while just this scar is characteristic of the individuality of my beloved.[94]

Paradoxically, it is love's blindness that reveals the scar—the blemish of the sacrificial institution. The scar is, furthermore, not a philosophical truth but an embodied feature of Jewish tradition; an indication that Hess's racial views are surfacing here again, for he compares animal sacrifice to the beautiful eyes "in other beautiful women," and finds the blemish more valuable because more distinctive. Recall Hess's account of intermarriages, in which Mongolian traits predominate in Russian children, yet the Jewish type shows no trace of such admixture. In that striking passage, Hess adds: "I showed an artist the beautiful picture known to you which would have honored the work of a Phidias. The artist could not admire it enough and finally, as if the light had suddenly shined on him, exclaimed: I wager that this is a picture of a Jewess."[95] There are no scars in that picture. Jewish women possess beautiful eyes precisely because they belong to the Jewish race. But in Hess's account of animal sacrifice, Jewish racial heritage is scarred and marked. Indeed, the Jewish race is scarred by its past traditions, and as with racial belonging, is defined and constricted by them. If the beautiful picture of the "Jewess" exposes Hess's romantic retrieval of pride in Jewish racial belonging, then in his love for the scar Hess accepts the disfigurings that are permanent features of his tradition. He simply refuses to replace the old scarred furniture with a more comfortable set. This is one aspect of what Stuart Hampshire calls the no-shopping principle: one cannot pick and choose from among competing conceptions of the good life, and construct a more holistic pattern of human flourishing by discarding undesirable features of one's tradition.[96] Hess is both embarrassed and sickened by the idea of animal sacrifice (the scar), yet appreciates how central it is to Jewish ritual observance. Sacrificial worship cannot be evaded, because it is stamped on the "face," however beautiful or distinctive, of Jewish memory and history.

The ancient sacrifices continue to influence Hess's understanding of Jewish identity. Hess had previously implied, in his refusal to "anticipate history," that Jews develop their own religious rituals according to contemporary needs. Thus Hess would not preclude the return to sacrificial worship. But those needs do not create, by themselves, a religion, much less a tradition. Instead, Jews struggle, as Hess does here, with a tradition that impinges upon, if not constricts the kind of choices and values they pursue. Traditions do not meaningfully answer fundamental questions so much as expose ambiguity and conflict. Hess's description of animal sacrifice as a "scar" reveals this tension quite well.

Hess's tradition is not Shils's furnished home in which one constructs a viable tradition from among its most appealing features. The old furniture remains, for a scar cannot simply be dismissed nor completely replaced. This is the force of Hess's racial theory, for the scars of the past are part of the permanent furniture of historical traditions. But given this account of sacrificial worship, moments of conflict are fundamental, indeed integral to a healthy and rich exploration of identity. Thus Hess's tradition is far more partial and fragmented than Taylor's "moral map" suggests. Although both Taylor and MacIntyre recognize that traditions are dynamic and often deeply conflicted, they both maintain that a strong narrative account will reconstruct, and thus reconstitute a coherent traditional identity. Hess is much more ambivalent about his past, and must negotiate among conflicting pressures and desires. Epistemological gains and coherent dramatic narratives do not give sufficient weight to Hess's continued ambivalence, powerfully expressed in his account of the scar.

A scarred tradition is an indeterminate one. Where racial belonging overcomes conflict, Hess's reading of the scar embraces it. And yet the love of the scar "just as it is" manifests another tension. National belonging cannot be justified nor scorned, but only affirmed as an inescapable feature of Jewish identity. It is to embrace the nation "just as it is." The scar represents one unavoidable aspect of that belonging, and suggests that racial heritage is both blessing and curse. Hess's racial theory betrays his struggle to belong, to feel at home in a tradition that often repels him. We see in Hess a person divided against himself, moved by multiple conflicting goods, devoted to past rituals that conflict with his modern sensibilities. He is a person not even at home in his own tradition. The Jewish tradition is a contextual battleground, a negotiated space in which Hess struggles with the complexity, ambiguity, and scars of his Jewish identity.[97]

Identity and Creativity: Hess's Critique of Jewish Orthodoxy

Hess's critique of German Orthodoxy reinforces this more fragmented and negotiated picture of Jewish tradition. Orthodox Judaism represents, to Hess, a secure insular community that shuns modern goods, aspirations, and enticements. To be sure, Hess shares much with the Orthodox reproach of Reform. In his *Nineteen Letters* (1836), the modern Orthodox rabbi Samson Raphael Hirsch (1808–1888) argues that emancipation should only be a means to gain basic civil rights.[98] The Reformers, however, made emancipation their *only* goal. Eighteen years later, in his *Religion Allied with Progress* (1854), Hirsch's criticisms are sharper and more caustic: "At the marketplace of politics, where emancipation was to be purchased, the sons of Judah could be seen everywhere, trading old-style Judaism for 'progress.' "[99] For both Hess and Hirsch, Reform Judaism represents a disgraceful abandonment of Jewish tradition, community, and identity.[100] But if Samuel Hirsch's

Reform dissolves Jewish identity altogether, then for Hess, Samson Raphael Hirsch's Orthodoxy is far too restrictive:

> It seems we must either side with the *Luxembourger* Hirsch [Samuel] that the goal and the primary essence of Judaism is humanity, and thus not a national but a human goal is worth striving for, as witnessed in freemasonry and Reform. But then Judaism, as well as every religious or political society, has the vocation to be devoured in general humanity. Or we side with the *Frankfurter* Hirsch [Samson Raphael] who sees in Judaism the exclusive salvation. But then we see a contradiction between the modern humanitarian movement and, like Orthodox Christianity, make little appeal to public opinion in our century. . . .
>
> There is absolutely nothing one can do with barren Orthodoxy and the uncritical reaction, for they still declare that the Polish fur cap is a law given to Moses on Sinai.[101]

As Samuel Hirsch represents Reform ideology for Hess, so Samson Raphael Hirsch exemplifies German Orthodoxy. Where the Reformers are "devoured" in German *Bildung*, the Orthodox prove too extreme as well: renouncing modernity outright, they reject legitimate public criticism and the value of pluralism. Hess denounces Orthodox "rigidity," exemplified most acutely in Samson Raphael Hirsch's symbolic interpretation of the commandments. S. R. Hirsch's symbolic reading, Hess concludes, suppresses competing interpretations. While securing a uniform and meaningful Jewish identity, Hirsch's symbolic account still cannot suppress the creative oral tradition that continually reinvents Jewish law.

Hess wishes to remove the "rigid forms" of German Jewish Orthodoxy and uncover its latent national spirit. This "rigid cover," which Hess calls *Rabbinismus*, will naturally dissipate in the wake of the national reawakening:

> The rigid forms of Orthodox Judaism, which were completely justified until the century of rebirth, will, from this time onward, be naturally ruptured through the vitality of the living idea of Jewish nationality and its historical tradition [*Geschichtskultus*]. Only out of a national rebirth will the Jewish religious genius, like a giant that touches its motherland, cultivate new powers and will again be inspired by the holy spirit of the prophets.[102]

Hess claims that only his critique can reconstruct Orthodox rabbinism without destroying the very essence of Judaism—the national historical tradition. His imagery is important. Hess imagines that within Orthodox rigidity there remains a vibrant Jewish tradition and a community yearning for a national rebirth. Yet this powerful "living idea" is hidden behind a wooden formalism that suppresses Jewish creativity. Hess's critique is meant to shatter the "rigid cover" and revitalize the historical interpretive tradition within an inflexible Orthodoxy.

The imagery of stagnation and rigidity is also found in Hess's critique of Christianity and Islam. Christianity is "the religion of death," its historical function completed now that modern nations have "returned to life." Both Christianity and Islam teach only resignation and submission, and their historical success is dependent on forced oppression: "Christianity and Islam are only inscriptions on the tombs which placed barbaric pressure on the graves of nations." France, the modern nation of freedom, will break the hold of Christian and Islamic barbarism, "rolling away the tombstones from the graves of the dead, and the nations will return to life."[103] The motif is striking, not only for what it says about Jewish and French supercessionism, but also for Hess's own critical project. Like rabbinism, Christianity and Islam are spiritually debilitating. But they lack a "living idea" resting within its "rigid forms." France, the savior of modern nations, must sweep aside entirely the Christian and Islamic "inscriptions on the tombs" in order to resurrect modern national consciousness. Within this context, Hess's revision takes on a larger, more global meaning. What France will do for Europe, Hess will do for Jewish Orthodoxy: he will remove the tombs ("rigid covers"), and reawaken the Jewish national tradition that sleeps within.

Hess exhibits little awareness of the religious reforms and genuine engagement with modernity then taking place within the Orthodox community in Germany.[104] He aligns himself with the burgeoning historical school critics—Rappoport, Frankel, Krochmal, and Sachs—citing their work to ridicule Orthodox practice and interpretation.[105] But just as the Reform community did not all support Samuel Hirsch's symbolic interpretation of religion, so too the Orthodox community in Germany was far more diverse and open to educational and hermeneutical reforms. Ismar Schorsch has argued persuasively that the modern, university-educated rabbi was not solely a Reform innovation. Isaac Bernays and Samson Raphael Hirsch, while not receiving doctorates, were both university-trained Orthodox rabbis.[106] David Ellenson has discussed how the Orthodox rabbi Esriel Hildesheimer endorsed *wissenschaftliche* scholarship and modern educational methods.[107] Through a singular lens, Hess focuses only on those aspects of Samson Raphael Hirsch's program that are most suspect.

Hess finds his target in Hirsch's symbolic reading of the commandments. Hirsch's theory is an audacious attempt to infuse precise and intricate meaning into Jewish religious observance; in effect, it attempts to provide an observant Jew with ready-made, irrefutable answers for religious observance. In his *Grundlinien einer jüdischen Symbolik* (1857),[108] Hirsch "draws up guidelines for a science [*Wissenschaft*]" of Jewish symbolic interpretation of the commandments.[109] Symbolic expression is natural, like bodily gestures, but not "ephemeral and fleeting" like spoken words. Serving as "constant reminders of the ideas they represent," symbols are more effective than language because "they set forth their meaning with deliberate sameness":

> [Symbolic acts are] sequences of physically perceptible gestures, all of which express one and the same idea, one and the same emotion. . . . [They evoke] a specific thought, a specific emotion, or a specific chain of thoughts and emotions.

The symbolic performance is, in Mendelssohn's language, a redemptive "living script."[110] The meaning of symbolic acts, however, does not proceed from the activity itself, but from "the intention [*Absicht*] of the one who instituted the symbol."[111] Only knowledge of God's intention will confer precise meaning to the symbol.[112] *Wissenschaft*, in Hirsch's theory of symbol, is the study of God's intentions.

Hirsch's discussion of tefillin provides a good illustration of his methodology at work.[113] Tefillin serve as an example of *Edoth*: a category of commandments in the Hebrew Bible that Hirsch calls "symbolic words and acts."[114] In *Horeb* (1837), a compendium of Jewish law and its meaning, Hirsch argues that wearing tefillin expresses four (and only four) essential Jewish beliefs: 1) God delivered the Jewish people from Egypt (the basis of Judaism), 2) service to God maintains human life (the implementation of Judaism), 3) Jews must take to heart (*Verherzigung*) the fulfillment of Israel's mission, and 4) tefillin have served as a memorial for Jews and non-Jews throughout history.[115] Both in *Horeb* and in Hirsch's biblical commentary we find intricate and detailed interpretations of the precise meaning of tefillin, even for their very shape and material.[116] For example, the shape of the *bayit* (the "house" which is worn on the forehead) is square and not round, because

> of all the creative organic forces it is only the energy of man, who thinks and acts freely, that constructs linear or angular forms. We therefore maintain that the circle characterizes the structures produced by organic forces not endowed with a free will, while angles and squares are hallmarks of man.

The "bayit" *must* be square, for human beings are endowed with freedom, and "the square is the mark of human freedom which masters the material world." God wishes to remind us of our human freedom, and our responsibility (to God) to exercise it.[117] As one scholar notes, "the more abstruse the rite and the more unintelligible its observance, the more complex and weighty is Hirsch's explanation."[118]

The precise meaning for each symbol and symbolic activity lies at the heart of Hirsch's defense of Jewish practice. In a long footnote to the eighteenth letter in *The Nineteen Letters,* Hirsch compares the study of nature with the study of Torah. Revealing the assumptions of Hirsch's hermeneutical theory, and the justification for his own symbolic reading, the passage is worth quoting at length:

> One word here concerning the proper method of Torah investigation. Two revelations are open before us; that is, nature and the Torah. (For both there is only one method of research.) In nature all phenomena stand before us as indisputable facts, and we can only endeavor *a posteriori* to ascertain the law of each and the connection of all. . . . The same principles must be applied to the investigation of the Torah. (Fact is Torah to us like heaven and earth; as fact the Torah's ordinances lie before us.) In the Torah, even as in nature, God is the ultimate cause. In the Torah, even as in nature, no fact may be denied, even though the reason and the connection may not be understood. What is true in nature is true also in the Torah; the traces of divine wisdom must ever be sought for. Its ordinances must be accepted in their entirety as undeniable phenomena. . . . So, too, the ordinances of the Torah must be law [*Gesetz*] for us, even if we do not comprehend the reason

and the purpose of a single one. Our fulfillment of the commandments must not depend upon our investigations. Only the commandments [*Gesetze*] belonging to the category of *Edoth,* which are designed to impress emotional and intellectual life, are incomplete without such research.[119]

Torah, like nature, is a compilation of undeniable facts.[120] But the written text requires the oral commentary for its own completion, and is itself not the source of its own authority.[121] Hirsch implies that the written Torah is not an integral, self-contained text, effectively reducing the written text to the background while positioning the oral tradition in the foreground. This is clear in his claim that the *Edoth* require "research" for their own intelligibility. Symbolic reading of the commandments completes what remains "incomplete." Hirsch's own detailed, symbolic commentary to the written text is a recovery of oral Torah. The symbolic reading reproduces the thoughts and intentions of God.

With this kind of symbolic interpretation in mind, Hess considers Hirsch's *Wissenschaft* to be, in truth, "a return to the old uncritical belief." It is, Hess emphasizes, "in *conscious* contradiction with reason."[122] Yet Hess's general appraisal of S. R. Hirsch's interpretation is imprecise and cavalier. He tells us that there are two fundamental tendencies in Judaism: the first is a radical individualism and subjectivism, which we find in Samuel Hirsch's interpretation of religion, and the second is S. R. Hirsch's need (*Bedürfnis*) to base Judaism on objective criteria. In the end, S. R. Hirsch's symbolic reading is nothing but a "desperate reaction." Hess admits that as an antidote (*Gegengift*) against Reform Judaism, German Jewish Orthodoxy may prove valuable, but it cannot substantiate the "valid norms" that it promises.[123]

What are we to make of Hess's critique? A clearer picture emerges from Hess's general appraisal of sacrificial worship (discussed above) and his own interpretation of tefillin. We have already observed Hess's ambivalence toward the return of sacrificial worship in a Jewish state, together with his insistence that the Jewish tradition of the future is open and indeterminate. One cannot predict or secure the future of the tradition, Hess argues, for each generation must discern the meaning of its own religious practice.[124] Hess reiterates this claim in the twelfth letter:

> I believe, as I have already remarked, that the future tradition of *all* reborn nations will be very different from the traditions of today.

> Finally I must stress again that our future tradition, like those of all other people, will not precede the national regeneration, but rather follow it.[125]

Refusing to offer *the* meaning of sacrificial worship, Hess cites a long list of alternative readings by medieval and modern rabbinic commentators. The multiple voices (all apparently authoritative) confirm Hess's claim that each generation must struggle to discover the significance of sacrificial worship in particular, and the meaning of the Jewish tradition in general. In a possible allusion to S. R. Hirsch, Hess admits that one might interpret sacrificial worship as "symbolic activity." But the "might discover" (*mag man erblicken*) suggests that Hirsch's symbolic reading is only one possible source. Hirsch's authoritative voice is relativized by the wealth of competing Jewish interpretations and the indeterminacy of the future Jewish historical tradition. The normative thrust of Hirsch's reading conflicts with Hess's belief that each generation must struggle for the religious meaning of the commandments.

Yet in his discussion of tefillin, Hess argues that meaning is too obscure even for the most perceptive of Jewish interpreters. He recalls an anecdote (which, he maintains, is quoted often by the Reform Jews) in which a Jewish man boasts before Moses Mendelssohn that his son no longer wears tefillin. After reporting the story, Hess cites both the biblical command to lay tefillin as a symbol of divine teaching, and the historical-critical research of his time that suggested wearing garments with fringes (tallit) was, in fact, an older custom than tefillin. But neither the symbolic biblical command nor the *wissenschaftliche* research are really at issue here between the observant Mendelssohn and the "enlightened Epicurus":

> The Berlin philosopher's attitude to Orthodox Judaism is in no way a strict consequence of his rationalistic thinking, although *even he* wants to persuade himself of this. Rather, it is a natural expression of his Jewish sensibility.[126]

Even Mendelssohn is unaware of the reasons for his commitment to tefillin! Hess does not justify Mendelssohn's observance by quoting biblical texts, nor criticize it with historical research. Rather, he appeals to a private and vague "sensibility," echoing the language of his racial theory. Due to the "natural expression," the enlightened Reformer would never understand Mendelssohn's emotional attachment to tradition. The point, I want to emphasize, is that neither could Mendelssohn.

Where Hess supports multiple meanings, or even replaces meaning with a vague "sensibility," Hirsch attaches fixed, immutable, and exacting interpretations to the commandments. Hess cites traditional Jewish authorities, yet claims that even they have no normative claim on future meanings. This approach contrasts sharply with Hirsch, who appears as *the* authority, the true and only revealer of God's intentions.[127] Jews need not struggle with textual ambiguity nor alternative readings, for Hirsch's revelation unveils the secrets of Torah, nature, and God. Yet Hess claims that even a traditionalist like Mendelssohn may be unaware of the real motivations for his observance. For Hirsch, to the contrary, the efficacy of the *Edoth* requires the full understanding of their deeper symbolic meaning. Hirsch's symbolism attempts to find "objective, valid norms" where none can be found. It is to purchase security at the price of obscurantism. Hirsch represents, for Hess, "the need for objective, valid norms, and the inability to create them."[128]

I have already commented that Hess exhibited little knowledge of the diversity and reforms within the Orthodox community in Germany. In Samson Raphael Hirsch, Hess had chosen an embattled leader, criticized by Orthodox and Reform alike, and one who envisioned himself as a lonely champion of traditional Judaism in a disbelieving age.[129] But Hess's claim that Orthodoxy is nothing but "uncritical reaction" is, like his critique of Reform, more than rhetoric. What Hess distrusts most about Hirsch is the finality of the interpretive enterprise. The oral tradition, Hess insists, continually develops and invigorates Judaism in exile. The creative capacity and adaptive techniques of the oral tradition ensure Judaism's very survival: "The national-legislative genius would have been extinguished if we had not engaged in the continuing development [*Fortbildung*] of the law." Not *Bildung*, but *Fortbildung* of Jewish law informs Jewish identity and continuity. Knowledge of God "develops," and is not "established once and for all." To Hess, the continuous, vibrant, and open activity of textual interpretation is "more holy work than merely standing by the written law." The future national rebirth, Hess tells us, will develop out of the fruits of the oral tradition.[130]

Hess's emphasis on the oral tradition is a polemical strategy designed to offset the excesses of Reform and Orthodox exegesis. He argues that his fight against Reform and Orthodoxy is analogous to the fight of the ancient rabbinical sages against "barren formalism." The rabbinical leaders of the past combated the stagnation and rigidity in religious thought and practice by refusing to write down the oral tradition. From *Mund zu Mund* the oral tradition continued as a living, changing, and creative spiritual instruction. The sages finally reduced the oral law to the written word due to the great danger that Jews in exile would forget the oral tradition completely. But this danger no longer exists, Hess argues. To avoid inscribing what should remain oral, we must

> awaken in ourselves both the spirit of critique against a paralyzing formalism, and the holy, patriotic spirit—which continually inspired our lawgiver, prophets and sages—against disintegrating rationalism.[131]

The paralyzing formalism and the disintegrating rationalism are terms that Hess elsewhere employs to describe the Orthodoxy and Reform of his day.[132] As the sages of old fought against freezing creative exegesis in fixed written language, so too Hess's appeal to the creativity and openness of oral law works in his generation to offset the "Luxembourg" and "Frankfurter" Hirsch. When oral law flourishes again, Hess promises, "we will again take part in the holy spirit," and Jewish law "will again develop and adapt according to the needs of the Jewish people." Then, Hess concludes, "when the end of the third exile comes, we will find ourselves prepared in the right way for the restoration of the Jewish state."[133]

Hess's appeal to indeterminacy, creativity, and pluralism rings hollow in the face of his racial theory. For just as S. R. Hirsch secures Jewish continuity in the metaphysics of symbolic discourse, so too does Hess protect Jewish identity in the narrative of racial belonging or Jewish "sensibility." Hess easily recognizes Hirsch's appeal to hermeneutical authority, yet is so utterly blind to his own counterclaims. But Hess's text comprises many voices, and one that emerges is his own ambivalence toward the Jewish tradition and its "scars." A strategy to overcome this anxiety is to appreciate how multiple and competing readings of texts inform and nourish Jewish identity. But an inexhaustible interpretive license may solve some problems even as it opens others. If creative hermeneutical strategies are required to combat Orthodox formalism, then a racial science might provide a reliable basis upon which to assess multiple readings. Hess recognizes the need for pluralism, but fears the "anarchy" and "nihilism" of the Reformers. He must therefore limit even while permitting conflicting textual voices. Hess uses race science to constrain those accounts that he believes will destroy the embodied, communal features of Jewish identity. Readings of texts shape identity, and so too the traditions that foster them. There are multiple pressures in *Rome and Jerusalem*, some visionary, others restrictive, but all operate in Hess's account of tradition. In Hess's defense of a Jewish tradition founded on racial heritage and creative textual readings, the reader witnesses again how negotiated strategies mark *Rome and Jerusalem* a singular work among Hess's texts, and such a modern one at that.

Taylor's account of strong and weak evaluation highlights what is most distinctive about Hess's ambivalent relation to the two divergent accounts of tradition in *Rome and Jerusalem*. Taylor draws upon Harry Frankfurt's influential essay, *Freedom of the Will and the Concept of a Person*. Frankfurt distinguishes between first-order and second-order desires. Someone has a first-order desire when he or she wants to *do* or not to *do* X, and a second-order desire when he or she wants to *have* or not to *have* a certain desire of the first order.[134] For example, John desires to be wealthy. But he also recognizes that wealth can lead to behavior and values he finds objectionable. If John were a person with only first-order desires, he would simply desire money for its own sake. But he would lack the reflective self-evaluation necessary for the formation of second-order desires. He would not reflect on consequences, on value, on the kind of being he wants to be. The "wanton" person, says Frankfurt, is simply indifferent to the "enterprise of evaluating his own desires and motives."[135]

The capacity to form second-order desires is what Taylor calls strong evaluation. If John's identity is in part defined by his goals, by what he desires to achieve or maintain, then John must ask: "do I really want to be what I am now? Is this the kind of being I want to be?"[136] Answering these questions requires contrastive language that ranks virtues, values, and commitments according to some standard of excellence (justice, equality, liberty, image of God). Second-order desires express what persons value most. At stake here, says Taylor, is "the definition of those inchoate evaluations which are sensed to be essential to our identity."[137] To be a strong evaluator, to form second-order desires, is to reflect upon the kind of person one wants to become.

Recall Taylor's "famous Sartrian example" discussed in the previous chapter. A young man is torn between two conflicting commitments: staying with his ailing mother or joining the French resistance. In Taylor's reading, the conflict cannot be recognized as an ethical one without appealing to some notion of strong evaluation. The young man must comparatively judge competing ethical claims, and determine how one alternative is superior to the other. Only a theory of strong evaluation as inescapable framework can make sense of a choice between conflicting claims. Taylor emphasizes that strong evaluation is "something inescapable in our conception of the agent and his experience."[138] Sartre's young man can act upon and defend his choice because he is, by virtue of being human, a strong evaluator. He can make sense of ethical conflicts because he can comparatively evaluate different commitments.

Persons with first-order desires lack the reflective capacity to decide which of those desires they would like to cultivate or abandon. They cannot articulate questions of value because they are indifferent to evaluating desires and motives. Similarly, Jews who identify through racial belonging will not ask whether they desire to be this kind of Jew: the "Jewish type," as Hess argues, is not open to reflective evaluation. It is not true that these persons are "indifferent to value," as Frankfurt would argue. But if asked why they *should* value the Jewish race, they can only appeal to a "true, natural feeling" that "can be neither demonstrated nor demonstrated to the contrary." It would not make sense for these Jews to ask Charles Taylor's question, Is this the kind of person I want to be? Yet the question is essential for strong evaluation, for it motivates a hierarchical ranking of the noble and base in order to express value. Hess's racial theory depends instead upon the "natural feeling" of Jewish continuity, stability, and racial harmony. It calls for weak rather than strong evaluation.

The problem for Hess is not that he fails to offer a ranking of values (he certainly does). His dilemma is, rather, that he cannot justify his strong evaluations.[139] It is this very inability to defend fundamental commitments that provokes the kind of ambivalence we see in Hess's account of tradition. This ambivalence is also responsible for his failure to assess coherently values and commitments. Taylor's theory of strong evaluation suggests that an agent can rank, from the ground up, as it were, those values that best express and shape his or her identity. The tensions between competing commitments are reduced, perhaps eliminated altogether, if a stronger ranking can show why one commitment is less valuable than the other. But does this mean that sufficient justifications are always readily available, such that every strong evaluation is rationally and coherently defensible? Hess's account of the "scar" and his ambivalent stance toward the Jewish tradition illustrate that while a ranking of values is always possible, reasons for that ranking are often unavailable.

This is why political philosopher Stuart Hampshire insists that "lack of sufficient reason is not ground for apology" because moral choices often are not rooted in a "comprehensive and reflexive" position.[140] Hampshire suggests, rightly I believe, that many of our most cherished values are like this. We cannot offer sufficient, grounding justifications for our commitments, and this because "our divided, and comparatively open, nature requires one to choose, without sufficient reason, between irreconcilable dispositions and contrary claims."[141] Hess's scarred account of tradition reflects this ambivalence, for even as he adopts the Jewish tradition as his own, he can only offer the beauty and singularity of the scar as the reason (insufficient, to be sure) for his choice. Hess implicitly recognizes this when he glosses his account with, "who knows?," and explicitly acknowledges it in his description of human desire—"the need for objective, valid norms, and the inability to create them."[142] These are not contrasting judgments of evaluation, yet Hess's explanation of them make up the most powerful and moving texts in *Rome and Jerusalem*.

Hess's analysis of tradition indicates that many strong judgments cannot be adequately defended. At some level, a claim simply cannot be demonstrated nor demonstrated to the contrary. There may be good reasons to accept or deny a principle or view, but just as often we do "plump for one rather than the other"[143] because not every strong evaluation is rationally defensible. This is certainly true in Hess's account of a traditional "scar." Unable to dismiss sacrificial worship entirely, Hess uneasily accepts it as part of the historical furniture of his tradition. The Reformers, by contrast, abandon that furniture for the empty ideal of German *Bildung*. Hess seeks to distance his account of tradition from the one he ascribes to Reform (even if, in his racial account of Jewish belonging, he remains very close to it). His commitment to sacrificial worship is not trumped or ranked lower in value, but is situated, side by side as it were, with other claims about the creativity of interpretation, historical contingency, racial attachments, and recognition of difference. Taylor's strong evaluator, however, would not give up so easily, and would attempt to "show up" Hess's confusion by refashioning a more stable hierarchy. But love is blind, Hess insists, and so the "lucidity" promised by strong evaluation will fall short. Hess is also blind to how much his two versions of Jewish tradition deviate from each other—the one scarred with ambivalence, creativity, and openness; the other marked by race, continuity, and difference. These two accounts are indeed signs of muddled thinking; but that is no ground for apology. Instead, they indicate that Jewish tradition, and the persons formed by it, are as uncertain, ambiguous, and fragmented as Hess suggests they should be.

Innocence and Experience
in *Rome and Jerusalem*

Bernard Williams distinguishes between two kinds of philosophers: those who believe in an underlying pattern and structure to human history and reason, and those who see no such order. While the comparison is overdrawn, it still offers a valuable guide to evaluate philosophical commitments:

> Plato, Aristotle, Kant, Hegel are all on the same side, all believing in one way or another that the universe or history or the structure of human reason can, when properly understood, yield a pattern that makes sense of human life and human aspirations. Sophocles and Thucydides, by contrast, are alike in leaving us with no such sense. Each of them represents human beings as dealing sensibly, foolishly, sometimes catastrophically, sometimes nobly, with a world that is only partially intelligible to human agency and in itself is not necessarily well adjusted to ethical aspirations.[1]

I have argued throughout this work that Moses Hess, even as he yearns for a pattern that makes sense of modern identity, often betrays the tragic sentiment that human agency is only partially intelligible to historical persons. It is this dynamic between openness and concealment, clarity and obscurity, and coherency and conflict that is most expressive in Hess's works. One detects a constant presence of revisionary forces that undermine dominant motifs. Here we find a coherent, unified narrative of national identity, yet elsewhere discover moments of chance encounters that challenge such totalizing, inescapable frameworks. If Hess at times reads like a Hegelian philosopher, the Sophoclean tragic vision is always present, too—revising, containing, challenging.

Charles Taylor's account of modern identity is a robust, persuasive, and highly influential contemporary revision of what Williams labels the "Plato, Aristotle, Kant, Hegel" school of philosophical analysis. Taylor, like Hegel before him, affirms that "human reason can, when properly understood, yield a pattern that makes sense of human life and human aspirations." His conceptual categories adopted here—narrative identity, inescapable frameworks, tradition, and strong evaluation—all work to uncover the moral and religious sources that inform a coherent, secure identity in the modern world. Hess, as we have seen, embraces much of Taylor's position. But as we trace those revisionary pressures that threaten Taylor's approach, Hess's works uncover features of modern identity that are left unexplored in Taylor's thesis.

One such feature is the role that conflict and ambiguous relations play in enriching notions of modern identity. In the middle chapters of this book, we have seen Hess struggling to balance conflicting commitments and values. Recall the discussion in chapter 3, where Hess attempts to integrate competing narrative accounts of his "return" to Judaism. The balance that Taylor seeks among various competing commitments cannot but minimize the serious disintegrating pressures that are produced by conflicting narrative accounts of return. When Hess affirms the one narrative, he only intensifies the pull of the other. Hess's return to Judaism is problematic because these countervailing stories disclose an identity in conflict. The notion of countervailing forces extends the self and broadens our notion of identity. Hess's works show us that identity relies upon the interplay and authority of multiple narratives. Taylor's hierarchy of values offers little solace for a modern Jew steeped in the ambiguity and pressures of conflicting accounts of identity.

Moses Hess is a conflicted and often tormented figure who defies exact categorization—religious Zionist, socialist, philosopher, Jew—precisely because he feels the narrative pull of each. He so often disappointed and angered friends, and still today confounds his interpreters, who look for the one category only to find that he fits so many others. But this is, to my mind, what makes his work so challenging and rewarding for contemporary Jewish thought. As I argued in chapter 2, Hess's early works express a singleness of purpose unmatched in his later texts. Only in *Rome and Jerusalem* (and later pieces) do we find other voices overtly, and sometimes covertly, threatening what once were secure and "scientific" claims. But those former commitments remain strong and defiant, resisting the displacement and authority of other narratives. They cannot be summarily resisted nor undermined by new portrayals of identity. Hess's construction of identity in *Rome and Jerusalem* is a contested site that continuously endangers the integrity of the work as a whole. This is so because Hess himself is sensitive (however unconsciously) to the multiple threads that interweave and complicate modern Jewish identity. *Rome and Jerusalem* is a testimony to the complexity, pressures, and disenchantment of the modern Jewish struggle for self-affirmation.

Ultimately, Williams's dichotomy between the comic Hegel and the tragic Sophocles forces Hess's notion of modern Jewish identity into a stifling *either/or*. I suggest, drawing upon the work of Stuart Hampshire, that Hess's works invite, instead, a nuanced *both/and*. Modern persons inevitably and continuously oscillate between moments of clarity and inconsistency, harmony and discord, purity and compromise. Jewish identity today is not a progressive gain in narrative clarity, as Taylor suggests, but instead an ever present struggle with the multiple and ambiguous scars of religious traditions.

Religious scars, in Hess's reading, are both exotic and repulsive. The scars of Jewish sacrificial worship attract Hess with their singular beauty, even as they offend his aesthetic and moral sensibilities. This dual relation mirrors what Stuart Hampshire perceives as an unavoidable split between "the acclaimed virtues of innocence" and the "undeniable virtues of experience." Hampshire's political philosophy attempts "to bring the rift, and the consequent ambivalence, into full view."[2] To illustrate this, he portrays two architectural models of innocence and experience:

the Quaker meeting house and the chapels of the Vatican. Hampshire wants us to imagine a meeting house with "freshly whitewashed walls," unadorned with pictures or alters, and a room without "designated spaces for rituals and sacraments":

> As soon as you open the heavy oak door and step inside, you are aware of stillness, purity of outline, and cleanness, of the absence of distractions and encumbrances, of the invitation to quiet reflection.[3]

Purged of all "pretence [*sic*] and all inherited conventions and authorities," the Quaker meeting house turns away from moral complexity and ambiguity, and represents a vision of the good that "sweeps away anything contaminated or corrupted or squalid." The virtues of innocence correspond to this vision of simplicity and cleanness: integrity, gentleness, generosity, and a sense of honor. Hess too appeals to these innocent virtues when describing ancient sacrificial worship. The Quaker meeting house, like those sacrifices, portrays a singular beauty uncorrupted by more complex and damaging emotions.

Not so the Vatican. If the Quaker meeting is the life of innocence, then the Vatican represents the conflicts and everyday drudgery of experience:

> The Church has lived through innumerable wars, periods of exile, negotiations, unwanted compromises, embarrassing alliances, distressing manoeuvres [*sic*], and secret betrayals.

> [Defending the Church] is a political activity and famously requires something of "the cunning of the serpent," the ingenuity of worldly wisdom, which Aristotle claimed that both rogues and statesmen need.[4]

In the corridors of the Vatican, "ideals of personal integrity and of moral innocence are kept in abeyance." This, because the virtues of experience—tenacity, courage, largesse of design and purpose, habits of leadership—disturb the more innocent virtues. Experience is "guilty knowledge" in which one accepts a life of "necessary disappointments and mixed results, of half success and half failure."[5] Hess's moral outrage and aesthetic disgust with sacrificial worship are rooted in this "guilty knowledge" where religious apologetics and identity politics are at play. The philosophical point, Hampshire insists, is that "there is no completeness and no perfection to be found in morality."[6]

The consequent human ambivalence surrounding innocence and experience arises from the desire to unite irreconcilable virtues within a unified model of the good. This desire, I have argued, is best represented in Taylor's philosophical program. But Hampshire's conception of the good, rather than integrative and harmonious, is instead a mosaic of "many distinct interests and commitments, usually exhibiting some general pattern, but probably not a very clear one."[7] The good is ambiguous and unclear because persons are drawn to both the virtues of innocence and experience, and are moved by these values in diverse ways. Hampshire insists that we experience conflict between competing moral requirements in our everyday lives. An established way of life "has its cost in repression," for certain dispositions and values must suffer at the expense of others. Conflicts are not signs of muddled thinking, Hampshire claims, but are instead fundamental to good ethical reasoning. Morality has its sources in conflict, and there is no assured resolution or harmony.[8] Practical reasoning and moral theory are neither tidy nor secure from ambiguity, conflict, and luck, and should not be if one values the peculiarities of individual character.

Hampshire doubts that practical reasoning can lead to an intelligible moral harmony. But if this were so, it would demand the repression of certain dispositions that do not fit the dominant moral order. When coherence is the ideal, then particular virtues and visions of the good become normative and thus divisive. Instead of yearning for security and harmony, Hampshire demands that we face our finitude nobly, and establish procedural accounts of justice that adjudicate between conflicting visions of the good. The life of innocence and experience—and the goods and virtues they foster—interweave, obscure, and continually revise, like a mosaic, the identity of modern persons.

The strategies employed by Hess to unify conflicting accounts of modern Jewish identity are movements of innocence and experience. The persistent oscillation between moments of clarity and discord is the most distinctive feature of Hess's works. Hess offers two dominant narrative depictions: the one rooted and secured in a racial theory developed out of his earlier socialist and scientific works, and the other a more contingent, conflicted, open view that is new to the pages of *Rome and Jerusalem.* These two narratives interweave in provocative ways, subverting and clarifying features of identity that, like Hampshire's mosaic, portray "many distinct interests and commitments, usually exhibiting some general pattern, but probably not a very clear one." Hess's texts are mosaics of many colors, exhibiting the tension of revisionary and conflicting strains that pull his works in competing directions. Hampshire tells us that his theory of innocence and experience arises from his interest in deceit, and he argues that "conflicts of feelings" are both natural and useful.[9] The dynamics of deceit and integrity play out before Hess's readers, but it is a serious play that raises important issues for modern Jewish identity.

Hess affirms, in various modes and in different contexts, the value of narrative continuity, the rootedness of racial belonging, the freedom of indeterminate meanings, and the interpretive authority of historical contingency. There are both clarity and deception in Hess's works, moments of innocence and experience that, taken singly, violate the supremacy and authority of other narratives. Hess's racial theory, for example, defies reflective critique, just as it spurns moral ambiguity. The Jewish "type," he argues, can neither be defended nor refuted, but is to be accepted as scientific, racial truth. Immune to practical reasoning, racial theory is an ideal of innocence. An innocent life, purified of the complexity and contrivances of experience, "allows the rays of sunlight to shine through clear windows on to clean walls."[10] Surely, the recollection of a lost purity, a moment of contentment, or a harmony of purpose can generate the most creative and hopeful ideals. They can also lead, however, to a story of perfection that undermines the complexity, ambiguity, and contingency of a human life. The temptation of an innocent narrative is strong precisely because, as even Hess admits, persons yearn to overcome the conflicts of their existence. Hess's racial theory is one such innocent account of Jewish identity. Unable to live solely with the ambiguity and conflicts in modern Judaism, Hess requires a coherent narrative account that justifies Jewish national politics and identity, and he finds it in a racial theory that is beyond rational critique. But this racial narrative minimizes, even obscures the complexity of relations and emotions that Hess reveals elsewhere in his account of identity and tradition.

It would be misguided and overtly apologetic to deny the significance of race and racial ideology in Hess's construction of modern identity. We should not labor to move beyond race in order to adopt only what is most compelling for contemporary readers. Instead, we should acknowledge Hess's racial theory as a powerful and persuasive narrative of self-affirmation. Racial theory remains an integral feature of *Rome and Jerusalem* and later essays. It represents Hess's attempt to restore the lost national heritage of the Jewish people. For this reason, betrayal is the most destructive vice in Hess's theory of the good. The Reformer is a traitor to his people, race, and family. To make sense of this, Hess relies on a racial history of purity and integrity. He does not defend his patriotism by exploring emotional attachments to the past, or obligations to family members, nor even how scars reveal unique beauty and attraction. Neither does he defend a national Jewish identity as the most plausible and defensible account of Jewish commitment in the modern world. All this would raise complex and delicate arguments that Hess can easily dismiss with a racial narrative that understands betrayal as impure blood. Hess still believes he can offer a defense for Jewish national identity based on foundational or scientific premises. If he were more convinced by his own insights into the ambiguity of Jewish identity and tradition, and the arguments that underlie them, perhaps he would see his racial theory as an innocent vision of the most vicious sort.

Deceit, betrayal, integrity, and loyalty are all features of an experienced and innocent life. Hess and his work manifest, at different times, these traits of human character. The text that best represents this ambiguity and conflict is worth quoting again here:

> True love, the love that dominates spirit and mind, is in actuality *blind*. Blind because it does not desire, philosophically or aesthetically, the perfection of the beloved being, but rather loves it just as it is with all its excellences and faults. . . . The scar on the face of my beloved does not harm my love, but rather makes it even the more precious—who knows?—perhaps more precious than her beautiful eyes, which can be found in other beautiful women, while just this scar is characteristic of the individuality of my beloved.[11]

The qualities of innocence and experience are all here: deceit, for love is not blind, but instead highlights the scars and beauty of Jewish tradition; betrayal, for in abandoning their national heritage, Reform Jews deny what is most precious, individual, and characteristic of Jewish history; integrity, for the rich expressive doubt, "who knows?" confesses all the inner conflict, uncertainty, and desire for a commanding Jewish identity; and loyalty, in the love and commitment to the whole, with all its excellences and faults. Hess expresses all these features as he struggles with and against unsettling commitments. In one honest moment, he admits that there is "a need for objective norms, and the inability to create them."[12] This is certainly evident in Hess's account of a scarred Jewish tradition. For even as he yearns for objective norms (more precious, more beautiful), Hess admits, however tentatively, that Jewish identity may be far more partial, fragmented, and conflicted. I have argued that Hess's works are scarred; they are texts that reveal the excellences and faults in Hess's struggle for a coherent narrative life, and the deceit and integrity that inform it. Yet Hess is right to say that beauty lies in imperfection. Hess's works are despite, or rather because of the scars, that much better and more valuable for the struggle.

NOTES

1. Moses Hess and Modern Jewish Identity

1. Philippson's criticism against Hess appeared in an anonymous article entitled "Zerstreute Bemerkungen" in the *Allgemeine Zeitung des Judentums*, #45 from Nov. 4, 1862, pp. 642–643. See Edmund Silberner, *Moses Hess: Geschichte Seines Lebens* (Leiden: E. J. Brill, 1966), pp. 426–427.

2. Moses Hess, "Rom und Jerusalem, die letzte Nationalitätsfrage," *Ausgewählte Schriften*, ed. Horst Lademacher (Köln: Joseph Melzer, 1962), p. 274 (hereafter Hess, *Rome and Jerusalem*, p. 274).

3. Silberner, *Moses Hess: Geschichte Seines Lebens.*

4. Jonathan Frankel, *Prophecy and Politics: Socialism, Nationalism, and the Russian Jews, 1862–1917* (Cambridge: Cambridge University Press, 1981), p. 21.

5. Isaiah Berlin, *The Life and Opinions of Moses Hess* (Cambridge: W. Heffer and Sons, 1959), p. 38.

6. Shlomo Avineri, *Moses Hess: Prophet of Communism and Zionism* (New York: New York University Press, 1985), p. 208.

7. Berlin, *The Life and Opinions of Moses Hess*, p. 38.

8. Emilie died in the beginning of 1860 as a mother to two small children, and Josephine raised these children and later became Samuel Hess's second wife. See *Moses Hess Briefwechsel*, ed. Edmund Silberner (The Hague: Mouton and Co., 1959), p. 374, fn. 1; and Silberner, *Moses Hess: Geschichte Seines Lebens*, p. 403.

9. Hess, *Rome and Jerusalem*, p. 224.

10. Even in Hess's personal correspondences, Hess signs his name "M. Hess." See Hess, *Moses Hess Briefwechsel*.

11. This brief account of Hess's life follows Silberner's definitive biography. See Silberner, *Moses Hess: Geschichte Seines Lebens.*

12. Avineri, *Moses Hess: Prophet of Communism and Zionism*, pp. 5–6.

13. Wolfgang Mönke, *Neue Quellen zur Hess Forschung* (Berlin: Akademie Verlag, 1964), Tagebuch, Sept. 16, 1836.

14. Hess, *Rome and Jerusalem*, p. 250.

15. Mönke, *Neue Quellen zur Hess Forschung*, Tagebuch, Sept. 16, 1836.

16. See John Efron, *Defenders of the Race: Jewish Doctors and Race Science in Fin-de-Siècle Europe* (New Haven: Yale University Press, 1994).

17. Hess, *Rome and Jerusalem*, p. 250.

18. Charles Taylor, *Sources of the Self: The Making of Modern Identity* (Cambridge: Cambridge University Press, 1989).

19. Charles Taylor, "What is Human Agency?" *Human Agency and Language: Philosophical Papers* 1 (Cambridge: Cambridge University Press, 1985), pp. 15–44.

20. Ibid., p. 19.

21. Ibid., p. 34.

22. Taylor, *Sources of the Self,* p. 106.

23. Silberner, *Moses Hess: Geschichte Seines Lebens,* pp. 425–426.

24. See Theodor Zlocisti, *Moses Hess: der Vorkämpfer des Sozialismus und Zionismus 1812–1875; eine Biographie* (Berlin: Welt-Verlag, 1921). Zlocisti's main concern is to counter the orthodox Marxist interpretation of Hess, a view that Georg Lukács, five years later (1926), would argue with force. See Lukács's famous article, one that has produced a steady stream of both positive and critical responses within Hess scholarship, *Moses Hess und die Probleme in der idealistischen Dialektik* (Leipzig: C. L. Hirschfeld, 1926). Zlocisti's biography is largely an apologetic work designed to bolster Hess's image in the face of Marxist criticism. Regarding Hess's religious thought, Zlocisti argues that one must understand his socialism (as well as Lassalle and Marx's, for that matter) as an outgrowth of his Judaism. "Jewish instincts" (*Antriebe*) inform all of Hess's works, and point to vague ideas of the messianic future and social justice. Zlocisti at one point claims that Hess does not separate religious from national Judaism, but the term *religious* has no other meaning than social justice in Zlocisti's schema. Silberner intends to shift Hess studies away from their dependence on Marxist polemics.

25. Silberner, *Moses Hess: Geschichte Seines Lebens,* p. 1.

26. See Jochanan Bloch, "Moses Hess: 'Rom und Jerusalem'-Jüdische und Menschliche Emanzipation," *Kölner Zeitschrift für Soziologie und Sozial Psychologie* 16/2 (1964), pp. 288–313; Julius Carlebach, "The Problem of Moses Hess's Influence on the Young Marx," *Leo Baeck Institute Year Book* 18 (1973), pp. 27–39; Horst Lademacher, *Moses Hess in seiner Zeit* (Bonn: Ludwig Röhrscheid, 1977); Lukács, *Moses Hess und die Probleme in der idealistischen Dialektik*; Mönke, *Neue Quellen zur Hess Forschung*; and Shlomo Na'aman, *Emanzipation und Messianismus: Leben und Werk des Moses Hess* (Frankfurt/Main: Campus Verlag, 1982).

27. For a good review of Hess studies, as well as critical appraisal, see Zevi Rosen, *Moses Hess und Karl Marx: Ein Beitrag zur Entstehung der Marxschen Theorie* (Hamburg: Christians, 1983), pp. 95–111.

28. Martha Nussbaum, "Non-Relative Virtues: An Aristotelian Approach," *The Quality of Life,* ed. Martha Nussbaum and Amartya Sen (Oxford: Clarendon Press, 1993), p. 245.

29. Hess, *Rome and Jerusalem,* p. 274.

30. Taylor, *Sources of the Self,* p. 31.

31. Nussbaum, "Non-Relative Virtues: An Aristotelian Approach," pp. 243, 263.

2. Conceptions of Self and Identity in Hess's Early Works and *Rome and Jerusalem*

1. Wigand was emphatic: "Die ganze Schrift ist meiner rein menschlichen Natur zuwider [the whole work is contrary to my pure human nature]." See Hess, *Rome and Jerusalem,* p. 234. Also see Silberner, *Moses Hess Briefwechsel,* p. 377.

2. Silberner, *Moses Hess Briefwechsel,* p. 376. Also Israel Cohen, "Moses Hess, Rebel and Prophet," *The Zionist Quarterly* (Fall 1951), p. 51.

3. Isaiah Berlin, *The Life and Opinions of Moses Hess.*

4. Ibid., pp. 26, 35.

5. Hess, *Rome and Jerusalem*, p. 227.

6. Berlin, *The Life and Opinions of Moses Hess*, p. 3.

7. Hess, *Rome and Jerusalem*, p. 286.

8. Frankel, *Prophecy and Politics*, p. 24.

9. Martin Buber, "Der erste der Letzten (Über Moses Hess)," in *Der Jude und sein Judentum: Gesammelte Aufsätze und Reden* (Köln: Joseph Melzer, 1963), pp. 406–419. The English translation can be found in Martin Buber, "Moses Hess," *Jewish Social Studies* 7/2 (1945), pp. 137–148.

10. Max Wiener argues that *Rome and Jerusalem* is a work written by a "religious socialist." He is the only other Hess scholar I am aware of who, along with Buber, regards Hess as a religious thinker. Yet Wiener's utter worship of Hess leads only to summaries of *Rome and Jerusalem*, and offers little analysis of Hess's *"religiöse Geschichtsauffassung."* See Max Wiener, *Jüdische Religion im Zeitalter der Emanzipation* (Berlin: Philo Verlag, 1933), pp. 262–266. Edmund Silberner calls Hess a "religious socialist" in 1951, although he rejects this description by the time he writes his biography (1966). See Edmund Silberner, "Moses Hess," *Historia Judaica* 13 (1951), p. 6; and Silberner, *Moses Hess: Geschichte Seines Lebens*, p. 421, where Silberner claims that, "In *Rom und Jerusalem* wird die Religion nicht mehr direkt bekampft, sie wird aber indirekt unterminiert."

11. Buber, *Der Jude und sein Judentum*, p. 414.

12. Samuel Blumenfeld, *Moses Hess, Dreamer of Realism* (New York: Department of Education and Culture of the American Zionist Council, 1962).

13. Gershon Winer, *The Founding Fathers of Israel* (New York: Bloch Publishing, 1971), p. 59.

14. Georg Lukács, "Moses Hess and the Problems of the Idealist Dialectic," *Telos* Winter 10 (1971), pp. 3–34. The original article in German, published in 1926, can be found as, *Moses Hess und die Probleme in der idealistischen Dialektik.*

15. Note Sidney Hook's claim that true socialists like Hess helped the reactionary nobility in its struggle to retain sole political supremacy in Germany. See Sidney Hook, "Karl Marx and Moses Hess," *New International* 1 (1934), p. 144.

16. Lukács claimed that Hess "remained trapped precisely in Feuerbach's weak and idealistic side: his love ethic." Hess could only "ally" himself with the revolutionary proletariat, "but was never able to think from their standpoint." Marx and Engels, however, "received from Feuerbach at best the stimulation to finally reject the last remnants of Hegelian idealism from their thinking, thus definitely and completely transforming the dialectic in a materialist direction." See Lukács, "Moses Hess and the Problems of the Idealist Dialectic," pp. 16–18. Simon Rawidowicz calls Hess a "modified Feuerbachian," and thinks Marx and Engels were right to see Hess as a follower of Feuerbach. See Simon Rawidowicz, *Ludwig Feuerbachs Philosophie: Ursprung und Schicksal* (Berlin: Reuther & Reichard, 1931), p. 463. Sidney Hook argues that true socialism was "a pseudo-political tendency among a certain group of literary men, publicists and philosophers in Germany, all of whom had been influenced by Feuerbach. It was not a system of thought." Hess, says Hook, was the recognized leader of this group. See Hook, "Karl Marx and Moses Hess," p. 140.

17. See Rawidowicz, *Ludwig Feuerbachs Philosophie: Ursprung und Schicksal*, pp. 458–464; and Silberner, *Moses Hess Briefwechsel*, pp. 105, 335–336, 342.

18. Hook goes so far as to say that Hess was completely unacquainted with the German working class: "the majority of the radical German intellectuals, however, were insen-

sitive to the existence and importance of social class divisions. Imbued with the ideals of a *perfect* society, they were unable to join the bureaucracy which administered *present* society." Again: "the only standpoint from which they passed criticism upon society was an allegedly classless ethics whose values expressed not the immediate need of this or that class but the essential needs of the whole of society. . . . But they had no conception of what constituted the proletariat. The proletariat was identified with an abstract category of distress." See Hook, "Karl Marx and Moses Hess," p. 141.

19. Lukács, "Moses Hess and the Problems of the Idealist Dialectic," p. 34.

20. Bruno Frei, *Im Schatten von Karl Marx. Moses Hess—Hundert Jahre nach seinem Tod* (Köln: Hermann Böhlau, 1977).

21. Ibid., p. 138.

22. Horst Lademacher, "Einleitung: Apostel und Philosoph," *Ausgewählte Schriften*, p. 16.

23. Ibid., p. 39.

24. Ibid., pp. 41, 42.

25. For a discussion of Hess's socialist works in relation to the socialist literature of the time, see chapter 1, n. 26.

26. Ibid., pp. 47, 53.

27. Horst Lademacher, "Die politische und soziale Theorie bei Moses Hess," *Archiv für Kulturgeschichte* 42/2 (1960), pp. 194–230, especially p. 197.

28. Hook, "Karl Marx and Moses Hess."

29. Irma Goitein, *Probleme der Gesellschaft und des Staates bei Moses Hess* (Leipzig: C. L. Hirschfeld, 1931).

30. Auguste Cornu and Wolfgang Mönke, "Einleitung," in Moses Hess, *Philosophische und Sozialistische Schriften (1837–1850),* ed. Auguste Cornu and Wolfgang Mönke (Berlin: Akademie Verlag, 1961), p. 67.

31. The first period is called "God the father," from Adam to the birth of Jesus; the second "God the son," from Jesus to the ascendancy of Spinoza; and the final period "the holy Spirit," the present age. Silberner argues that this trichotomy recalls the philosophy of Joachim of Fiore (1130/35–1201/02). Fiore, like Hess, divides historical periods into the *"Reich des Vaters, des Sohnes und des heiligen Geistes,"* yet Silberner doubts that Hess ever read Fiore. Alexander Altmann believes that Fiore's tripartite theory of history influenced Schelling, and through Schelling infiltrated the historical thinking of later German Christian and Jewish idealists. It is therefore possible that Hess, too, copied Fiore's division of history through his reading of Schelling. See Alexander Altmann, "Franz Rosenzweig on History," *Studies in Religious Philosophy and Mysticism* (Ithaca: Cornell University Press, 1969), pp. 276–277; Silberner, *Moses Hess: Geschichte Seines Lebens,* p. 40; and Hans Liebeschütz, "German Radicalism and the Formation of Jewish Political Attitudes during the Earlier Part of the Nineteenth Century," *Studies in Nineteenth-Century Jewish Intellectual History,* ed. Alexander Altmann (Cambridge, Mass.: Harvard University Press, 1964), pp. 161, 169–170.

32. Hess liberally appropriated Hegel's philosophy of history, but how much he actually studied himself, or merely absorbed from the philosophical culture around him, cannot be known. See Silberner's discussion of *Die Heilige Geschichte* and its philosophical sources in his, *Moses Hess: Geschichte Seines Lebens,* pp. 36–52. Berlin ridicules Hess's *Geschichte* as "pretentious, tedious, badly written metaphysics of history, full of Hegelian clichés." See Berlin, *The Life and Opinions of Moses Hess,* p. 6. Shlomo Na'aman calls it *"Ideengeschichte,"* tying it directly to Hegelian metaphysics rather than to Marxist dialectics. See Na'aman, *Emanzipation und Messianismus: Leben und Werk des Moses Hess,* p. 75. Also see Nathan

Rotenstreich, *Jews and German Philosophy* (New York: Schocken Books, 1984), pp. 160–169, and Nathan Rotenstreich, "Moses Hess and Karl Ludwig Michelet," *Leo Baeck Institute Year Book* 7 (1962), pp. 283–286, for his discussion of Hess's relationship to Hegelian philosophy.

33. Moses Hess, "Die heilige Geschichte," *Philosophische und Sozialistische Schriften (1837–1850)*, p. 18.

34. For an excellent account of the Trinitarian roots of Hegel's philosophy, see Cyril O'Regan, *The Heterodox Hegel* (Albany: State University of New York Press, 1994), pp. 63–80, especially p. 70.

35. Hess, "Die heilige Geschichte," p. 60.

36. Ibid., p. 37.

37. Ibid., p. 31.

38. Ibid., p. 71.

39. Ibid., pp. 72, 37.

40. Frankel, *Prophecy and Politics*, p. 10.

41. Hess, "Die heilige Geschichte," pp. 21–22. For helpful discussions of Jewish and Christian attitudes toward Islam, see Susannah Heschel, *Abraham Geiger and the Jewish Jesus* (Chicago: University of Chicago Press, 1998), pp. 50–61.

42. Hess's discussion of Adam's fall from Eden follows closely Hegel's lectures. See G. W. F. Hegel, *Lectures on the Philosophy of Religion*, ed. Peter Hodgson (Berkeley: University of California Press, 1988), pp. 439–452.

43. Hess, "Die heilige Geschichte," p. 6.

44. Ibid., p. 37.

45. Ibid., p. 6.

46. Ibid., p. 7.

47. Ibid., p. 68.

48. Frankel, *Prophecy and Politics*, p. 8.

49. Hegel, *Lectures on the Philosophy of Religion*, pp. 439–440. Also note Cyril O'Regan's claim that Hegel sought to undermine the "naive Enlightenment view of human being's aboriginal goodness." To Hegel, "human being as such, that is, human being as spirit, who supposes differentiation from the natural environment, is aboriginally evil." O'Regan recognizes Gnostic roots in Hegel's account of creation as fall. See O'Regan, *The Heterodox Hegel*, pp. 151–169, especially pp. 153, 158.

50. For general accounts of Hess's *Triarchy*, which I forgo here, see Silberner, *Moses Hess: Geschichte Seines Lebens*, pp. 67–90; Na'aman, *Emanzipation und Messianismus: Leben und Werk des Moses Hess*, pp. 85–101; and Avineri, *Moses Hess: Prophet of Communism and Zionism*, pp. 47–75. These scholars each offer fair and sound overviews of the book, although they disagree on the importance of Jewish history (Avineri), the work's relation to Hess's first book (Na'aman), and its social and political agenda (Silberner).

51. Moses Hess, "Die europäische Triarchie," *Philosophische und Sozialistische Schriften (1837–1850)*, p. 90.

52. Ibid., p. 116.

53. Ibid., pp. 97, 165. Otto Wigand, Hess's publisher, wrote a book himself in 1839 called *Die europäische Pentarchie*—counting Prussia, Austria, Russia, England, and France as the dominant political and social powers. For Wigand, Russia and Austria were supreme. Silberner thinks that Hess's work is an indirect polemic against and answer to Wigand's thesis. See Silberner, *Moses Hess: Geschichte Seines Lebens*, p. 79.

54. Hess, "Die europäische Triarchie," pp. 105, 150.

55. Ibid., p. 102.

56. Moses Hess, "Religion und Sittlichkeit," *Moses Hess: Sozialistische Aufsätze (1841–1847)*, ed. Theodor Zlocisti (Berlin: Welt Verlag, 1921), pp. 27–30. Hess employed the then popular Hegelian distinction between religion and ethical life (*Sittlichkeit*). For an excellent analysis of Hegel's use of these terms, see Charles Taylor, *Hegel and Modern Society* (Cambridge: Cambridge University Press, 1979); and John Edward Toews, *Hegelianism: The Path toward Dialectical Humanism, 1805–1841* (Cambridge: Cambridge University Press, 1980).

57. See Svante Lundgren's discussion of "Religion und Sittlichkeit," in his *Moses Hess on Religion, Judaism and the Bible* (Aobo: Aobo Akademis Förlag, 1992), pp. 56, 60, 107–109. Lundgren distinguishes between Hess's interpretation of religion as established religion and *Sittlichkeit* as pure ideal religion. He claims that only Hess's attitude toward established religion had changed, yet he remained remarkably consistent about the value of *Sittlichkeit*. But Hess himself did not divide religion from the ethical life in this fashion, and, as we shall see, he altogether rejected this dichotomy a year later in his article, "Über das Geldwesen." But Lundgren seeks a pattern, and thinks he finds it when he describes Hess's interpretation of religion and the ethical life as, "no to religion, yes to Sittlichkeit."

58. Hess, "Religion und Sittlichkeit," p. 27.

59. Moses Hess, "Über Staat und Religion," *Philosophische und Sozialistische Schriften (1837–1850)*, p. 187.

60. For an important study of the differing interpretations of the "left Hegelian" school concerning religion and politics, see Toews, *Hegelianism: The Path toward Dialectical Humanism, 1805–1841;* and Avineri, *Moses Hess: Prophet of Communism and Zionism,* pp. 134–139.

61. See Frankel, *Prophecy and Politics,* pp. 16–17.

62. Moses Hess, "Die eine und ganze Freiheit!" *Philosophische und Sozialistische Schriften (1837–1850),* pp. 227–228.

63. Moses Hess, "Socialismus und Communismus," *Philosophische und Sozialistische Schriften (1837–1850),* p. 202.

64. Hess's shift in his critique of religion and state is certainly indebted to his discussions with Marx between 1842 and 1843. In 1842, Hess was the first editor of the *Rheinische Zeitung.* Deemed too radical for the journal, he became the chief correspondent in Paris, only to return to Köln in 1844. While working for the journal, Hess met Marx for the first time. His glowing admiration of Marx in his letter to Berthold Auerbach in 1841 is now part of Marxist lore: "Dr. Marx-this is the name of my idol [*mein Abgott*]-is still a very young man, hardly twenty-four years old; but he will give the final blow to all medieval religion and politics; he combines deepest philosophical seriousness with cutting wit. Can you imagine Rousseau, Voltaire, Holbach, Lessing, Heine and Hegel combined-not thrown together-in one person? If you can, you have Dr. Marx." Quote taken from Avineri, *Moses Hess: Prophet of Communism and Zionism,* p. 15. See also Silberner, *Moses Hess Briefwechsel,* pp. 79–80. A great deal of scholarly research has focused on the character and content of Hess and Marx's relationship. There are some—Silberner, Avineri, and McLellan—who argue persuasively that Hess influenced Marx's understanding of socialism and the left Hegelian movement. Others—Lukács is the most prominent example—find the influence moving in the opposite direction. In my view, this is not a question of influence so much as witness to how new ideas develop out of fruitful and engaging debate.

65. For an excellent discussion on the background to "Über das Geldwesen" and its relationship to Marx's *On the Jewish Question,* see Julius Carlebach, *Karl Marx and the Radical Critique of Judaism* (London: Routledge and Kegan Paul, 1978), especially pp. 109–123, and Carlebach, "The Problem of Moses Hess's Influence on the Young Marx," pp. 27–39.

Also see Lundgren's analysis in his *Moses Hess on Religion, Judaism and the Bible*, p. 60, as well as Avineri, *Moses Hess: Prophet of Communism and Zionism*, pp. 115–133.

66. Moses Hess, "Über das Geldwesen," *Philosophische und Sozialistische Schriften (1837–1850)*, p. 331.

67. Ibid., p. 335.

68. Ibid., p. 336.

69. Ibid., p. 339.

70. Ibid., pp. 339–340.

71. Ibid., p. 344.

72. Silberner, *Moses Hess: Geschichte Seines Lebens*, pp. 333–351.

73. Ibid., p. 347.

74. Moses Hess, "Zur Entwicklungsgeschichte von Natur und Gesellschaft," *Neue Quellen zur Hess Forschung*, ed. Wolfgang Mönke (Berlin: Akademie Verlag, 1964), pp. 56–68.

75. Ibid., pp. 59–60.

76. Ibid., p. 64.

77. Ibid., pp. 57–59.

78. Moses Hess, "Prolegomena zu einer Entstehungs-und Entwicklungsgeschichte des kosmischen, organischen und sozialen Lebens," *Neue Quellen zur Hess Forschung*, p. 78.

79. Hess, *Rome and Jerusalem*, p. 269.

80. Ibid., pp. 269–270.

81. Frankel, *Prophecy and Politics*, p. 21.

82. Hess, *Rome and Jerusalem*, p. 270.

83. Ibid., p. 270.

84. Ibid., p. 270.

85. Ibid., p. 271.

86. Ibid., p. 270. See also the Epilogue, "Der letzte Antagonismus," p. 314, for a similar description and analysis of the creation story in Genesis.

87. See Moses Hess, "Mein Messiasglaube," *Moses Hess Jüdische Schriften*, ed. Theodor Zlocisti (Berlin: Louis Lamm, 1905), p. 6; Moses Hess, "Briefe über Israels Mission in der Geschichte der Menschheit," *Moses Hess Jüdische Schriften*, pp. 45–46.

88. Moses Hess, *Dynamische Stofflehre* (Paris: Syb. M. Hess, 1877). Adolphe Reiff printed the book for Sybille Hess, who after Moses's death labored vigorously to find a publisher for her husband's last work. On the title page, the author is "M. Hess."

89. Ibid., pp. 21, 15.

90. Ibid., p. 13.

91. Silberner, *Moses Hess Briefwechsel*, p. 381.

92. Ibid., p. 384. For a general account of Hess's search for a publisher for *Rome and Jerusalem*, see Edmund Silberner, "Heinrich Graetz' Briefe an Moses Hess 1861–1872," *Annali* 4 (1961), pp. 326–400, especially p. 335.

93. Hess, *Rome and Jerusalem*, p. 223.

94. See Benedict Anderson's excellent discussion of nations and nationality in his *Imagined Communities* (London: Verso, 1983), especially the Introduction, pp. 1–7.

95. Hess, *Rome and Jerusalem*, pp. 223–224.

96. Ibid., p. 224.

97. Hess, "Mein Messiasglaube," pp. 23–24.

98. Hess, *Rome and Jerusalem*, p. 235.

99. See Avineri's discussion of Hess's conception of a national homeland in his *Moses Hess: Prophet of Communism and Zionism*, pp. 248–253, and "Socialism and Nationalism in

Moses Hess," *Midstream* 22/4 (1976), pp. 36–44, especially p. 43, where Avineri claims that for Hess, "nationalism constitutes a mediating factor, analogous to the family, between the individual and the universal commonalty. In a nation the individual learns to move beyond his individuality, to consider himself interwoven into society, to be firmly tied to other people and to act on the basis of this relationship."

100. Hess, *Rome and Jerusalem*, p. 224.

101. Ibid., p. 224.

102. Ibid., p. 225.

103. See Kurt Bayertz, "Naturwissenschaft und Sozialismus: Tendenzen der Naturwissenschafts-Rezeption in der deutschen Arbeiterbewegung des 19. Jahrhunderts," *Social Studies of Science* 13/3 (1983), pp. 355–394.

104. Avineri, *Moses Hess: Prophet of Communism and Zionism*, pp. 236–237.

105. Hess, *Rome and Jerusalem*, p. 232.

3. Hess's "Return" to Judaism and Narrative Identity

1. See Frank Kermode, *The Sense of an Ending: Studies in the Theory of Fiction* (New York: Oxford University Press, 1967).

2. Peter Brooks, *Reading for the Plot: Design and Intention in Narrative* (New York: Alfred A. Knopf, 1984), pp. 107–109.

3. For a narrative reading of Hegel's philosophical theology, see O'Regan, *The Heterodox Hegel*.

4. Edmund Silberner argues that Hess writes the letters to Josephine Hirsch, whose sister Emilie married Hess's brother Samuel. Emilie died in the beginning of 1860 as a mother to two small children. Josephine took in the two children and later became Samuel Hess's second wife. See Hess, *Moses Hess Briefwechsel*, p. 374, fn. 1; and Silberner, *Moses Hess: Geschichte Seines Lebens*, p. 403.

5. Hess, *Rome and Jerusalem*, p. 227.

6. Hess criticized the Reform movement for not recognizing how Jewish religious commitments complicate, perhaps even conflict with Jewish emancipation in nineteenth-century Germany. Religious expression, on Hess's account, can flourish freely and openly only in a society that values religious pluralism without demanding conformity to social standards of conduct. It is in part for this reason that Hess argues for the establishment of a Jewish state in Palestine.

7. On the Damascus affair, see Heinrich Graetz, *History of the Jews* 5 (Philadelphia: Jewish Publication Society of America, 1945), pp. 632–666; and Jonathan Frankel, *The Damascus Affair: "Ritual Murder," Politics, and the Jews in 1840* (Cambridge: Cambridge University Press, 1997).

8. See Silberner, *Moses Hess: Geschichte Seines Lebens*, pp. 62–65.

9. Quoted from Frankel, *The Damascus Affair*, p. 325. For the German, see Silberner, *Moses Hess: Geschichte Seines Lebens*, p. 63; and Hess, "Die Polen und die Juden," ms. (Central Zionist Archives: A49, file 18/4), pp. 61–68.

10. Hess, *Rome and Jerusalem*, p. 227. According to Silberner, Hess had considered entitling his work "Wiedergeburt Israels," the rebirth of Israel, perhaps implying the rebirth of Hess as well. See Silberner, *Moses Hess: Geschichte Seines Lebens*, p. 391; and Hess, *Rome and Jerusalem*, p. 224.

11. Hess, *Rome and Jerusalem*, p. 227.

12. Michael Graetz argues that *Rome and Jerusalem* is best understood as Hess's at-

tempt to unify Jewish philosophy and the universal-socialist ideal. See Michael Graetz, "Le-shivato shel Moshe Hes la-yahadut—ha-reka le-hibur 'romi vi-yerushalayim'" [Hebrew], *Zion* 42/2 (1980), pp. 133–153. For an English translation see Michael Graetz, "On the Return of Moses Hess to Judaism: The Background to 'Rome and Jerusalem,'" *Binah: Studies in Jewish History* 1, ed. Joseph Dan (New York, Westport, and London: Praeger, 1989), pp. 159–171.

13. Hess, *Rome and Jerusalem*, p. 232.

14. James Sheehan, "The Problem of the Nation in German History," *Die Rolle der Nation in der Deutschen Geschichte und Gegenwart*, ed. James Sheehan and Otto Busch (Berlin: Colloquium Verlag, 1985), p. 6. Also see Isaiah Berlin, *Vico and Herder: Two Studies in the History of Ideas* (New York: The Viking Press, 1976), pp. 145–216.

15. Johann Gottfried von Herder, *Reflections on the Philosophy of the History of Mankind* (Chicago: University of Chicago Press, 1968), p. 77. For the German, see Johann Gottfried Herder, "Ideen zur Philosophie der Geschichte der Menschheit," *Werke* 6, ed. Martin Bollacher (Frankfurt am Main: Deutscher Klassiker, 1989), p. 334.

16. Sheehan, "The Problem of the Nation in German History," pp. 6–8.

17. Ibid., pp. 8–9.

18. George Mosse argues that "Volkish thought" in the nineteenth century is characterized by its animosity toward cities and urban industrialized development, its glorification of the agrarian peasant, its desire for rootedness in the land and the historical continuity of a people. In this context, "the Jew was identified with modern industrial society, which uprooted the peasant, deprived him of his land, caused his death [through industrial progress], and thereby destroyed the most genuine part of the Volk." See George Mosse, *The Crisis of German Ideology: Intellectual Origins of the Third Reich* (New York: Grosset and Dunlap, 1964), pp. 13–30, especially p. 27.

19. Hess, *Rome and Jerusalem*, p. 230.

20. Hess, "Socialismus und Communismus," p. 202.

21. Hess, *Rome and Jerusalem*, pp. 254–255.

22. Shulamit Volkov, "Moses Hess: Problems of Religion and Faith," *Zionism* 3 (1981), pp. 14–15.

23. Hess, *Rome and Jerusalem*, p. 227.

24. The standard English edition translates the opening phrase as, "is it mere chance" for the German, "Ist es Zufall," thereby adding rhetorical force to the question. See Moses Hess, *Rome and Jerusalem: A Study in Jewish Nationalism* (New York: Bloch Publishing Co., 1943), p. 44.

25. Shlomo Na'aman believes that there were three great women in Hess's life—Lena (Hess's first love), Sybille Pesch (Hess's Christian wife) and Josephine Hirsch (the wife of Hess's brother). Na'aman contends that Hess refers to Josephine Hirsch in this passage. See Na'aman, *Emanzipation und Messianismus: Leben und Werk des Moses Hess*, p. 299; and Silberner, *Moses Hess: Geschichte Seines Lebens*, p. 374.

26. For theories of autobiography, and the need for telling a continuous, coherent narrative in autobiography, see Steven Kepnes, *The Text as Thou: Martin Buber's Dialogical Hermeneutics and Narrative Theology* (Bloomington and Indianapolis: Indiana University Press, 1992), pp. 104–109; and James Olney, ed., *Autobiography: Essays Theoretical and Critical* (Princeton: Princeton University Press, 1980). Note especially Georges Gusdorf's claim that autobiography "calls up the past for the present and in the present, and it brings back from earlier times that which preserves a meaning and value today; it asserts a kind of tradition between myself and me that establishes an ancient and new fidelity, for the past drawn up

into the present is also a pledge and a prophecy of the future." See Georges Gusdorf, "Conditions and Limits of Autobiography," *Autobiography: Essays Theoretical and Critical*, p. 44.

27. Abraham Geiger, "Alte Romantik, neue Reaktion," *Jüdische Zeitschrift für Wissenschaft und Leben* 1/Sept. 10 (1862), pp. 245–252.

28. Hess, *Rome and Jerusalem*, p. 241.

29. Silberner, *Moses Hess: Geschichte Seines Lebens*, p. 62; also Frankel, *The Damascus Affair*, pp. 323–325.

30. Na'aman, *Emanzipation und Messianismus: Leben und Werk des Moses Hess*, p. 307.

31. Lundgren, *Moses Hess on Religion, Judaism and the Bible*, p. 73.

32. Silberner, *Moses Hess: Geschichte Seines Lebens*, p. 62.

33. On this point, see Frankel, *The Damascus Affair*, p. 323.

34. Moses Hess, *Rom und Jerusalem: Die letzte Nationalitätsfrage* (Jerusalem: The Schocken Library, 1862).

35. See Silberner, *Moses Hess: Geschichte Seines Lebens*, pp. 85–86.

36. Brooks, *Reading for the Plot*, p. 110.

37. See Harold Bloom, *The Anxiety of Influence: A Theory of Poetry* (New York: Oxford University Press, 1973).

38. Ibid., pp. 15, 141.

39. Harold Bloom, *A Map of Misreading* (New York: Oxford University Press, 1975), p. 19.

40. Bloom, *The Anxiety of Influence*, p. 78.

41. Ibid., p. 139.

42. Bloom, *A Map of Misreading*, p. 19.

43. Frankel, *Prophecy and Politics*, pp. 7–28.

44. Ibid., pp. 22, 24.

45. Ibid., p. 11.

46. In his most recent book on the Damascus Affair, Frankel has this to say about the unpublished document of 1840 in *Rome and Jerusalem:* "He there included a long passage from a manuscript that he had composed (or so he said) at the time of the ritual-murder case. The original manuscript, though, has never been found, and it is impossible to tell what (if anything) was written during the period of the affair and what was written or rewritten some twenty years later." See Frankel, *The Damascus Affair*, p. 323.

47. Frankel, *Prophecy and Politics*, p. 27.

48. Felix Weltsch, "'Rom und Jerusalem'—nach 100 Jahren," *Bulletin des Leo Baeck Instituts* 5/20 (1962), p. 239.

49. Winer, *The Founding Fathers of Israel*, p. 50.

50. See David Vital, *The Origins of Zionism* (Oxford: Clarendon Press, 1975), pp. 3–4: "The idea of the Return and the idea of Redemption came to be dissolved into each other. The restoration of the Jews to their ancestral Land, when it occurred, would be a matter of extraordinary and universal significance auguring or even instituting a millennial situation in which something like the harmony between man and his Creator that had obtained before the Fall would be restored."

51. Robert Wistrich, *Socialism and the Jews: The Dilemmas of Assimilation in Germany and Austria-Hungary* (London and Toronto: Associated University Press, 1982), p. 37.

52. Na'aman, *Emanzipation und Messianismus: Leben und Werk des Moses Hess*, p. 30.

53. Paula Fredriksen, "Paul and Augustine: Conversion Narratives, Orthodox Traditions, and the Retrospective Self," *Journal of Theological Studies* 37/1 (1986), p. 33.

54. Taylor, *Sources of the Self*, p. 47.

55. Alasdair MacIntyre, *After Virtue* (Notre Dame: University of Notre Dame Press, 1981), pp. 205–219.

56. Taylor, *Sources of the Self,* p. 52.

57. Ibid., p. 94.

58. Arnold Eisen, *Rethinking Modern Judaism* (Chicago: University of Chicago Press, 1998).

59. Lenn Goodman, *God of Abraham* (New York and Oxford: Oxford University Press, 1996).

60. Ibid., pp. 9–10.

61. Ibid., p. 11.

62. Ibid., pp. 21–23.

63. David Hartman, *A Living Covenant* (New York: The Free Press, 1985), pp. 44–45.

64. Goodman, *God of Abraham,* pp. 11–12.

65. Ibid., p. 28.

66. Ibid., p. 12.

67. Ibid., p. 33.

4. Inescapable Frameworks: Emotions, Race, and the Rhetoric of Jewish Identity

1. Recall Jonathan Frankel's assessment that "the personal, fragmented, often emotional form in which the book is put together gives it a unique place among his works. It is the closest he comes to writing his confessions." See Frankel, *Prophecy and Politics,* p. 21.

2. Berlin, *The Life and Opinions of Moses Hess,* p. 38.

3. Silberner, *Moses Hess: Geschichte Seines Lebens,* pp. 392–393. See also Silberner, "Moses Hess," *Historia Judaica,* p.11, where Silberner claims, "there is no semblance of logical order in the work." Note Israel Cohen's remark that Hess's "exposition of Jewish nationalism is rather discursive than methodical, as he often goes off at a tangent to make observations on persons and events not directly concerned with the subject," in his "Moses Hess, Rebel and Prophet," *The Zionist Quarterly,* p. 49. Cornu and Mönke argue that the theoretical confusions in *Rome and Jerusalem* result from Hess's return to "the representational world of his childhood and youth," in their *Philosophische und sozialistische Schriften (1837–1850),* p. lxvii. Avineri claims that "the highly sentimental tone thus creeping into the book did not make it a very happy medium for a serious political tract," in his *Moses Hess: Prophet of Communism and Zionism,* p. 175.

4. Martha Nussbaum argues persuasively that all philosophical and literary projects express through their form and style particular conceptions of value and truth: "Conception and form are bound together; finding and shaping the words is a matter of finding the appropriate and, so to speak, the honorable, fit between conception and expression." A view of life, she argues, is told: "The telling itself—the selection of genre, formal structures, sentences, vocabulary, of the whole manner of addressing the reader's sense of life—all of this expresses a sense of life and of value, a sense of what matters and what does not, of what learning and communicating are, of life's relations and connections." Shlomo Na'aman claims that Hess's style changes with the topic at hand. If, for example, he writes about the Hebrew Bible, then his style reflects biblical grammar and idiom. His style in all cases fits the content of his message. Hess is certainly aware that style and form must fit his philosophical project. In 1849 or 1850, Hess wrote *Röter Katechismus für das deutsche Volk.* In this summary of socialist principles, Hess employs the standard question and answer format of

religious catechisms in the nineteenth century. I contend that Hess's passionate and intimate style in the twelve letters in *Rome and Jerusalem,* rather than undermining his philosophical message, is instead a critical feature of it. See Martha Nussbaum, *Love's Knowledge: Essays on Philosophy and Literature* (New York: Oxford University Press, 1990), pp. 3–53, especially p. 5; and Na'aman, *Emanzipation und Messianismus: Leben und Werk des Moses Hess,* p. 86. For a discussion of Jewish religious catechisms in nineteenth-century Germany, see Jakob Petuchowski, "Manuals and Catechisms of the Jewish Religion in the Early Period of Emancipation," *Studies in Nineteenth-Century Jewish Intellectual History,* ed. Alexander Altmann (Cambridge, Mass.: Harvard University Press, 1964); Steven Lowenstein, "The 1840s and the Creation of the German Jewish Religious Reform Movement," *Revolution and Evolution: 1848 in German-Jewish History,* ed. Werner Mosse, Arnold Paucker and Reinhard Rurup (Tübingen: J. C. B. Mohr, 1981), pp. 255–297; and Michael Meyer, *The Origins of the Modern Jew: Jewish Identity and European Culture in Germany, 1749–1824* (Detroit: Wayne State University Press, 1967), pp. 125–126.

5. See Taylor, *Sources of the Self,* pp. 3–24.

6. Hess translated from French into German large portions of Ernest Laharanne's "The new oriental Question" (1860), which argued for a Jewish presence in Palestine to introduce French culture to the "uncivilized" Orient. He inserted these sections between the eleventh and twelfth letter.

7. Hess, *Rome and Jerusalem,* pp. 229, 231, 236, 240, 284.

8. For helpful articles on the relation between textual meaning and reading, see *The Critical Tradition,* ed. David H. Richter (New York: Bedford Books, 1989), especially ch. 7, pp. 1158–1173; and Mary Louise Pratt, "Interpretive Strategies/Strategic Interpretations: On Anglo-American Reader Response Criticism," *Postmodernism and Politics,* ed. Jonathan Arac (Minneapolis: University of Minnesota Press, 1986), pp. 26–54.

9. Yosef Hayim Yerushalmi, *Zakhor: Jewish History and Jewish Memory* (Seattle and London: University of Washington Press, 1982), p. 100; Arnold Eisen, *Taking Hold of Torah: Jewish Commitment and Community in America* (Bloomington: Indiana University Press, 1997).

10. Hess claims that Mercier's translation in *Essai sur la Littérature Juive* "attracted the attention of the French press to the Jewish people." Yet Hess shows no interest in the translation itself nor its reception in the French press, and only comments on Mercier's interpretation of Judaism. See Hess, *Rome and Jerusalem,* sixth letter.

11. Hess, *Rome and Jerusalem,* pp. 248–249.

12. Ibid., p. 249.

13. See Kepnes, *The Text as Thou,* pp. 104–119. Kepnes's chapter on Buber's "Autobiographical Fragments" is an insightful and especially relevant text for recognizing conceptions of self in autobiographical writings. He concludes that "the self, in Buber's view, only grows to selfhood through relation to another" (p. 109), and this view accounts for the particular form and content of Buber's own autobiographical sketches.

14. As we shall see below, the label "Spinozist" became what one author has called a *Schimpfwort* (a term of abuse or invective) in eighteenth- and nineteenth-century Germany. See Hong Han-Ding, *Spinoza und die Deutsche Philosophie* (Darmstadt: Scientia Verlag Aalen, 1989), p. 46.

15. Avineri, *Moses Hess: Prophet of Communism and Zionism,* pp. 21, 26.

16. Scholars disagree, however, on the nature of this appeal. Avineri believes that Hess always looks to Spinoza as a "Jewish" philosopher, and thus draws his "spiritual nourishment

from the Jewish tradition." See Avineri, *Moses Hess: Prophet of Communism and Zionism,* p. 45. Silberner, however, argues that in Hess's earlier writings his identification with Judaism is minimal, or at least ambiguous. See Silberner, *Moses Hess: Geschichte Seines Lebens,* pp. 24–25. Michael Graetz claims that only with *Rome and Jerusalem* does Hess view Spinoza as a "Jewish" philosopher with a distinctly Jewish vision of world history. See Graetz, "Le-shivato shel Moshe Hes la-yahadut—ha-reka le-hibur 'romi vi-yerushalayim'" [Hebrew], p. 151.

17. Moses Hess, "Die heilige Geschichte," p. 31.

18. See Stuart Hampshire, *Spinoza* (London: Penguin Books, 1951), pp. 105–108. Hampshire argues that the primary passions (pleasure, pain, and desire) in Spinoza's philosophy are "by definition 'confused' perceptions, in which the mind is not aware of the causes of its ideas. In experiencing these passions, we are merely reacting to external causes; our conscious life is proceeding at the level of sense-perception and imagination, and not at the level of logical thought or active intellect" (p. 106). For background to Spinoza's life, see Steven Nadler, *Spinoza: A Life* (Cambridge: Cambridge University Press, 1999).

19. Benedict de Spinoza, *Ethics,* ed. James Gutmann (New York: Hafner Press, 1949), pp. 215–216.

20. Hess, *Rome and Jerusalem,* pp. 309–312. For an analysis of Luzzatto's understanding of Judaism as a "religion of the heart," see Noah Rosenbloom, *Luzzatto's Ethico-Psychological Interpretation of Judaism* (New York: Balshon Printing and Offset Co., 1965), pp. 27–39, especially pp. 36–38 for Luzzatto's interpretation of Spinoza. Luzzatto criticized Spinoza's "detached rational attitude" and his fear of the emotions. Also see Wiener, *Jüdische Religion im Zeitalter der Emanzipation,* pp. 59–69, for an overview of Luzzatto's religious thought.

21. Hess, *Rome and Jerusalem,* p. 310.

22. See Friedrich Schleiermacher, *On the Glaubenslehre* (Chico, Calif.: Scholars Press, 1981), p. 100, fn. 15.

23. Alexander Altmann, *Moses Mendelssohn: A Biographical Study* (Tuscaloosa: University of Alabama Press, 1973), pp. 604, 620. The term *pantheism* first referred to English Deism, and only toward the end of the eighteenth century, due in large part to Jacobi's criticism of Spinoza, were deism and pantheism contrasted. Under Jacobi's influence, *pantheism* was used polemically to refer to neo-Spinozists, Lessing, Goethe, Schleiermacher, and, indeed, to most German philosophers in the nineteenth century. See Schleiermacher, *On the Glaubenslehre,* p. 114, fn. 78.

24. David Bell, *Spinoza in Germany from 1670 to the Age of Goethe* (London: Institute of Germanic Studies, University of London, 1984), p. 84.

25. I am indebted to Hong Han-Ding's *Spinoza und die Deutsche Philosophie,* and Alexander Altmann's *Moses Mendelssohn: A Biographical Study,* for the history of Spinoza's reception in Germany. I follow closely Han-Ding's account, while not ascribing to his more general assessment of Spinoza's influence on specific German philosophers. I am less concerned, as Han-Ding is, to show how such philosophers incorporate Spinoza's insights into their own philosophy. Instead, my interest here is to outline the German philosophical preoccupation with Spinoza and the critique of his philosophy.

26. Altmann, *Moses Mendelssohn: A Biographical Study,* p. 35.

27. Ibid., pp. 50–52, 33.

28. Han-Ding, *Spinoza und die Deutsche Philosophie,* pp. 46–48.

29. In a section entitled "Spinoza" in his *Grundsätze der Philosophie* (1769), Herder

denounced the uncritical acceptance of Spinoza's philosophy as pure atheism. Instead of atheism or pantheism, Herder called Spinozism "panentheism": God is not only in the world, but the world is also in God. To Herder, Spinoza was a "God-intoxicated man," to use Novalis's famous description, who did not, as Jacobi would have it, worship an abstract, rational God. In his *Gott, Einige Gespräche über Spinozas System*, Herder again challenged Jacobi's reading of Spinoza, and reinterpreted Spinoza's concept of substance as a dynamic, immanent, and ever present power in the world. See F. C. Copleston, "Pantheism in Spinoza and the German Idealists," *Philosophy* 21 (1946), p. 45; and Han-Ding, *Spinoza und die Deutsche Philosophie*, pp. 87–90.

30. Han-Ding, *Spinoza und die Deutsche Philosophie*, p. 95.

31. One can readily see the influence of Hegel's interpretation on the young Hegelian movement. For example, Ludwig Feuerbach at first praised Spinoza's philosophy for finally moving beyond the traditional western theological context. But in his study of Leibnitz in *Exposition, Development and Critique of Leibnitzian Philosophy* (1836), Feuerbach described seventeenth-century philosophy in Amsterdam: "Here grinds the lens grinder [*Augengläser*], in order to see more clearly and distinctly. Here, there was a pure and true image of itself. But the stuff with which it reflected itself was hard and unsuitable. It was only a lithograph in black and white [*Steindruck*], and not a picture of living colors [*farbenlebendiges Bild*]." Feuerbach's claim that Spinoza's philosophy still remained abstract in "black and white" foreshadowed his later critique in 1847 that Spinoza's *Substance* was still metaphysically obscure. Even in 1843, as Feuerbach called Spinoza "der Moses der modernen Freigeister und Materialisten," he also criticized Spinoza's conception of matter as a "metaphysical object [*ein metaphysisches Ding*]" and a "pure entity of the mind." According to one Feuerbach scholar, "Feuerbach's objection is Hegel's: Substance has no principle of self-differentiation in itself." By 1847, Feuerbach believed that Jacobi's charge of atheism against Spinoza's philosophy was justified. See Ludwig Feuerbach, *Principles of the Philosophy of the Future* (Indianapolis: Hackett Publishing Co., 1986), pp. 24, 32; *Ludwig Feuerbachs Sämmtliche Werke* 2, ed. Friedrich Jodl (Stüttgart: Fromann Verlag, 1903–1911), pp. 266, 275; Marx Wartofsky, *Feuerbach* (Cambridge: Cambridge University Press, 1977), pp. 49, 87. Quote taken from Wartofsky, *Feuerbach*, p. 95. I have altered the English translation somewhat so that it reflects the original German.

32. G. W. F. Hegel, *Phenomenology of Spirit* (Oxford: Oxford University Press, 1977), Preface, p. 10; G. W. F. Hegel, *Werke* 3 (Frankfurt am Main: Suhrkamp Taschenbuch Verlag, 1986), p. 23. The first collection of Spinoza's works had been published in Jena in 1802–3 by Professor of Theology H. E. Gottlob Paulus (1761–1851). Hegel collaborated with Paulus in the preparation of the text by comparing the German and French translations. Paulus's edition, according to Parkinson, "failed to meet the most elementary critical standards—and it appears that Hegel's part in the work was only a modest one." Carl Gebhardt, the editor of the now standard text of Spinoza's complete works, complained that Paulus's edition was little more than a reprint of what had previously been published separately and contained many errors. Valentin Schmidt, the third German translator of Spinoza's *Ethics*, made careful citations in order to overcome Paulus's errors. But Gebhardt praised Berthold Auerbach's translation (1841) as an improvement on Schmidt's. See Spinoza, *Opera* 2, ed. Carl Gebhardt (Heidelberg: Carl Winters, 1925), pp. 343–344; G. H. R. Parkinson, "Hegel, Pantheism, and Spinoza," *Journal of the History of Ideas* 38/3 (1977), p. 449; Han-Ding, *Spinoza und die Deutsche Philosophie*, p. 158; Hegel tells us about his work with Paulus in his *Geschichte der Philosophie* 3, p. 371, in G. W. F. Hegel, *Werke*.

33. Hegel, *Phenomenology of Spirit*, Preface, p. 10.

34. Parkinson, "Hegel, Pantheism, and Spinoza," p. 453; and O'Regan, *The Heterodox Hegel,* pp. 48–49.

35. Hess, *Rome and Jerusalem,* p. 311. The quotation is in Hebrew and then translated into German.

36. Ibid., p. 312.

37. Ibid., pp. 237–238.

38. In the third chapter to his *Tractatus,* Spinoza suggests that God "may a second time" elect the Jews and re-establish the Jewish state. See Benedict de Spinoza, *A Theologico-Political Treatise* (New York: Dover Publications, 1951), p. 56. Hess's appeal to the *Tractatus* rather than Spinoza's *Ethics* is indicative of what Michael Graetz notices as a shift in his evaluation of the "Jewish" Spinoza.

39. Hess, *Rome and Jerusalem,* p. 251

40. Nussbaum, *Love's Knowledge,* p. 3.

41. See Martha Nussbaum, *The Therapy of Desire: Theory and Practice in Hellenistic Ethics* (Princeton: Princeton University Press, 1994), p. 79. Nussbaum offers an insightful critique of those who understand emotions as irrational in what she calls the "normative sense, that is, inappropriate and illegitimate in discourse that claims to engage in persuasive reasoning."

42. During the 1850s, Hess studied physics, chemistry, natural sciences and racial theory. See Silberner, *Moses Hess: Geschichte Seines Lebens,* p. 333.

43. See Silberner, *Moses Hess: Geschichte Seines Lebens,* pp. 404–405, where he blames Hess's "confused terminology" and lack of precision for conflating nation with race. Silberner defends Hess's account of race, arguing that we should replace the term *nation* for every instance of *race,* even as he admits that Hess fails to hold one clear definition of race. See also Silberner, "Moses Hess," *Historia Judaica,* p. 17. Eliezer Schweid describes Hess's view as a "biological interpretation of Spinoza" in which a nation or people is a political unit. These national characteristics are peculiar to every people and provide a basis for political unification. See Eliezer Schweid, *A History of Jewish Thought in Modern Times* [Hebrew] (Jerusalem: Keter, 1977), pp. 389–390. For a critique of "nation" as a fixed category, see E. J. Hobsbawm, *Nations and Nationalism since 1780: Programme, Myth, Reality* (Cambridge: Cambridge University Press, 1990).

44. Weltsch, "'Rom und Jerusalem'—nach 100 Jahren," p. 252: "jeder Rasse eine besondere spezifische Begabung innewohnt [every race maintains a special and specific gift]." The Jews have a "besondere Begabung für Geschichtsbewußtsein und für soziale Gesetzgebung [special gift for historical consciousness and for social legislation]." Weltsch cites Hess's claim in the ninth letter to *Rome and Jerusalem* that every modern community has its own "special calling as an organ of humanity." Isaiah Berlin offers a similar account: "Each race has different and incommensurable gifts, and they can all contribute to the enrichment of mankind." See Berlin, *The Life and Opinions of Moses Hess,* p. 29.

45. Blumenfield, *Moses Hess, Dreamer of Realism,* p. 9.

46. Frankel, *Prophecy and Politics,* p. 24.

47. Hess, *Rome and Jerusalem,* p. 237.

48. Ibid., pp. 294–295.

49. Claude Blanckaert, "On the Origins of French Ethnology: William Edwards and the Doctrine of Race," *Bones, Bodies, Behavior: Essays on Biological Anthropology* 5, ed. George W. Stocking Jr. (Madison: University of Wisconsin Press, 1988), pp. 25–28. For an account of polygenesis and the anthropological and religious background to the polygenesis/monogenesis debate, see Michael Banton, *Racial Theories* (Cambridge: Cambridge Univer-

sity Press, 1987), especially pp. 38–43; Silberner, *Moses Hess: Geschichte Seines Lebens*, p. 406; and Jayne Chong-Soon Lee, "Navigating the Topology of Race," *Stanford Law Review* 46/3 (1994), pp. 747–780, especially p. 766.

50. Hess, *Rome and Jerusalem*, pp. 294–295. Hess does not clarify the distinction between "Menschenrassen" and "Volksstämme." My sense is that they are interchangeable terms for him.

51. Ibid., p. 265. On the language of "type" in anthropological research in the nineteenth century, see Banton, *Racial Theories*, pp. 38–43.

52. Hess, *Rome and Jerusalem*, p. 265.

53. Ibid., pp. 293–296. Also see Avineri's discussion in his *Moses Hess: Prophet of Communism and Zionism*, pp. 201–208.

54. Hess shared this account of two original and distinctive groups of people with many Jewish intellectuals of his time. See Michael Graetz, *The Jews in Nineteenth-Century France* (Stanford: Stanford University Press, 1996), p. 241.

55. Hess, *Dynamische Stofflehre*, p. 38.

56. Compare Hess's account with Matthew Arnold's 1869 essay, "Hebraism and Hellenism." Arnold, much like Hess, describes Hebraism as the energy of practice, the obligation of duty that focuses upon conduct and obedience—in short, the domain of practical action and moral virtue. Hellenism, by contrast, is the impulse to know, to "see things as they really are"—the domain of knowledge and the intellectual virtues. "To get rid of one's ignorance, to see things as they really are, and by seeing them as they are to see them in their beauty, is the simple and attractive ideal which Hellenism holds out before human nature. . . . Difficulties are kept out of view, and the beauty and rationalness of the ideal have all our thoughts." "Hebraism,—and here is the source of its wonderful strength,—has always been severely preoccupied with an awful sense of the impossibility of being at ease in Zion; of the difficulties which oppose themselves to man's pursuit or attainments of that perfection of which Socrates talks so hopefully." Yet Arnold adds that Christianity is "the more spiritual, the more attractive development of Hebraism," while for Hess, Christianity evolves from Hellenism. See Matthew Arnold, "Hebraism and Hellenism," *The Works of Matthew Arnold* 6 (London: Macmillan and Co., 1903), pp. 120–140, especially pp. 127–128, 130. For a broader account of the dichotomy of Hebraism and Hellenism in English thought, see David DeLaura, *Hebrew and Hellene in Victorian England* (Austin: University of Texas Press, 1969).

57. Hess might have adopted from Heine the very notion that the ancient world was divided by "Hebrews and Hellenes." See Peter Gay, *The Enlightenment: An Interpretation—The Rise of Modern Paganism* (New York: Alfred Knopf, 1966), p. 33, where Gay attributes to Heine the division between Hebrews and Hellenes as historical and philosophical "patterns of life."

58. S. S. Prawer, *Heine: The Tragic Satirist* (Cambridge: Cambridge University Press, 1961), p. 63.

59. Jeffrey Sammons, *Heinrich Heine: A Modern Biography* (Princeton: Princeton University Press, 1979), p. 271.

60. Heinrich Heine, "Atta Troll. Ein Sommernachtstraum," in *Sämmtliche Werke* 4, ed. Manfred Windfuhr (Hamburg: Hoffmann und Campe, 1985), pp. 56–58, 63. For an English translation, see *The Poems of Heine*, ed. Edgar Alfred Bowring (London: George Bell and Sons, 1878).

61. Heine claims that he began *Atta Troll* in late fall 1841, although he mentions the poem for the first time in his letters in 1842, and only in early 1843 do sections of it appear

in Laube's *Zeitung für die elegante Welt*. At this time (1842), both Hess and Heine were living in Paris. Sometime at the end of that year Hess met Heine, and, when Karl Marx moved to Paris in October, 1843, there developed a discussion group that included Marx, Ruge, Bakunin, Hess, and Heine. See Sammons, *Heinrich Heine: A Modern Biography,* p. 269; and Silberner, *Moses Hess: Geschichte Seines Lebens,* pp. 152, 164.

62. Hess, "Die europäische Triarchie," pp. 130–131. Schleiermacher's infamous characterization that Judaism is "long since dead" while modern Jews sit "lamenting beside the imperishable mummy, bewailing its departure and its sad legacy," finds echoes in both Heine's *Atta Troll* and Hess's *Triarchie*. Hegel too criticizes the abstract universality of the Jewish God. The Jewish commandments, Hegel claims, are "something given by God, as something prescribed and immutable, something eternally and firmly posited." Judaism lacks the historical development, the suffering and work of Substance as Subject. Hegel's Judaism, like his Spinoza, is cold, abstract, and passionless. See Friedrich Schleiermacher, *On Religion: Speeches to its Cultured Despisers* (San Francisco: Harper and Row, 1958), p. 238; and G. W. F. Hegel, *Lectures on the Philosophy of Religion,* ed. Peter Hodgson (Berkeley: University of California Press, 1988), pp. 371, 374. Also see Emil Fackenheim, *The Religious Dimension in Hegel's Thought* (Bloomington: Indiana University Press, 1967).

63. Michael Graetz argues that when French Christian socialists removed Judaism from the process of socialist redemption, it awoke in Hess's heart a "feeling of discrimination" and set in motion a response against Christian supercessionism. See his "Le-shivato shel Moshe Hes la-yahadut—ha-reka le-hibur 'romi vi-yerushalayim'" [Hebrew], p. 149.

64. Although he is best known for his ground-breaking work *A History of Art among the Ancients* (1764), Winckelmann's earlier essay, *Thought on the Imitation of Greek Works in Painting and Sculpture* (1755), contains in embryo his revolutionary approach to Greek art. See E. M. Butler, *The Tyranny of Greece over Germany* (Cambridge: Cambridge University Press, 1935), p. 45. Butler claims it was this work, and not his *History of Art,* that "exerted such an overwhelming inspirational force on his literary contemporaries."

65. Butler, *The Tyranny of Greece over Germany,* p. 46.

66. Ibid., pp. 47, 59.

67. Gotthold Ephraim Lessing, *Laocoon: An Essay upon the Limits of Painting and Poetry* (New York: The Noonday Press, 1961), pp. 1–2.

68. Ibid., p. 4.

69. Ibid., pp. 7, 11–12, 39.

70. Where Lessing and Winckelmann wished to return to the grandeur and nobility of Greek citizenship, aesthetic beauty, and ethical life, Herder, Schiller, Hegel, and Heine all believed that Greece represented an innocent perfection that moderns could never recover. Herder's eloquent critique of lost innocence goes to the heart of the German conflicted appreciation of Greek society: "Absurd as it would be, to endeavor to transport ourselves back to this period of youthful levity, which is now past, and to skip as a hobbling graybeard [*lahmer Greis*] among boys; why should the graybeard be offended with youth for being lively, and dancing?" Charles Taylor described this general trend among late eighteenth- and early nineteenth-century German thinkers as the "spiral vision of history, where we return not to our starting point but to a higher variant of unity": "The Greeks represented for many Germans of the late eighteenth century a paradigm of expressivist perfection. . . . Ancient Greece had supposedly achieved the most perfect unity between nature and the highest human expressive form. To be human came naturally, as it were. But this beautiful unity died. And moreover, it had to, for this was the price of the development of reason to that higher stage of self-clarity which is essential to our realization as radically

free beings." See Taylor, *Hegel and Modern Society,* pp. 7, 8; and Herder, *Reflections on the Philosophy of the History of Mankind,* pp. 177–178; for the original German, see Herder, "Ideen zur Philosophie der Geschichte der Menschheit," *Werke,* p. 578.

71. Quote taken from Butler, *The Tyranny of Greece over Germany,* p. 268.

72. Schiller, for example, encountered German society as "ingenious clock-work, in which, out of the piecing together of innumerable but lifeless parts, a mechanical kind of collective life ensued." See Friedrich Schiller, *On the Aesthetic Education of Man,* eds. Elizabeth Wilkinson and L. A. Willoughby (Oxford: Clarendon Press, 1982), p. 35.

73. Hess, *Rome and Jerusalem,* pp. 294–295.

74. Jacob Katz cites an anonymous review of Hess's *Rome and Jerusalem* in the *Berliner Revue.* According to Katz, the author was Bruno Bauer, a frequent contributor to this journal. Bauer argued that Hess's *Rome and Jerusalem* was not original, for Bauer himself had earlier described the Jews as a race with a particular spirit and destiny. Bauer therefore regarded his conception of Judaism as identical with Hess's. See Katz's chapter entitled "Zionism versus Anti-Semitism" in his *Jewish Emancipation and Self-Emancipation* (New York: Jewish Publication Society, 1986), pp. 145–146. This essay was first published, under the same title, in *Commentary* 73/1 (1982), pp. 34–41. Also see Bauer's 1863 article, "Das Judentum in der Fremde" [The Jews as Aliens], published originally in the first volume of the conservative *Political and Social Encyclopedia* edited by Hermann Wagener. Moving beyond his 1843 article, Bauer emphasized in "The Jews as Aliens" (1863) that Jewish racial peculiarities, unaffected by changing circumstances or geography, would prevent Jewish emancipation into German society. Nathan Rotenstreich, in his article on the reaction of Jews and non-Jews to Bauer's articles, noted that, "it is an interesting coincidence that Bauer wrote these statements in the same year in which Moses Hess's *Rome and Jerusalem* was published," yet "Hess could not, at the time of writing, have known Bauer's essay." See Nathan Rotenstreich, "The Bruno Bauer Controversy," *Leo Baeck Institute Year Book* 4 (1959), pp. 3–36, especially pp. 32–36.

75. Hess could quite naturally assume that his racial theory would be understood and embraced by European Jews and non-Jews alike. The weekly *Leipziger Illustrierte* (founded 1843) published more articles on people, art, and nature than traditional politics and diplomacy. And with the *Augsburger Allgemeine Zeitung* (1840s), science was seeping into weekly journals once devoted solely to politics. *Die Gartenlaube* (founded 1853) saw its circulation increase to about four hundred thousand within twenty years. Together with poetry and novels, each issue devoted whole sections to scientific essays written by Carl Vogt and other well-known scientists. Ernst Keil, the founder of *Die Gartenlaube,* dedicated his journal to "the progressive bourgeoisie whose aspirations had been shattered in 1848." E. A. Rossmassler, co-founder of *Die Natur* in 1852, and a former liberal representative of the Frankfurt parliament, published his journal in order to educate mass culture in material science, "which would break the chains of superstition and bring the freedom promised in 1848." The journal *Das Jahrhundert* (founded 1856) disseminated scientific studies to mass audiences. Most of Hess's articles on the natural sciences were published between 1855–1858, and many of them appeared in this journal. See Alfred Kelly, *The Descent of Darwin: The Popularization of Darwinism in Germany, 1860–1914* (Chapel Hill: University of North Carolina Press, 1981), pp. 14–18, and Silberner, *Moses Hess: Geschichte Seines Lebens,* p. 344.

76. Blanckaert, "On the Origins of French Ethnology," pp. 30–31; Leon Poliakov, *The Aryan Myth: A History of Racist and Nationalist Ideas in Europe* (London: Sussex University Press, 1974), pp. 180–182.

77. Blanckaert, "On the Origins of French Ethnology," p. 35; Poliakov, *The Aryan Myth*, p. 226.

78. John Efron, "Defining the Jewish Race: The Self-Perceptions and Responses of Jewish Scientists to Scientific Racism in Europe, 1882–1933." Dissertation submitted to Columbia University, 1991, pp. 16–18.

79. Quote taken from Efron, "Defining the Jewish Race," p. 19.

80. See Zlocisti, *Moses Hess: der Vorkämpfer des Sozialismus und Zionismus 1812–1875; eine Biographie*, pp. 281–286.

81. Hess aligns himself politically and scientifically with Moleschott, the Dutch natural scientist, whose *Der Kreislauf des Lebens* (1852) became an instant classic in nineteenth-century *Naturwissenschaft*. Moleschott, argues Hess, unites philosophy and science in a "positive knowledge" that promotes a radical socialist agenda. In his 1855 essay, *Zur Entwicklungsgeschichte von Natur und Gesellschaft*, Hess argues that idealist philosophers and materialist scientists must forge common bonds in order to uproot the social and political inequalities in modern society. In his last work, *Dynamische Stofflehre*, he explores the "scientific synthesis" in the cosmic, organic, and human spheres in order to breach and heal the gap between philosophy and science. For Hess, such healing is spiritual healing, as it initiates the social and political culture necessary for a Jewish return to Palestine and ultimately the messianic age. James Sheehan argues that for many liberals in nineteenth-century Germany, politics was a spiritual practice in which "the proper end of political action remained popular enlightenment." The popularization of science was part of the liberal educational strategy associated with *Bildung*. See James Sheehan, *German Liberalism in the Nineteenth Century* (Atlantic Highlands, N.J.: Humanities Press, 1978), pp. 14–17, 86–88, and especially p. 104; Silberner, *Moses Hess: Geschichte Seines Lebens*, chapter 12, "Naturwissenschaftliche Periode," pp. 333–357, especially pp. 331–334; Hess, "Zur Entwicklungsgeschichte von Natur und Gesellschaft"; and Hess, *Dynamische Stofflehre*, pp. 7–8.

82. Bayertz specifically mentions Hess's role in translating French socialist thought for his German contemporaries. See Silberner, *Moses Hess: Geschichte Seines Lebens*, pp. 134–151, where Silberner discusses Hess's review of Lorenz von Stein's work *Der Sozialismus und Kommunismus des heutigen Frankreichs: Ein Beitrag zur Zeitgeschichte*. Von Stein's essay brought French socialist and communist thought to the attention of German radical thinkers.

83. Bayertz, "Naturwissenschaft und Sozialismus," pp. 359, 361, 378, 383.

84. Hermann von Helmholtz, "On the Relation of Natural Science to Science in General," *Popular Lectures on Scientific Subjects*, trans. E. Atkinson (London: Longmans, Green, and Co., 1873); for the original German, see Helmholtz, "Über das Verhältniss der Naturwissenschaften zur Gesammtheit der Wissenschaften," *Vorträge und Reden* (Braunschweig: Friedrich Vieweg und Sohn, 1903).

85. Helmholtz, "On the Relation," pp. 16–17; Helmholtz, "Über das Verhältniss," pp. 171–173.

86. Helmholtz, "On the Relation," pp. 23–24, 26–27; Helmholtz, "Über das Verhältniss," pp. 178, 180.

87. Helmholtz distinguishes between *Gebote* (laws established "through a foreign authority") and *Gesetze* (laws proper that are "generalizations which comprise the wealth of facts"). *Gesetze* witness to the autonomy of human reason. See his "Über das Verhältniss," p. 173.

88. Hess, *Rome and Jerusalem*, p. 247.

89. Ibid., p. 236. According to George Mosse, this argument for racial superiority is quite rare in nineteenth-century Jewish thinkers. Although the writers we have considered —Heine, Lessing, Winckelmann, Hegel, and Schleiermacher—all qualitatively compare Greeks to Germans or Jews, none to my knowledge make a claim similar to Hess, in which Jews maintain a *biological* superiority that is evident in exceptional ethical and social traits. See George Mosse, *Toward the Final Solution: A History of European Racism* (New York: Howard Fertig, 1978), p. 123: "A belief in the reality of race did not mean that any one race was necessarily superior to another. . . . It was possible to believe in pure races and still not be a racist; indeed, this was a trait shared by most Jews who believed in a Jewish race, and by many Gentiles as well."

90. German Orthodox Jews employed the term *Neumodische* to refer to Reform Jews who belonged to the Hamburg Temple (1818). Eduard Kley and Gotthold Salomon, two young rabbis in Hamburg influenced by Christian preaching and ritual, instituted changes in the liturgy and decorum of the prayer service, thereby drawing condemnation by the *Altmodische* Orthodox community. See Heinrich Graetz, *Geschichte der Juden* 11 (Leipzig: Oskar Leiner, 1900), pp. 377–379; Michael Meyer, *Response to Modernity: A History of the Reform Movement in Judaism* (Oxford: Oxford University Press, 1988), pp. 53–61; and David Philipson, *The Reform Movement in Judaism* (New York: Ktav Publishing House, 1967), pp. 29–35.

91. Hess, *Rome and Jerusalem*, p. 237.

92. Ibid., p. 236.

93. Taylor, *Sources of the Self,* pp. 18, 26–32. For Taylor's account of transcendental arguments, and their force and limits, see Charles Taylor, "The Validity of Transcendental Arguments," *Proceedings of the Aristotelian Society* 79 (1978–79), pp. 151–165.

94. Taylor, *Sources of the Self,* p. 27.

95. Ibid., pp. 29–30.

96. See Taylor, "What Is Human Agency?" pp. 29–33.

97. Ibid., p. 30.

98. Taylor, *Sources of the Self,* p. 29.

99. Charles Taylor, "Self-Interpreting Animals," *Human Agency and Language: Philosophical Papers* 1 (Cambridge: Cambridge University Press, 1985), p. 67.

100. Taylor, *Sources of the Self,* p. 11.

101. John Efron argues that "in the wake of the perceived failures of emancipation and assimilation, anthropology is used as a political tool to free Jews from the humiliation brought on by the loss of Jewish identity. Race science is, in this context, race-affirming." This is true for Hess, although his racial theory is more than just a reaction to the failure of Jewish emancipation in Germany. See John Efron, "Defining the Jewish Race," p. 36.

102. Hess, *Rome and Jerusalem*, p. 235.

103. See *Insider/Outsider: American Jews and Multiculturalism,* ed. David Biale, Michael Galchinsky, and Susannah Heschel (Berkeley, Los Angeles, and London: University of California Press, 1998), pp. 1–12.

104. Ibid., p. 8.

105. For a discussion of identity politics and essentialism, see Michael Eric Dyson, "Essentialism and the Complexities of Racial Identity," *Multiculturalism: A Critical Reader,* ed. David Theo Goldberg (Oxford and Cambridge: Basil Blackwell, 1994), pp. 218–229.

106. For the notion of a protective strategy, see Wayne Proudfoot, *Religious Experience* (Berkeley: University of California Press, 1985).

107. Martha Nussbaum, *The Fragility of Goodness: Luck and Ethics in Greek Tragedy and Philosophy* (Cambridge: Cambridge University Press, 1986), pp. 55–58.

5. Traditions and Scars: Hess's Critique of Reform and Orthodox Judaism

1. Avineri, "Socialism and Nationalism in Moses Hess," p. 40.

2. Hess, *Rome and Jerusalem*, p. 225.

3. Charles Taylor, "Responsibility for Self," *The Identities of Persons*, ed. Amelie Rorty (Berkeley: University of California Press, 1969), p. 299.

4. Hess's critique echoed the left Hegelian criticism of the bourgeoisie and Hegelian philosophy. According to many disenchanted Hegelians, the German state did not embody free, expressive spirits (as Hegel argued), but rather produced abstract, enslaved human beings. See *The Young Hegelians*, ed. Lawrence Stepelevich (Cambridge: Cambridge University Press, 1983); and Toews, *Hegelianism*.

5. This is a radical reversal from Hess's earlier claim, made in *The European Triarchy*, that the Jews, and *not* the Germans, were "soulless mummies" (*entseelte Mumien*) who wandered the world like ghosts "who cannot die, yet cannot be resurrected." See Hess, "Die europäische Triarchie," pp. 130–131.

6. Hess, *Rome and Jerusalem*, p. 421.

7. Moses Hess, *Rome and Jerusalem* (Jerusalem: Schocken Library, 1862), p. 35. In the Leipzig German publication (1862), and the more recent scholarly edition by Lademacher (1962), the midrash is unrelated to Hess's critique of Reform Jewry (so too the English translation by Meyer Waxman). Yet in the original manuscript, Hess inserts a reference to this midrash when condemning Reform Jewry.

8. Hess, *Rome and Jerusalem*, p. 243.

9. The political theorist Wilhelm von Humboldt's conception of *Bildung* was the most influential for later nineteenth-century Germany. For the history of the term, and Humboldt's conception of *Bildung*, see David Sorkin, "Wilhelm von Humboldt: The Theory and Practice of Self-Formation (*Bildung*), 1791–1810," *Journal of the History of Ideas* 44 (January 1983), pp. 55–73; Hans-Georg Gadamer, *Truth and Method* (New York: The Seabury Press, 1975), pp. 11–12; and Jacob Katz, *Out of the Ghetto: The Social Background of Jewish Emancipation, 1770–1870* (New York: Schocken Books, 1978), pp. 77–78.

10. George Mosse, *German Jews Beyond Judaism* (Cincinnati: Hebrew Union College Press, 1985), p. 3.

11. Ibid., p. 4. See also Monika Richarz, *Der Eintritt der Juden in akademischen Berufe* (Tübingen: J. C. B. Mohr, 1974), pp. 1–9, for her account of the changes in Jewish education in eighteenth- and nineteenth-century Germany, and the new *Bildungsidee* in Jewish thought. Of particular interest is her discussion of German-Jewish reaction to the excess of Sabbataism, and her account of Mendelssohn as a positive model for the *gebildeter Jude*.

12. For a good overview of Auerbach's life and work, see David Sorkin, *The Transformation of German Jewry, 1780–1840* (Oxford: Oxford University Press, 1987), pp. 140–155.

13. Quote taken from Mosse, *German Jews beyond Judaism*, p. 4.

14. Sorkin, *The Transformation of German Jewry, 1780–1840*, pp. 17–18.

15. Sorkin, "Wilhelm von Humboldt," p. 66. Also see David Sorkin, "The Genesis of the Ideology of Emancipation: 1806–1840," *Leo Baeck Institute Year Book* 32 (1987), pp. 11–40, especially pp. 21–35. For the Romantic conception of *Bildung* as aesthetic ideal,

see Tzvetan Todorov, *Theories of the Symbol* (Ithaca: Cornell University Press, 1982), pp. 167–173.

16. Mosse, *German Jews beyond Judaism*, p. 3.

17. Jacob Katz, *Tradition and Crisis: Jewish Society at the End of the Middle Ages* (New York: New York University Press, 1993), p. 215. The philosophical and educational approach of the *maskilim* can be found in their journal *Ha-Measef* [*The Gatherer*], first published at the end of the eighteenth century. It was written almost entirely in Hebrew, and edited by Isaac Euchel (1756–1804) and Mendel Bresselau (1760–1827). In 1806 a second journal, *Sulamith* (written in German), edited by David Fränkel (1779–1865) and Joseph Wolf (1762–1826), appeared as the new vehicle for the elaboration and dissemination of the maskilic agenda. Its original title, *Sulamith, eine Zeitschrift zur Beförderung der Kultur und Humanität unter der jüdischen Nation*, changed with the third volume (1810), to *Sulamith, eine Zeitschrift zur Beförderung der Kultur und Humanität unter den Israeliten*, a sign that the *maskilim* were more concerned with Jewish political, economic, and social emancipation. The Westphalian Consistory, the center of the Reform movement in early nineteenth-century Germany, made the *Sulamith* its "veritable organ." See Sorkin, *The Transformation of German Jewry, 1780–1840*, pp. 58, 85; Meyer, *Response to Modernity*, pp. 28–29; and Meyer, *The Origins of the Modern Jew*, pp. 116–118, 208 (fn. 10).

18. Katz, *Tradition and Crisis*, p. 221.

19. Meyer, *Response to Modernity*, p. 30. For a discussion of replacing *Judaism* with *Mosaic religion*, and *Jew* with *Israelite* in Jewish Enlightenment literature, see Meyer, *The Origins of the Modern Jew*, pp. 121–127. *Mosaic faith* and *Israelite* were common terms in the maskilic literature of late eighteenth- and early nineteenth-century Germany. Meyer notes that Jewish catechisms, which employed this new terminology, reproduced the natural theology of the eighteenth century in order to stress Judaism's compatibility with citizenship.

20. See Silberner, "Moses Hess," *Historia Judaica*, p. 20, for a similar interpretation of Hess's view of emancipation.

21. For background on Gabriel Riesser, see Moshe Rinott, "Gabriel Riesser: Fighter for Jewish Emancipation," *Leo Baeck Institute Year Book* 7 (1962), pp. 11–38. The journal *Der Jude* served two purposes according to Riesser: to discuss religious questions, and to carry forward the struggle for equal rights. The first volume appeared in 1832, the second in 1833, and one further volume in 1835. The journal provoked angry protests by those who felt that "Israelites" or "members of the Mosaic Faith" would be a title better suited for Riesser's agenda. Only a year before the publication of *Der Jude*, Riesser himself published an essay entitled: "Über die Stellung der Bekenner des mosaischen Glaubens in Deutschland" ("On the Condition of those Professing the Mosaic Faith in Germany"). See Rinott, "Gabriel Riesser," pp. 32–33, 16.

22. Hess, *Rome and Jerusalem*, p. 252.

23. Hess, "Mein Messiasglaube," p. 5.

24. Moses Hess, "Lettres sur la Mission d'Israël dans l'Histoire de l'Humanité," *Archives Israélites* 25 (1864), p. 202; for the German translation, see Moses Hess, "Briefe über Israels Mission in der Geschichte der Menschheit," *Moses Hess Jüdische Schriften*, p. 28. On his return to Paris in 1863 from Germany, Hess began writing for the *Archives Israélites*. His *Lettres sur la Mission d'Israël* (1864) was his first article that appeared in the journal. Silberner claims, somewhat naively, that this was fundamentally a French translation of *Rome and Jerusalem*. See Silberner, *Moses Hess: Geschichte Seines Lebens*, p. 474.

25. Hess's critique against Reform Judaism would only be reinforced by his colleague and friend Heinrich Graetz. Like Hess, Graetz's early works can be read as an extended

polemic against the Reform movement in Germany. Hess revered Graetz, and maintained an active correspondence with him. After Geiger's critical review of Hirsch's *The Nineteen Letters,* which Graetz called *undenkbar,* Graetz harbored a profound hatred for Geiger that would last the rest of his life. Schorsch claims that "Graetz quickly received the notoriety he sought as a talented and uncompromising critic of Geiger and his movement. His articles were personal, passionate, and pugnacious. In short, long before Graetz was to make his mark as a scholar he had developed a profound abhorrence for the Reform movement, fed by an envious dislike for the man who embodied and led it." See Ismar Schorsch, "Ideology and History in the Age of Emancipation," *Heinrich Graetz: The Structure of Jewish History and Other Essays,* ed. Ismar Schorsch (New York: Jewish Theological Seminary of America, 1975), pp. 33–35; Philipp Bloch, "Heinrich Graetz: A Memoir," *Heinrich Graetz: History of the Jews* 6 (Philadelphia: Jewish Publication Society of America, 1956), pp. 12–13; Noah Rosenbloom, *Tradition in an Age of Reform: The Religious Philosophy of Samson Raphael Hirsch* (Philadelphia: The Jewish Publication Society of America, 1976), pp. 70–71; Jay Harris, *How Do We Know This?: Midrash and the Fragmentation of Modern Judaism* (Albany: State University of New York Press, 1995), p. 175; Hans Liebeschütz, *Das Judentum in deutschen Geschichtsbild von Hegel bis Max Weber* (Tübingen: J. C. B. Mohr, 1967), pp. 132–135; and *Heinrich Graetz: Tagebuch und Briefe,* ed. Reuven Michael (Tübingen: J. C. B. Mohr, 1977), p. 135, diary entry dated August 28, 1844.

26. Hess, *Rome and Jerusalem,* pp. 266–267.

27. Ludwig Philippson and Berthold Auerbach challenged Hess's claim to be a spokesperson for the German Jewish community. See Silberner, *Moses Hess Briefwechsel,* pp. 415, 375–376.

28. See Michael Graetz, "Le-shivato shel Moshe Hes la-yahadut."

29. Hess, *Rome and Jerusalem,* p. 250.

30. Hess, "Die europäische Triarchie," pp. 98, 108, 117, 150.

31. Silberner, *Moses Hess: Geschichte Seines Lebens,* p. 76.

32. See Reuven Michael, "Vier unveröffentlichte Manuskripte von Moses Hess," *Bulletin des Leo Baeck Instituts* 7 (1964), pp. 312–344.

33. This text is reminiscent of Hess's *Religion und Sittlichkeit,* with its sharp division between private religion and public politics. It was probably written at the same time (1841–1842).

34. Michael, "Vier unveröffentlichte Manuskripte von Moses Hess," p. 315.

35. Michael agrees with Silberner that the Damascus Affair (1840) influenced Hess's argument in "The Poles and the Jews," and this text was probably written shortly thereafter. See Silberner, *Moses Hess: Geschichte Seines Lebens,* p. 62.

36. Michael, "Vier unveröffentlichte Manuskripte von Moses Hess," pp. 330–331.

37. See Silberner, *Moses Hess: Geschichte Seines Lebens,* p. 424.

38. According to James Sheehan, German liberals in the nineteenth century viewed politics as moral, spiritual improvement: "In the minds of many liberals, therefore, politics was closely associated with *Bildung.*" Reconciliation of the citizen with the state was the goal of political education. See Sheehan, *German Liberalism in the Nineteenth Century,* p. 14.

39. Hess, *Rome and Jerusalem,* p. 234.

40. Ibid., p. 234.

41. In Note VI, Hess argues that Christianity recognizes only abstract persons but not subjects essentially connected to "nature and history, family and fatherland." *Bildung,* Hess argues, reflects this kind of Christian spiritualism. See Hess, *Rome and Jerusalem,* Note VI, p. 427.

42. Silberner, *Moses Hess Briefwechsel,* p. 376, fn. 233.
43. Hess, *Rome and Jerusalem,* p. 424.
44. Ibid., p. 242.
45. Hess claims that "even for the German patriot Börne, Christianizing his family name from Baruch to Börne was of no avail. He himself admits this: 'Whenever my opponents run aground on Börne,' he says somewhere in his writings, 'they throw out, as an anchor of security, the name *Baruch.*'" Ibid., p. 250.
46. Ibid., p. 234.
47. Ibid., p. 235.
48. For a critique of liberalism that follows Hess's strategy, see Laura Levitt, *Jews and Feminism: The Ambivalent Search for Home* (New York: Routledge, 1997). Although Levitt's postmodern sympathies move beyond Hess, she shares with him a distrust for liberal claims to equality.
49. For a concise biographical sketch of Hirsch's life and works, see Gershon Greenberg, "Samuel Hirsch: Jewish Hegelian," *Revue des études juives* 129 (1970), pp. 205–215. Hirsch was born in the village of Thalfang near Trier in Rhenish Prussia. He graduated from Gymnasium at Mainz, and attended university in Bonn from 1835 to 1837. Appointed permanent rabbi of Dessau in 1840, he received ordination from Samuel Holdheim soon thereafter in 1841. Hirsch's major work is his *Religionsphilosophie* (1842), a 884-page Hegelian defense of Judaism that is the only completed part of a larger work he never finished. In the secondary literature, this work has received enormous attention, including Emil Fackenheim's well-known study, "Samuel Hirsch and Hegel," *Studies in Nineteenth-Century Jewish Intellectual History,* ed. Alexander Altmann (Cambridge, Mass.: Harvard University Press, 1964), pp. 171–201 (see also Wiener, *Jüdische Religion im Zeitalter der Emanzipation,* pp. 131–147). From 1843 to 1866 Hirsch was the Chief Rabbi in Luxembourg, and there he wrote his 1854 lectures, *Die Humanität als Religion.* In 1866 Hirsch moved to the United States, succeeding David Einhorn as rabbi of Keneseth Israel in Philadelphia.
50. Samuel Hirsch, *Die Humanität als Religion* (Trier: C. Troschel, 1854), hereafter "Hirsch, *Religion.*" In the Central Zionist Archives in Jerusalem there is a manuscript of Hess's notes on *Religion.* Most of these notes are quotations or summaries of the text, and unfortunately provide little additional evidence for Hess's critique of the work. See Moses Hess, "Bemerkungen von Hess zur Humanität als Religion von Samuel Hirsch (Luxembourg)," The Central Zionist Archives (Jerusalem: #8).
51. For a history of Jewish participation in Masonic Lodges, see Jacob Katz, "Freemasons and Jews," *Jewish Journal of Sociology* 9 (1967), pp. 137–148; and Jacob Katz, *Jews and Freemasons in Europe 1723–1939* (Cambridge, Mass.: Harvard University Press, 1970). Prussian lodges were the most reactionary, denying Jewish membership from the very beginning. This is significant, because by 1840, there were 164 Prussian lodges with a membership of 13,000, accounting for roughly two thirds of the entire membership in Germany. The Luxembourg lodge imposed no restrictions against Jews. Hirsch joined the fraternity after he had been appointed Communal Rabbi of Luxembourg (1843). For Hirsch's relationship to the Freemasons, see Jacob Katz, "Samuel Hirsch—Rabbi, Philosopher and Freemason," *Revue des études juives* 125 (1966), pp. 113–126.
52. Katz, "Samuel Hirsch—Rabbi, Philosopher and Freemason," p. 113.
53. Hess and Hirsch did meet once in Luxembourg in 1860 or 1861, but it is not clear whether they in fact knew each other very well. See Gershon Greenberg, "The Reformers'

First Attack upon Hess' Rome and Jerusalem: An Unpublished Manuscript of Samuel Hirsch," *Jewish Social Studies* 35/3 (1973), p. 175; and Silberner, *Moses Hess: Geschichte Seines Lebens*, p. 422.

54. Hess, *Rome and Jerusalem*, p. 262.

55. Hirsch, *Religion*, p. 54.

56. Ibid., pp. 127–130.

57. "To us, it does not matter how the truth is expressed, but only what has been proclaimed as the truth, and whether the truth has issued forth from the correct or the false interpretation of the data of our heart." Ibid., p. 213.

58. Ibid., p. 214.

59. Ibid., pp. 226–227. Hirsch, like Heinrich Graetz, Abraham Geiger, and Moses Hess, believes that Paul's interpretation of Christianity leads to the historical break of Christianity from Judaism. The pure teaching of Judaism is the pure teaching of Jesus. But Paul reinterprets Jesus' teaching and wrongly emphasizes original sin. Thus, "not Jesus, but Paul must be understood as the real founder of the Christian Church." Paul is a pagan thinker, and the Christian Church a pagan Church. See Hirsch, *Religion*, pp. 11–13, 145, 223, 230–231, 237; Samuel Hirsch, *Die Religionsphilosophie der Juden* (Leipzig: Heinrich Hunger, 1842), pp. 43, 722–767; and Fackenheim, "Samuel Hirsch and Hegel," pp. 187, 197–200. For Geiger's view of Paul and Christianity, see Abraham Geiger, *Das Judentum und seine Geschichte* (Breslau: Wilhelm Jacobsohn & Co., 1910). Susannah Heschel claims that Abraham Geiger "repeats the formulation of Samuel Hirsch" in his analysis of Judaism and Christianity. Geiger's study draws heavily from the Tübingen School and Ferdinand Christian Baur's distinction between Jewish and Pauline Christianity. It is likely that the Tübingen school played an influential role in Samuel Hirsch's understanding of Christianity as well. See Susannah Heschel, "Abraham Geiger on the Origins of Christianity" (Doctoral dissertation, University of Pennsylvania, 1989), pp. 126–129, 178–181, 189–202, 234–235, 343–360, and her more recent book, *Abraham Geiger and the Jewish Jesus*, notably p. 135; also note Liebeschütz, *Das Judentum in deutschen Geschichtsbild von Hegel bis Max Weber*, pp. 123–125. For Graetz's appraisal of Judaism, Christianity, and Paul, see Heinrich Graetz, *Geschichte der Juden* 3 (Leipzig: Oskar Leiner, 1905), pp. 271–316. Hess copied significant parts of this chapter into his *Rome and Jerusalem*, and later translated into French an expanded version of Graetz's discussion, entitled *Sinai et Golgotha*. For Hess's review of Graetz's *Geschichte*, originally published in French in *Archives Israélites* (1864), see Moses Hess, "Studien zur heiligen und profanen Geschichte," *Moses Hess Jüdische Schriften*, pp. 56–67, especially pp. 60–61 for Hess's account of Graetz's view of Christianity.

60. Hirsch, *Religion*, pp. 199–200.

61. Ibid., pp. 210–211. Note Jacob Katz's appraisal: "What Hirsch's theory amounted to was the identification of freemasonry with the Judeo-Christian teachings. Theoretically this would have entailed the exclusion of the adherents of other religions from the Masonic order. The tolerance achieved by his theory was not, then, absolute, but limited to Jews and Christians only." See Katz, "Samuel Hirsch—Rabbi, Philosopher and Freemason," p. 125.

62. Moses Hess, "Du dernier Article de M. Hirsch," *Archives Israélites* 26 (1865), pp. 248–249; see the German translation in Moses Hess, "Noch ein Wort über meine Missionsauffassung," *Moses Hess Jüdische Schriften*, pp. 68–69. Hirsch, so Hess claims, had misunderstood his criticism, for he argued that Christian philosophy, and not Christian practice, provoked Hirsch's move away from the Jewish "Kultus": "Imitation of the pure negative work of the Christian rationalists is completely different, in my opinion, than what Mr.

Hirsch believes: imitating the Church" (p. 248). See Samuel Hirsch, "La Vérité du Dieu-Un et la Mission d'Israël," *Archives Israelites* 26 (1865), pp. 194–200, especially p. 197; and Greenberg, "The Reformers' First Attack," pp. 175–197.

63. Moses Hess, "Die Einheit des Judentums innerhalb der heutigen religiösen Anarchie," *Moses Hess Jüdische Schriften,* pp. 115–116.

64. Hess, "Lettres," p. 202; Hess, "Briefe über Israels Mission," p. 28.

65. Hess, "Lettres," p. 241; Hess, "Briefe über Israels Mission," p. 29.

66. Hess, *Rome and Jerusalem,* pp. 261–262.

67. Ibid., p. 263.

68. It is in this context, as a critique of Reform Judaism, that we should understand Hess's guarded praise of Hassidism. The eastern European Jews have two alternatives, "either to fall away from Judaism, like the Reformers, as a result of the infiltrating modern culture [*Kultur*], or to prevent this disaffection through a regeneration, of which Hassidism is certainly only a forerunner." Samuel Hirsch too understands Hess's appeal to Hassidism as part of his attack on the German Reform movement. See Greenberg, "The Reformers' First Attack," p. 197; Hess, *Rome and Jerusalem,* Note V, p. 426. Hess is somewhat more critical of Hassidism in his sixth letter, where he perceives a one-sided spirituality that neglects material goods (p. 247).

69. This is a direct reference to Hirsch's *Religion.* On the last page of his work, Hirsch claims: "The religion of love and tolerance is certainly the religion of the future." See Hirsch, *Religion,* p. 248.

70. Hess, *Rome and Jerusalem,* p. 253.

71. Greenberg, "The Reformers' First Attack," p. 195.

72. Hess, *Rome and Jerusalem,* pp. 232–233, 256–257, 272–273.

73. Gotthold Salomon, "Vertrautes Schreiben an einen Rabbi," *Wissenschaftliche Zeitschrift für jüdische Theologie* 2 (1836), p. 422.

74. Silberner, *Moses Hess Briefwechsel,* p. 415.

75. Moses Hess, "Ein charakteristischer Psalm," *Moses Hess Jüdische Schriften,* pp. 124–127.

76. Hess, "Lettres," p. 242; Hess, "Briefe über Israels Mission," p. 30.

77. Hess, *Rome and Jerusalem,* p. 285.

78. Ibid., p. 255. Elsewhere, Hess argues that "the modern religious Reformers are sectarians without sects. Each one of our Jewish Protestants has his own code" (p. 261).

79. Hess, "Lettres," pp. 147–148; Hess, "Briefe über Israels Mission," pp. 23–24.

80. See Hess, *Rome and Jerusalem,* p. 252, for a similar critique of the Reformers, who, unlike Mendelssohn, attempt to reform "the basis, the tradition, itself."

81. See Moses Mendelssohn, *Jerusalem* (Hanover: Brandeis University Press, 1983), p. 90, for his distinction between *geöffenbarte Religion* (revealed religion) and *geöffenbarte Gesetzgebung* (revealed legislation).

82. Mendelssohn argued this very point in the first part of his *Jerusalem!*

83. Hess, *Rome and Jerusalem,* pp. 253–254.

84. Taylor, "Self-Interpreting Animals," p. 67.

85. Alasdair MacIntyre, "Epistemological Crisis, Dramatic Narrative and the Philosophy of Science," *The Monist* 60/4 (1977), p. 455.

86. Edward Shils, *Tradition* (Chicago: University of Chicago Press, 1981).

87. Ibid., p. 213.

88. Ibid., pp. 229–230.

89. See *The Zionist Writings of Rabbi Zvi Kalisher* [Hebrew], ed. Israel Klausner (Je-

rusalem: Mossad Harav Kook, 1947); and Jakob Petuchowski, *Prayerbook Reform in Europe: The Liturgy of European Liberal and Reform Judaism* (New York: The World Union for Progressive Judaism, 1968).

90. Löw reviewed *Rome and Jerusalem* in *Ben Chananja,* 5 (1862).

91. Hess, "Mein Messiasglaube," pp. 3–4. This essay is, in part, Hess's response to Löw's review of *Rome and Jerusalem.*

92. Hess, *Rome and Jerusalem,* p. 274.

93. Ibid., p. 276.

94. Ibid., p. 274.

95. Ibid., p. 236.

96. Stuart Hampshire, *Morality and Conflict* (Cambridge, Mass.: Harvard University Press, 1983), p. 148.

97. For a discussion of tradition as a negotiated space within which participants construct identity, see Delwin Brown, *Boundaries of Our Habitations: Tradition and Theological Construction* (Albany: State University of New York Press, 1994), pp. 83–92, especially pp. 83–86.

98. Samson Raphael Hirsch, *The Nineteen Letters,* ed. Jacob Breuer (Jerusalem and New York: Feldheim Publishers, 1969), pp. 110, 113; Samson Raphael Hirsch, *Igerot Tzafon: Neunzehn Briefe über Judenthum* (Altona: J. F. Hammerische, 1836), pp. 82, 84. For an analysis of Hirsch's critique of Jewish emancipation as a means and not an end of reform, see Isaac Heinemann, *Ta'amei ha-Mitzvot in Jewish Literature* [Hebrew] 2 (Jerusalem: Horev, 1993), p. 156. Also see Sorkin, *The Transformation of German Jewry, 1780–1840,* pp. 156–170. For biographical information on Hirsch's life, see Isaac Heinemann, "Samson Raphael Hirsch: The Formative Years of the Leader of Modern Orthodoxy," *Historia Judaica* 13 (1951), pp. 29–54; Robert Liberles, *Religious Conflict in Social Context: The Resurgence of Orthodox Judaism in Frankfurt am Main, 1838–1877* (Westport: Greenwood Press, 1985); and Rosenbloom, *Tradition in an Age of Reform,* pp. 3–120. Rosenbloom claims that, on the whole, Hirsch's literary work is an extended polemic against the Reform movement. For Geiger's response to Hirsch, see his "Neunzehn Briefe über Judenthum, von Ben Uziel: eine Recension," *Wissenschaftliche Zeitschrift für jüdische Theologie* 2 (1836). Geiger argues that Hirsch does not fully appreciate the motivations behind the Jewish Reform movement. Jewish civil and political equality will allow "all spiritual and ethical powers" to fully flourish, and thus lead to a more vibrant and fulfilling Jewish religious life.

99. Samson Raphael Hirsch, "Religion Allied with Progress," *The Collected Writings* 6 (New York: Feldheim Publishers, 1990), p. 108.

100. For an account (though uncritical) of Hirsch's conception of *Torah im derekh eretz,* see Mordechai Breuer, *The "Torah-Im-Derekh-Eretz" of Samson Raphael Hirsch* (New York: Feldheim Publishers, 1970). Also see Isaac Heinemann's more critical yet sympathetic account, "Studies on R. Samson Raphael Hirsch" [Hebrew], *Sinai* 24 (1949), pp. 249–271; and Julius Carlebach, "The Foundation of German-Jewish Orthodoxy: An Interpretation," *Leo Baeck Institute Year Book* 33 (1988), pp. 67–91. Zacharias Frankel also wished to charter a middle course between traditional Jewish observance and commitments to modern scientific research (*Wissenschaft*). Frankel described his reform in his *Über Reformen in Judenthume* (1844) as a "gemäßigten Reform" (moderate Reform), in which "Erhaltung und Fortschritt" (preservation and progress) are the marks of the "regeneration of Judaism." As an active, engaged religion, Judaism must have a practical influence on life, but present Reform "has, in general, little to do with life, and takes as its starting point a completely abstract conception." Frankel thus concluded his article: "True representation of the general will

[*Gesammtwillens*] and science [*Wissenschaft*], they will lead to the goal, they will discover the measure for reforms, which does not live in abstraction only but passes over into reality; through science and the general will the word *moderate Reform* [gemäßigte Reform] will be the salvation, and the advancement of Judaism and its eternal longevity will be recognized." See Zacharias Frankel, "Über Reformen in Judenthume," *Zeitschrift für die religiösen Interessen des Judenthums* 1 (1844), pp. 3–27. For an overview of Frankel's interpretation of Judaism, see Ismar Schorsch, "Zacharias Frankel and the European Origins of Conservative Judaism," *Judaism* 30/119 (1981), pp. 344–354. A review of Frankel's interpretation of the Jewish commandments, and his critique of Reform, can be found in Harris, *How Do We Know This?*, pp. 190–202.

101. Hess, *Rome and Jerusalem*, pp. 264, 251.

102. Ibid., p. 244.

103. Ibid., p. 243.

104. One can readily ascertain the Orthodox interest in modern scholarly debates and European social issues by perusing the burgeoning Orthodox press at the time. The very existence of Orthodox journals in the German language attests to their broadening concerns. The Orthodox could no longer afford to remain outside the public and academic discussions concerning Jewish identity and tradition. See Judith Bleich, "The Emergence of an Orthodox Press in Nineteenth-Century Germany," *Jewish Social Studies* 42 (1980), pp. 323–344.

105. Hess, *Rome and Jerusalem*, pp. 258–259.

106. Ismar Schorsch, "Emancipation and the Crisis of Religious Authority: The Emergence of the Modern Rabbinate," *Revolution and Evolution: 1848 in German-Jewish History*, ed. Werner Mosse, Arnold Paucker and Reinhard Rurup (Tübingen: J. C. B. Mohr, 1981), pp. 205–247.

107. David Ellenson, *Rabbi Esriel Hildesheimer and the Creation of a Modern Jewish Orthodoxy* (Tuscaloosa: University of Alabama Press, 1990).

108. Hirsch's essays on symbolic interpretation were published over the course of a number of years in the 1850s. The ground-breaking methodological essays were published in 1857. See Samson Raphael Hirsch, "Grundlinien einer jüdischen Symbolik," *Jeschurun* 3 (1856/57), pp. 615–630, and *Jeschurun* 4 (1857/58), pp. 19–32. For an English translation, see Samson Raphael Hirsch, *The Collected Writings: Jewish Symbolism* 3 (New York: Philipp Feldheim Publishers, 1984). Quotations will be taken from the English translation, with reference to specific German terminology from *Jeschurun*.

109. See Wiener, *Jüdische Religion im Zeitalter der Emanzipation*, pp. 76–77, for a general review of S. R. Hirsch's symbolic interpretation.

110. "[Symbols are] not the signs by which man expresses his changing thoughts and feelings, but the script in which God has set forth the truths by which the world is redeemed and established."

111. Hirsch, *The Collected Writings: Jewish Symbolism*, pp. 3–8. Hirsch argues that in order to understand the meaning of a symbol, the interpreter must understand, in addition to the intention of the author, the person to whom it is addressed, the time and place of its origin, and the local and historical background. A symbol, "considered by itself," could have many possible interpretations, but only when studied "in context" will the fitting interpretation be revealed. This is Hirsch's claim to hermeneutical authority—that only he, with the required university and rabbinic training to understand historical context and authorial intent, can deliver the one true meaning for particular symbols.

112. David Sorkin argues that Hirsch's symbolic reading of the commandments was influenced by the eighteenth- and nineteenth-century expressivist traditions. Neo-humanists

believed that through a "close study of the literary remains of classical Greece the student could encounter the 'spirit' (*Geist*) of the Greeks." Schleiermacher, in his hermeneutical theory, claimed that "all communication, written as well as oral, was a dialogue in which the listener tried to understand the speaker's thought." Understanding, therefore, "meant reconstructing the 'spirit' (*Geist*) of the speaker, his ideas and intentions, through the comprehension of his language." See Sorkin, *The Transformation of German Jewry, 1780–1840*, pp. 156–167; and Isaac Heinemann, "The Relationship between S. R. Hirsch and his Teacher Isaac Bernays" [Hebrew], *Zion* 16 (1951), pp. 60–69. For a discussion of the Romantic conception of symbol in eighteenth- and nineteenth-century Germany, see Gadamer, *Truth and Method*, pp. 147–173; and Andrew Louth, "Return to Allegory," *Discerning the Mystery: An Essay on the Nature of Theology* (Oxford: Clarendon Press, 1983), pp. 96–131, especially p. 102. On Schleiermacher's hermeneutical theory, see Hans Frei, *The Eclipse of Biblical Narrative: A Study in Eighteenth and Nineteenth Century Hermeneutics* (New Haven and London: Yale University Press, 1974), pp. 290–300. For an important critique of Romantic conceptions of symbol as "an act of ontological bad faith," see Paul de Man, "The Rhetoric of Temporality," *Blindness and Insight: Essays in the Rhetoric of Contemporary Criticism* (Minneapolis: University of Minnesota Press, 1983), pp. 187–228. De Man privileges what he sees as the indeterminacy of allegory over the precise meaning of symbol. For background to the nineteenth-century debate over symbol and allegory, see David Dawson, *Allegorical Readers and Cultural Revision in Ancient Alexandria* (Berkeley and Los Angeles: University of California Press, 1992), pp. 11–17; John Gatta Jr., "Coleridge and Allegory," *Modern Language Quarterly* 38 (March 1977), pp. 62–77; and Todorov, *Theories of the Symbol*, pp. 198–221. Dawson nicely summarizes the romantic preference for symbol: "Reflecting culturally dominant literary and aesthetic judgments about the value of the symbol's intrinsic and 'organic' relationship to that which is symbolized over allegory's artificial, sterile, or merely 'mechanical' juxtaposition of image and meaning, Romantic theorists consistently denigrated allegory and praised the symbol. Unlike allegory's allegedly wooden translation of abstract ideas into sensuous images to which those ideas bore no essential resemblance, the literary symbol supposedly fused the idea and image into an 'organic' whole with quasi-sacramental significance" (p. 14). These distinctions are found in Jewish sources as well. See Frank Talmage, "Apples of Gold: The Inner Meaning of Sacred Texts in Medieval Judaism," *Jewish Spirituality* 1, ed. Arthur Green (New York: The Crossroad Publishing Co., 1987), pp. 313–355. Talmage, like Dawson, finds the medieval and modern distinction between symbol and allegory to be ideologically motivated. An example of this can be found in Isaac Heinemann's defense of S. R. Hirsch's symbolic interpretation. See Heinemann, *Ta'amei ha-Mitzvot in Jewish Literature* [Hebrew], pp. 111, 269 fn. 114.

113. Hirsch, *The Collected Writings: Jewish Symbolism*, pp. 140–161.

114. Hirsch, *The Nineteen Letters*, p. 83; Hirsch, *Igerot Tzafon: Neunzehn Briefe über Judenthum*, p. 59.

115. Samson Raphael Hirsch, *Horeb* (New York: Soncino Press, 1962), p. 176, paragraph #271; Samson Raphael Hirsch, *Horeb: Versuche über Jissroels Pflichten in der Zerstreuung* (Frankfurt am Main: J. Kauffmann, 1921), p. 153, paragraph #271.

116. See Samson Raphael Hirsch, *The Pentateuch* 1 and 5 (Gateshead: Judaica Press, 1989), pp. 160–174 in volume one, and pp. 88–114, 182–192 in volume five.

117. Hirsch, *The Collected Writings: Jewish Symbolism*, p. 152.

118. Rosenbloom, *Tradition in an Age of Reform: The Religious Philosophy of Samson Raphael Hirsch*, p. 203. It is interesting to note, in this context, one of Abraham Geiger's criticisms of Hirsch's symbolic theory in *The Nineteen Letters*. Geiger questions whether we

will really believe in the divine source of the commandments if they depend upon the support that Hirsch gives even to the "geringsten Theile der Ceremonian" (the smallest/petty part of the ceremonies). The more convoluted the symbolic interpretation, Geiger believes, the less plausible it becomes. Arnold Eisen, a century later, offers a similar critique of Hirsch. Also note Nathan Rotenstreich's response that S. R. Hirsch formulated his symbolic readings for what had come to be seen as "irrational religious activity." See Abraham Geiger, "Neunzehn Briefe über Judenthum, von Ben Uziel: eine Recension," *Wissenschaftliche Zeitschrift für jüdische Theologie* 3 (1837), p. 87; Arnold Eisen, "Divine Legislation as 'Ceremonial Script': Mendelssohn on the Commandments," *AJS Review* 15/2 (Fall 1990), p. 264; and Nathan Rotenstreich, *Ha-mahashavah ha-yehudit be-et ha-hadashah* 1 [Hebrew] (Tel-Aviv: Am Oved, 1966), p. 120.

119. Hirsch, *The Nineteen Letters*, pp. 143–144, fn. 6; Hirsch, *Igerot Tzafon: Neunzehn Briefe über Judenthum*, p. 96. Sentences in parentheses ( ) appear in the original German but not in the English translation.

120. For a similar description of Torah as factual data that is unchangeable and permanent, see Hirsch, *Horeb*, p. 20, paragraph #34; Hirsch, *Horeb: Versuche über Jissroels Pflichten in der Zerstreuung*, p. 17, paragraph #34.

121. In his discussion of Jewish tradition, Hirsch describes the relationship between the written and oral Torah: "Thus the Written Law seeks to be celebrated only in a company of men who are permeated by the living breath of the Oral Law, which is Divine like the written word; and in this way the Written Law itself makes it clear that its very being depends on the existence of the Oral Law." See Hirsch, *The Collected Writings* 1, pp. 195–196. Jay Harris understands Hirsch's interpretation of oral Torah as a response to the burgeoning historical school and the partial relativization of midrash halakhah by Frankel, Graetz and Geiger. See Harris, *How Do We Know This?*, pp. 157–210, 223–228, especially pp. 225–227 on Hirsch's understanding of oral Torah.

122. Hess, *Rome and Jerusalem*, p. 261.

123. Ibid., p. 261.

124. Ibid., pp. 274–275.

125. Ibid., p. 285.

126. Ibid., p. 260. Emphasis added.

127. See Hirsch, "Grundlinien einer jüdischen Symbolik," p. 628, and Hirsch, *The Collected Writings: Jewish Symbolism*, p. 14, where he admits that ten commentators can offer ten different interpretations of the same text, but only one of them will be correct, namely, Hirsch's own reading. Also note a review of Hirsch's *The Nineteen Letters* in Geiger's journal by Gotthold Salomon (1784–1862). He found the work to have "eine prophetische Richtung" with an "arrogant tone." See Salomon, "Vertrautes Schreiben an einen Rabbi," pp. 417–418.

128. Hess, *Rome and Jerusalem*, p. 261.

129. See Liberles's account in his, *Religious Conflict in Social Context*.

130. Hess, *Rome and Jerusalem*, p. 256.

131. Ibid., p. 256. Arnold Eisen argues that Moses Mendelssohn's discussion of the commandments as "living script" is a strategy to infuse personal meaning that is flexible and dynamic into ritual activity. Hess, I believe, is following Mendelssohn on this point. He is fearful, like Mendelssohn, that fixing the oral law in writing may lead to its own demise. See Eisen, "Divine Legislation," pp. 242–243, 253–254, 258–259, and the relevant passages in Mendelssohn, *Jerusalem*, pp. 102–104.

132. See, for example, the twelfth letter in *Rome and Jerusalem*, pp. 285–286, where

Hess interprets his mission as liberating the Jewish masses from the "spiritually deadening formalism" of the Orthodox, and the "most superficial rationalism" of the Reform Jews.

133. Hess, *Rome and Jerusalem,* p. 257.

134. Harry Frankfurt, "Freedom of the Will and the Concept of a Person," *The Journal of Philosophy* 68/1 (1971), p. 7.

135. Ibid., p. 13.

136. Taylor, "Responsibility for Self," p. 281.

137. Ibid., p. 299.

138. Taylor, "What is Human Agency?" p. 33.

139. Stuart Hampshire argues that even after serious deliberation among competing options, sufficient reasons for choices are often missing: "No sufficient reason of any kind is on occasion available to explain a decision made after careful reflection in a situation of moral conflict; and that this lack of sufficient reason is not ground for apology, because our divided, and comparatively open, nature requires one to choose, without sufficient reason, between irreconcilable dispositions and contrary claims." See Stuart Hampshire, "Public and Private Morality," *Public and Private Morality,* ed. Stuart Hampshire (Cambridge: Cambridge University Press, 1978), p. 44.

140. Ibid., p. 44. The phrase "comprehensive and reflexive" comes from Seyla Benhabib, *Situating the Self: Gender, Community and Postmodernism in Contemporary Ethics* (New York: Routledge, 1992), p. 43.

141. Hampshire, "Public and Private Morality," p. 44.

142. Hess, *Rome and Jerusalem,* p. 261.

143. Taylor, "What is Human Agency?," p. 32.

6. Innocence and Experience in *Rome and Jerusalem*

1. Bernard Williams, *Shame and Necessity* (Berkeley: University of California Press, 1993), pp. 163–164.

2. Stuart Hampshire, *Innocence and Experience* (Cambridge, Mass.: Harvard University Press, 1989), p. 12.

3. Ibid., p. 172.

4. Ibid., p. 174.

5. Ibid., p. 170.

6. Ibid., p. 177.

7. Ibid., p. 103.

8. Hampshire, "Morality and Conflict," p. 152.

9. Hampshire, *Innocence and Experience,* p. 11.

10. Ibid., p. 173.

11. Hess, *Rome and Jerusalem,* p. 274.

12. Ibid., p. 261.

Bibliography

Albert, Phyllis Cohen. *The Modernization of French Jewry: Consistory and Community in the Nineteenth Century.* Hanover, N.H.: University Press of New England, 1977.

Altmann, Alexander. *Essays in Jewish Intellectual History.* Hanover, N.H.: University Press of New England, 1981.

———. "Franz Rosenzweig on History." In *Studies in Religious Philosophy and Mysticism,* 275–291. Ithaca: Cornell University Press, 1969.

———. *Moses Mendelssohn: A Biographical Study.* Tuscaloosa: University of Alabama Press, 1973.

———. "The New Style Preaching in Nineteenth-Century German Jewry." In *Essays in Jewish Intellectual History,* 190–245. Hanover, N.H.: University Press of New England, 1981.

———. *Studies in Nineteenth-Century Jewish Intellectual History.* Cambridge, Mass.: Harvard University Press, 1964.

Anderson, Benedict. *Imagined Communities.* London: Verso, 1983.

Andrew, E. "Marx and the Jews." *European Judaism* 3/1 (1968): 9–14.

Arnold, Matthew. "Hebraism and Hellenism." In *The Works of Matthew Arnold,* 120–140. London: Macmillan and Co., 1903.

Avineri, Shlomo. "Marx and Jewish Emancipation." *Journal of the History of Ideas* 25/3 (1964): 445–450.

———. *Moses Hess: Prophet of Communism and Zionism.* New York: New York University Press, 1985.

———. *The Social and Political Thought of Karl Marx.* Cambridge: Cambridge University Press, 1968.

———. "Socialism and Judaism in Moses Hess's 'Holy History of Mankind.'" *The Review of Politics* 45/2 (1983): 234–253.

———. "Socialism and Nationalism in Moses Hess." *Midstream* 22/4 (1976): 36–44.

Banton, Michael. *Racial Theories.* Cambridge: Cambridge University Press, 1987.

Bar-Nir, Dov. "The Modernism of Moses Hess" [Hebrew]. *Me'asef* 16 (1986): 51–60.

Baron, Salo. "Ghetto and Emancipation." *The Menorah Journal* 14/6 (1928): 515–526.

———. "Jewish Studies at Universities: An Early Project." *Hebrew Union College Annual* 46 (1975): 357–376.

Bartsch, Christian. "Martin Buber über Moses Hess, Anmerkungen zu einem Denkanstoss." In *Leben als Begegnung,* edited by P. Osten-Sachen, 55–62. Berlin: Institut Kirche und Judentum, 1978.

Barzilay, Eisig. "Perez Smolenskin and Moses Hess" [Hebrew]. *Bitzaron,* no. 49–51 (1992): 57–79.

Bayertz, Kurt. "Naturwissenschaft und Sozialismus: Tendenzen der Naturwissenschafts-Rezeption in der deutschen Arbeiterbewegung des 19. Jahrhunderts." *Social Studies of Science* 13/3 (1983): 355–394.

Bell, David. *Spinoza in Germany from 1670 to the Age of Goethe.* London: Institute of Germanic Studies, University of London, 1984.

Benhabib, Seyla. *Situating the Self: Gender, Community and Postmodernism in Contemporary Ethics.* New York: Routledge, 1992.

Bensussan, Gérard. *Moses Hess: la philosophie, le socialisme (1836–1845).* Paris: Presses Universitaires de France, 1985.

Berkovitz, Jay. *The Shaping of Jewish Identity in Nineteenth-Century France.* Detroit: Wayne State University Press, 1989.

Berlin, Isaiah. "Benjamin Disraeli, Karl Marx and the Search for Identity." *Midstream* 16/7 (1970): 29–49.

———. "Introduction." In *Philosophy in an Age of Pluralism: The Philosophy of Charles Taylor in Question,* edited by James Tully, 1–3. Cambridge: Cambridge University Press, 1994.

———. *The Life and Opinions of Moses Hess.* Cambridge: W. Heffer and Sons, 1959.

———. *Vico and Herder: Two Studies in the History of Ideas.* New York: The Viking Press, 1976.

Bernstein, Richard. "Nietzsche or Aristotle?: Reflections on Alasdair MacIntyre's *After Virtue.*" *Soundings* 67/1 (1984): 6–29.

Biale, David, Michael Galchinsky, and Susannah Heschel, eds. *Insider/Outsider: American Jews and Multiculturalism.* Berkeley, Los Angeles, and London: University of California Press, 1998.

Birnbaum, Pierre, and Ira Katznelson, eds. *Paths of Emancipation: Jews, States, and Citizenship.* Princeton: Princeton University Press, 1995.

Blanckaert, Claude. "On the Origins of French Ethnology: William Edwards and the Doctrine of Race." In *Bones, Bodies, Behavior: Essays on Biological Anthropology,* edited by George W. Stocking Jr., 18–55. Madison: University of Wisconsin Press, 1988.

Bleich, Judith. "The Emergence of an Orthodox Press in Nineteenth-Century Germany." *Jewish Social Studies* 42 (1980): 323–344.

Bloch, Jochanan. "Moses Hess: 'Rom und Jerusalem'—Jüdische und Menschliche Emanzipation." *Kölner Zeitschrift für Soziologie und Sozial Psychologie* 16/2 (1964): 288–313.

Bloch, Philipp. "Heinrich Graetz: A Memoir." In *Heinrich Graetz: History of the Jews.* Philadelphia: Jewish Publication Society of America, 1956.

Bloom, Harold. *The Anxiety of Influence: A Theory of Poetry.* New York: Oxford University Press, 1973.

———. *A Map of Misreading.* New York: Oxford University Press, 1975.

Bloom, Solomon. "Karl Marx and the Jews." *JSS* 4/1 (1942): 3–16.

Blumenbach, Johann Friedrich. *On the Natural Varieties of Mankind.* New York: Berman Publishers, 1969.

Blumenfield, Samuel. *Moses Hess, Dreamer of Realism.* New York: The Department of Education and Culture of the American Zionist Council, 1962.

Breuer, Mordechai. *The "Torah-Im-Derekh-Eretz" of Samson Raphael Hirsch.* New York: Feldheim Publishers, 1970.

Brooks, Peter. *Reading for the Plot: Design and Intention in Narrative.* New York: Alfred A. Knopf, 1984.

Brown, Delwin. *Boundaries of Our Habitations: Tradition and Theological Construction.* Albany: State University of New York Press, 1994.

Buber, Martin. *Der Jude und sein Judentum: Gesammelte Aufsätze und Reden.* Köln: Joseph Melzer, 1963.

———. "Moses Hess." *Jewish Social Studies* 7/2 (1945): 137–148.

Butler, E. M. *The Saint-Simonian Religion in Germany: A Study of the Young German Movement.* Cambridge: Cambridge University Press, 1926.

———. *The Tyranny of Greece over Germany.* Cambridge: Cambridge University Press, 1935.

Carlebach, Julius. "The Foundation of German-Jewish Orthodoxy—An Interpretation." *Leo Baeck Institute Year Book* 33 (1988): 67–91.

———. *Karl Marx and the Radical Critique of Judaism.* London: Routledge and Kegan Paul, 1978.

———. "The Problem of Moses Hess's Influence on the Young Marx." *Leo Baeck Institute Year Book* 18 (1973): 27–39.

Chadwick, Owen. *The Secularization of the European Mind in the Nineteenth Century.* Cambridge: Cambridge University Press, 1975.

Christ, Kurt. *Jacobi und Mendelssohn: eine Analyse des Spinozastreits.* Wurzburg: Königshausen & Neuman, 1988.

Cohen, Israel. "Moses Hess, Rebel and Prophet." *The Zionist Quarterly,* Fall (1951).

Cole, G. D. H. *Socialist Thought: The Forerunners 1789–1850.* Vol. 1. New York: St Martin's Press, 1953.

Comstock, Gary. "Two Types of Narrative Theology." *Journal of the American Academy of Religion* 55/4 (1987): 687–717.

Copleston, F. C. "Pantheism in Spinoza and the German Idealists." *Philosophy* 21 (1946): 42–56.

Cornu, Auguste. *Moses Hess et la gauche hegelienne.* Paris: Presses Universitaires de France, 1934.

———, and Wolfgang Mönke. "Einleitung." In *Philosophische und Sozialistische Schriften (1837–1850),* edited by Auguste Cornu and Wolfgang Mönke, ix–lxix. Berlin: Akademie Verlag, 1961.

Craig, Gordon. "Frederick the Great and Moses Mendelssohn: Thoughts on Jewish Emancipation." *Leo Baeck Institute Year Book* 32 (1987): 3–10.

Dawson, David. *Allegorical Readers and Cultural Revision in Ancient Alexandria.* Berkeley and Los Angeles: University of California Press, 1992.

———. "Against the Divine Ventriloquist: Coleridge and De Man on Symbol, Allegory and Scripture." *Literature and Theology* 4/3 (1990): 293–310.

De Man, Paul. "The Rhetoric of Temporality." In *Blindness and Insight: Essays in the Rhetoric of Contemporary Criticism,* 187–228. Minneapolis: University of Minnesota Press, 1983.

DeLaura, David. *Hebrew and Hellene in Victorian England.* Austin: University of Texas, 1969.

Descombes, Vincent. "Is there an Objective Spirit?" In *Philosophy in an Age of Pluralism: The Philosophy of Charles Taylor in Question,* edited by James Tully, 96–118. Cambridge: Cambridge University Press, 1994.

Dumont, Louis. *German Ideology: From France to Germany and Back.* Chicago: University of Chicago Press, 1994.

Dyson, Michael Eric. "Essentialism and the Complexities of Racial Identity." In *Multicul-*

turalism: A Critical Reader, edited by David Theo Goldberg, 218–229. Oxford and Cambridge: Basil Blackwell, 1994.

Edelheim-Muhsam, Margaret. "The Jewish Press in Germany." *Leo Baeck Institute Year Book* 1 (1956): 163–176.

Efron, John. *Defenders of the Race: Jewish Doctors and Race Science in Fin-de-Siècle Europe.* New Haven: Yale University Press, 1994.

———. "Defining the Jewish Race: The Self-Perceptions and Responses of Jewish Scientists to Scientific Racism in Europe, 1882–1933." Doctoral dissertation, Columbia University Department of History, 1991.

———. "Scientific Racism and the Mystique of Sephardic Racial Superiority." *Leo Baeck Institute Year Book* 38 (1993): 75– 96.

Eisen, Arnold. "Divine Legislation as "Ceremonial Script": Mendelssohn on the Commandments." *AJS Review* 15/2 (Fall 1990): 239–267.

———. *Rethinking Modern Judaism.* Chicago: University of Chicago Press, 1998.

———. *Taking Hold of Torah: Jewish Commitment and Community in America.* Bloomington: Indiana University Press, 1997.

Ellenson, David. *Between Tradition and Culture: The Dialectics of Modern Jewish Religion and Identity.* Atlanta: Scholars Press, 1994.

———. *Rabbi Esriel Hildesheimer and the Creation of a Modern Jewish Orthodoxy.* Tuscaloosa: University of Alabama Press, 1990.

Fackenheim, Emil. *The Religious Dimension in Hegel's Thought.* Bloomington: Indiana University Press, 1967.

———. "Samuel Hirsch and Hegel." In *Studies in Nineteenth-Century Jewish Intellectual History,* edited by Alexander Altmann, 171–201. Cambridge, Mass.: Harvard University Press, 1964.

Feuerbach, Ludwig. *Principles of the Philosophy of the Future.* Translated by Manfred H. Vogel. Indianapolis: Hackett Publishing Co., 1986.

———. *Sämtliche Werke.* Edited by Friedrich Jodl. Stüttgart: Fromann Verlag, 1903–1911.

Fishman, Aryei. "Moses Hess on Judaism and Its Aptness for a Socialist Civilization." *The Journal of Religion* 63 (1983): 143–158.

Frankel, Jonathan. "Assimilation and the Jews in Nineteenth-Century Europe: Towards a New Historiography." In *Assimilation and Community: The Jews in Nineteenth-Century Europe,* edited by Jonathan Frankel and Steven J. Zipperstein, 1–37. Cambridge: Cambridge University Press, 1992.

———. "The Communist Rabbi." *Commentary* June (1966): 77–80.

———. *The Damascus Affair: "Ritual Murder," Politics, and the Jews in 1840.* Cambridge: Cambridge University Press, 1997.

———. *Prophecy and Politics: Socialism, Nationalism, and the Russian Jews, 1862–1917.* Cambridge: Cambridge University Press, 1981.

Frankel, Zecharias. "Über Reformen in Judenthume." *Zeitschrift für die religiösen Interessen des Judenthums* 1 (1844): 3–27.

Frankfurt, Harry. "Freedom of the Will and the Concept of a Person." *The Journal of Philosophy* 68/1 (1971): 5–20.

Fredriksen, Paula. "Paul and Augustine: Conversion Narratives, Orthodox Traditions, and the Retrospective Self." *Journal of Theological Studies* 37/1 (1986): 3–34.

Frei, Bruno. *Im Schatten von Karl Marx. Moses Hess—Hundert Jahre nach seinem Tod.* Köln: Hermann Böhlau, 1977.

Frei, Hans. *The Eclipse of Biblical Narrative: A Study in Eighteenth and Nineteenth Century Hermeneutics.* New Haven and London: Yale University Press, 1974.

Gadamer, Hans-Georg. *Truth and Method.* New York: The Seabury Press, 1975.

Gatta, John, Jr. "Coleridge and Allegory." *Modern Language Quarterly* 38 (March 1977): 62–77.

Gay, Peter. *The Bourgeois Experience: Victoria to Freud.* Vol. 1, Education of the Senses. New York: Oxford University Press, 1984.

———. *The Enlightenment, an Interpretation: The Rise of Modern Paganism.* New York: Alfred Knopf, 1966.

Geiger, Abraham. "Alte Romantik, neue Reaktion." *Jüdische Zeitschrift für Wissenschaft und Leben* 1/Sept. 10 (1862): 245–252.

———. *Judaism and Its History in Two Parts.* Translated by Charles Newburgh. Lanham, Md.: University Press of America, 1985.

———. *Das Judentum und seine Geschichte.* Breslau: Wilhelm Jacobsohn & Co., 1910.

———. *Nachgelassene Schriften.* Edited by Ludwig Geiger. Berlin: Louis Gerschel, 1875.

———. "Neunzehn Briefe über Judenthum, von Ben Uziel: eine Recension." *Wissenschaftliche Zeitschrift für jüdische Theologie* 2 (1836): 351–359, 518–548.

———. "Neunzehn Briefe über Judenthum, von Ben Uziel: eine Recension." *Wissenschaftliche Zeitschrift für jüdische Theologie* 3 (1837): 74–91.

Gellner, Ernest. *Nations and Nationalism.* Ithaca: Cornell University Press, 1983.

Goitein, Irma. *Probleme der Gesellschaft und des Staates bei Moses Hess.* Leipzig: C. L. Hirschfeld, 1931.

Goldberg, David, and Michael Krausz, eds. *Jewish Identity.* Philadelphia: Temple University Press, 1993.

Goldberg, Michael. "God, Action, and Narrative: *Which* Narrative? *Which* Action? *Which* God?" In *Why Narrative? Readings in Narrative Theology,* edited by Stanley Hauerwas and L. Gregory Jones, 348–365. Grand Rapids: William B. Eerdmans, 1989.

Goodman, Lenn. *God of Abraham.* New York and Oxford: Oxford University Press, 1996.

Graetz, Heinrich. "Die Construction der jüdischen Geschichte." *Zeitschrift für die religiösen Interessen des Judenthums* 3 (1846): 81–97, 121–132, 361–381, 413–421.

———. *Geschichte der Juden.* 2nd ed. Leipzig: Oskar Leiner, 1905.

———. *History of the Jews.* 6 vols. Philadelphia: Jewish Publication Society of America, 1945.

———. "Jüdisch-geschichtliche Studien." *Monatsschrift für Geschichte und Wissenschaft des Judentums* 1 (1852): 112–120, 156–162, 192–202, 307–322.

———. *The Structure of Jewish History and Other Essays.* Edited by Ismar Schorsch. New York: Jewish Theological Seminary of America, 1975.

Graetz, Michael. "The History of Estrangement between Two Jewish Communities: German and French Jewry during the Nineteenth Century." In *Toward Modernity: The European Jewish Model,* edited by Jacob Katz, 159–169. New Brunswick, N.J.: Transaction Books, 1987.

———. *The Jews in Nineteenth-Century France.* Stanford: Stanford University Press, 1996.

———. "On the Return of Moses Hess to Judaism: The Background to 'Rome and Jerusalem.'" In *Binah: Studies in Jewish History,* edited by Joseph Dan, 159–171. New York, Westport, and London: Praeger, 1989.

———. "Le-shivato shel Moshe Hes la-yahadut—ha-reka le-hibur 'romi vi-yerushalayim.'" *Zion* 42/2 (1980): 133–153.

Gray, Alexander. *The Socialist Tradition: Moses to Lenin.* London: Longmans, Green and Co., 1946.

Greenberg, Gershon. "The Historical Origins of God and Man: Samuel Hirsch's Luxembourg Writings." *Leo Baeck Institute Year Book* 20 (1975): 129–148.

———. "The Reformers' First Attack upon Hess' Rome and Jerusalem: An Unpublished Manuscript of Samuel Hirsch." *Jewish Social Studies* 35/3 (1973): 175–197.

———. "Samuel Hirsch: Jewish Hegelian." *Revue des études juives* 129 (1970): 205–215.

Grégoire, Henri Baptiste. *An Essay on the Physical, Moral, and Political Reformation of the Jews.* London: C. Forster, 1791.

Gregory, Frederick. *Nature Lost?: Natural Science and the German Theological Traditions of the Nineteenth Century.* Cambridge, Mass.: Harvard University Press, 1992.

———. *Scientific Materialism in Nineteenth Century Germany.* Dordrecht: D. Reidel Publishing Co., 1977.

Gusdorf, Georges. "Conditions and Limits of Autobiography." In *Autobiography: Essays Theoretical and Critical,* edited by James Olney, 28–48. Princeton: Princeton University Press, 1980.

Guttman, Nachum. *Herzl, Hess and Histadrut.* New York: National Committee for Labor Israel, 1975.

Hamburger, Ernest. "One Hundred Years of Emancipation." *Leo Baeck Institute Year Book* 14 (1969): 3–66.

Hampshire, Stuart. *Innocence and Experience.* Cambridge, Mass.: Harvard University Press, 1989.

———. *Morality and Conflict.* Cambridge, Mass.: Harvard University Press, 1983.

———. "Public and Private Morality." In *Public and Private Morality,* edited by Stuart Hampshire, 23–53. Cambridge: Cambridge University Press, 1978.

———. *Spinoza.* London: Penguin Books, 1951.

Han-Ding, Hong. *Spinoza und die Deutsche Philosophie.* Darmstadt: Scientia Verlag Aalen, 1989.

Harris, Horton. *The Tübingen School.* Oxford: Oxford University Press, 1975.

Harris, Jay. *How Do We Know This?: Midrash and the Fragmentation of Modern Judaism.* Albany: State University of New York Press, 1995.

———. *Nachman Krochmal: Guiding the Perplexed of the Modern Age.* New York: New York University Press, 1991.

Hartman, David. *A Living Covenant.* New York: The Free Press, 1985.

Hauerwas, Stanley, and L. Gregory Jones, eds. *Why Narrative? Readings in Narrative Theology.* Grand Rapids: William B. Eerdmans Publishing Co., 1989.

Hegel, G. W. F. *Lectures on the Philosophy of Religion.* Edited by Peter Hodgson. Berkeley: University of California Press, 1988.

———. *Phenomenology of Spirit.* Oxford: Oxford University Press, 1977.

———. *Werke.* 20 vols. Frankfurt am Main: Suhrkamp Taschenbuch Verlag, 1986.

Heine, Heinrich. *The Poems of Heine.* Translated by Edgar Alfred Bowring. Edited by Edgar Alfred Bowring. London: George Bell and Sons, 1878.

———. *Sämtliche Werke.* Edited by Manfred Windfuhr. Hamburg: Hoffmann und Campe, 1985.

Heinemann, Isaac. "The Relationship between S. R. Hirsch and his Teacher Isaac Bernays" [Hebrew]. *Zion* 16 (1951): 44–90.

———. "Samson Raphael Hirsch: The Formative Years of the Leader of Modern Orthodoxy." *Historia Judaica* 13 (1951): 29–54.

———. "Studies on R. Samson Raphael Hirsch" [Hebrew]. *Sinai* 24 (1949): 249–271.

———. *Ta'amei ha-Mitzvot in Jewish Literature* [Hebrew]. 2nd ed. 2 vols. Jerusalem: Horev, 1993.

Helmholtz, Hermann von. "On the Relation of Natural Science to Science in General." In *Popular Lectures on Scientific Subjects.* London: Longmans, Green, and Co., 1873.

———. "Über das Verhältniss der Naturwissenschaften zur Gesammtheit der Wissenschaften." In *Vorträge und Reden,* 157–185. Braunschweig: Friedrich Vieweg und Sohn, 1903.

Herder, Johann Gottfried. "Ideen zur Philosophie der Geschichte der Menschheit." In *Werke,* edited by Martin Bollacher. Frankfurt am Main: Deutscher Klassiker, 1989.

———. *Reflections on the Philosophy of the History of Mankind.* Chicago: University of Chicago Press, 1968.

Heschel, Susannah. *Abraham Geiger and the Jewish Jesus.* Chicago: University of Chicago Press, 1998.

———. "Abraham Geiger on the Origins of Christianity." Doctoral Dissertation, University of Pennsylvania, 1989.

Hess, Moses. *Ausgewählte Schriften.* Edited by Horst Lademacher. Köln: Joseph Melzer, 1962.

———. "Bemerkungen von Hess zur Humanität als Religion von Samuel Hirsch (Luxemburg)." Jerusalem: The Central Zionist Archives.

———. "Betrachtungen über die Juden in Deutschland." Jerusalem: The Central Zionist Archives.

———. "Briefe über Israels Mission in der Geschichte der Menschheit." In *Moses Hess Jüdische Schriften,* edited by Theodor Zlocisti, 16–49. Berlin: Louis Lamm, 1905.

———. "Ein charakteristischer Psalm." In *Moses Hess Jüdische Schriften,* edited by Theodor Zlocisti, 124–127. Berlin: Louis Lamm, 1905.

———. "Du dernier Article de M. Hirsch." *Archives Israélites* 26 (1865): 248–249.

———. "La Doctrine Mosaique est-elle Matérialiste ou Spiritualiste?" *Archives Israélites* 27 (1866): 295–296.

———. *Dynamische Stofflehre.* Paris: Syb. M. Hess, 1877.

———. "Die eine und ganze Freiheit!" In *Philosophische und Sozialistische Schriften (1837–1850),* edited by Auguste Cornu and Wolfgang Mönke. Berlin: Akademie Verlag, 1961.

———. "Die Einheit des Judentums innerhalb der heutigen religiösen Anarchie." In *Moses Hess Jüdische Schriften,* edited by Theodor Zlocisti, 112–119. Berlin: Louis Lamm, 1905.

———. *Die europäische Triarchie.* Leipzig: Otto Wigand, 1841.

———. "Die europäische Triarchie." In *Philosophische und Sozialistische Schriften (1837–1850),* edited by Auguste Cornu and Wolfgang Mönke. Berlin: Akademie Verlag, 1961.

———. *Die heilige Geschichte der Menschheit.* Stuttgart: Hallberger, 1837.

———. "Die heilige Geschichte." In *Philosophische und Sozialistische Schriften (1837–1850),* edited by Auguste Cornu and Wolfgang Mönke. Berlin: Akademie Verlag, 1961.

———. "Die ideale Grundlage des neuen Jerusalem." Jerusalem: The Central Zionist Archives.

———. "Ist die mosaische Lehre materialistisch oder spiritualistisch?" In *Moses Hess Jüdische Schriften,* edited by Theodor Zlocisti, 79–80. Berlin: Louis Lamm, 1905.

———. "Die Jüdisch-Theologische Fakultät." Jerusalem: The Central Zionist Archives.

———. "Letters from Hess to Rabbi Joseph Natonek." Jerusalem: The Central Zionist Archive, 1862.

———. "Lettres sur la Mission d'Israël dans l'Histoire de l'Humanité." *Archives Israélites* 25 (1864): 14–17, 102–106, 145–149, 198–202, 240–244, 287–292, 336–340, 377–382, 432–436, 472–477.

———. "Die letzte Nationalitätsfrage." Jerusalem: The Central Zionist Archives, 1862.

———. "Mein Messiasglaube." In *Moses Hess Jüdische Schriften*, edited by Theodor Zlocisti, 1–8. Berlin: Louis Lamm, 1905.

———. "Meine Aussicht vom Judentum." Jerusalem: The Central Zionist Archives.

———. "Noch ein Wort über meine Missionsauffassung." In *Moses Hess Jüdische Schriften*, edited by Theodor Zlocisti, 68–69. Berlin: Louis Lamm, 1905.

———. "Ökonomische Schriften." In *Ökonomische Schriften*, Edited by Detlef Horster. Darmstadt: Melzer Verlag, 1972.

———. *Philosophische und sozialistische Schriften (1837–1850).* Edited by Auguste Cornu and Wolfgang Mönke. Berlin: Akademie Verlag, 1961.

———. "Die Polen und die Juden." Jerusalem: The Central Zionist Archives, 1840.

———. "Prolegomena zu einer Entstehungs-und Entwicklungsgeschichte des kosmischen, organischen und sozialen Lebens." In *Neue Quellen zur Hess Forschung*, edited by Wolfgang Mönke, 68–78. Berlin: Akademie Verlag, 1964.

———. "Religion und Sittlichkeit." In *Moses Hess: Sozialistische Aufsätze (1841–1847)*, edited by Theodor Zlocisti, 27–30. Berlin: Welt Verlag, 1921.

———. *Rom und Jerusalem: Die letzte Nationalitätsfrage.* Jerusalem: The Schocken Library, 1862.

———. "Rom und Jerusalem, die letzte Nationalitätsfrage." In *Ausgewählte Schriften*, edited by Horst Lademacher. Köln: Joseph Melzer, 1962.

———. *Rome and Jerusalem: A Study in Jewish Nationalism.* Translated by Meyer Waxman. New York: Bloch Publishing Co., 1943.

———. "Socialismus und Communismus." In *Philosophische und Sozialistische Schriften (1837–1850)*, edited by Auguste Cornu and Wolfgang Mönke. Berlin: Akademie Verlag, 1961.

———. "Studien zur heiligen und profanen Geschichte." In *Moses Hess Jüdische Schriften*, edited by Theodor Zlocisti, 56–67. Berlin: Louis Lamm, 1905.

———. "Über das Geldwesen." In *Philosophische und Sozialistische Schriften (1837–1850)*, edited by Auguste Cornu and Wolfgang Mönke. Berlin: Akademie Verlag, 1961.

———. *Über Socialokonomische Reformen. Eine Rede.* Hamburg: I. E. W. Kohler's Buch und Steinbruderei, 1863.

———. "Über Staat und Religion." In *Philosophische und Sozialistische Schriften (1837–1850)*, edited by Auguste Cornu and Wolfgang Mönke. Berlin: Akademie Verlag, 1961.

———. "Zur Entwicklungsgeschichte von Natur und Gesellschaft." In *Neue Quellen zur Hess Forschung*, edited by Wolfang Mönke, 56–68. Berlin: Akademie Verlag, 1964.

Hirsch, Helmut. *Moses Hess: Vorkämpfer der Freiheit.* Köln: Nachrichtenamt der Stadt Köln, 1975.

———. "Moses Hess, Vorläufer des Sozialismus und Zionismus." In *Freiheitsliebende Rheinländer: Neue beiträge zur deutschen Sozialgeschichte.* Düsseldorf: Econ Verlag, 1977.

Hirsch, Samson Raphael. *The Collected Writings.* IV vols. New York: Feldheim Publishers, 1984.

———. "Grundlinien einer jüdischen Symbolik." *Jeschurun* 3 (1856/57): 615–630.

———. "Grundlinien einer jüdischen Symbolik." *Jeschurun* 4 (1857/58): 19–32, 184–200, 352–387, 450–473, 621–633.

———. *Horeb.* New York: The Soncino Press, 1962.

———. *Horeb: Versuche über Jissroels Pflichten in der Zerstreuung.* 5th ed. Frankfurt am Main: J. Kauffmann, 1921.

———. *Igerot Tzafon: Neunzehn Briefe über Judenthum.* Altona: J. F. Hammerische, 1836.

———. *The Nineteen Letters.* Edited by Jacob Breuer. Jerusalem and New York: Feldheim Publishers, 1969.

———. *The Pentateuch.* 2nd ed. Gateshead: Judaica Press, 1989.

———. "Religion Allied with Progress." In *The Collected Writings,* 107–150. New York: Feldheim Publishers, 1990.

Hirsch, Samuel. *Die Humanität als Religion.* Trier: C. Troschel, 1854.

———. *Die Religionsphilosophie der Juden.* Leipzig: Heinrich Hunger, 1842.

———. "La Vérité du Dieu-Un et la Mission d'Israël." *Archives Israélites* 26 (1865): 194–200.

Hobsbawm, Eric, and Terence Ranger, eds. *The Invention of Tradition.* Cambridge: Cambridge University Press, 1992.

———. *Nations and Nationalism since 1780: Programme, Myth, Reality.* Cambridge: Cambridge University Press, 1990.

Hook, Sidney. "Karl Marx and Moses Hess." *New International* 1 (1934): 140–144.

Israel, Gérard. "The Adventure of the Alliance Israélite Universelle." *The Wiener Library Bulletin* 27 (1973/74): 49– 58.

Kansteiner, Wulf. "Hayden White's Critique of the Writing of History." *History and Theory* 32 (1993): 273–295.

Katz, Jacob. *Emancipation and Assimilation:* Farnborough: Gregg International, 1972.

———. "The Fight for Admission to Masonic Lodges." *Leo Baeck Institute Year Book* 11 (1966): 171–209.

———. "Freemasons and Jews." *Jewish Journal of Sociology* 9 (1967): 137–148.

———. "The Jewish National Movement." In *Jewish Emancipation and Self-Emancipation.* New York: Jewish Publication Society, 1986.

———. *Jews and Freemasons in Europe 1723–1939.* Cambridge, Mass.: Harvard University Press, 1970.

———. *Out of the Ghetto: The Social Background of Jewish Emancipation, 1770–1870.* New York: Schocken Books, 1978.

———. "Samuel Hirsch—Rabbi, Philosopher and Freemason." *Revue des études juives* 125 (1966): 113–126.

———. "The Term 'Jewish Emancipation': Its Origin and Historical Impact." In *Studies in Nineteenth-Century Jewish Intellectual History,* edited by Alexander Altmann, 1–25. Cambridge, Mass.: Harvard University Press, 1964.

———. *Tradition and Crisis: Jewish Society at the End of the Middle Ages.* New York: New York University Press, 1993.

———. "Zionism vs. Anti-Semitism." *Commentary* 73/1 (1982): 34–41.

Kelly, Alfred. *The Descent of Darwin: The Popularization of Darwinism in Germany, 1860–1914.* Chapel Hill: University of North Carolina Press, 1981.

Kepnes, Steven. *The Text as Thou: Martin Buber's Dialogical Hermeneutics and Narrative Theology.* Bloomington and Indianapolis: Indiana University Press, 1992.

Kermode, Frank. *The Sense of an Ending: Studies in the Theory of Fiction.* New York: Oxford University Press, 1967.

Klausner, Israel, ed. *The Zionist Writings of Rabbi Zvi Kalisher* [Hebrew]. Jerusalem: Mossad Harav Kook, 1947.

Lademacher, Horst. "Einleitung: Apostel und Philosoph." In *Ausgewählte Schriften,* edited by Horst Lademacher, 5–53. Köln: Joseph Melzer, 1962.

———. *Moses Hess in seiner Zeit.* Bonn: Ludwig Röhrscheid, 1977.

———. "Die politische und soziale Theorie bei Moses Hess." *Archiv für Kulturgeschichte* 42/2 (1960): 194–230.

Larmore, Charles. "Review of *Sources of the Self.*" *Ethics* 102/1 (1991): 158–162.

Lee, Jayne Chong-Soon. "Navigating the Topology of Race." *Stanford Law Review* 46/3 (1994): 747–780.

Lefkovits, Maurice. "Samuel Hirsch." *Year book of the Central Conference of American Rabbis* 25 (1915): 174–190.

Legters, Lyman. "Between Marxism and Zionism: Moses Hess." *Proceedings of the Sixth World Congress of Jewish Studies* 2 (1975): 169–183.

Lessing, Gotthold Ephraim. *Laocoon: An Essay upon the Limits of Painting and Poetry.* Translated by Ellen Frothingham. New York: The Noonday Press, 1961.

Leveen, Jacob. *Moses Hess.* London: English Zionist Federation, 1926.

Levitt, Laura. *Jews and Feminism: The Ambivalent Search for Home.* New York: Routledge, 1997.

Liberles, Robert. "Emancipation and the Structure of the Jewish Community in the Nineteenth Century." *Leo Baeck Institute Year Book* 31 (1986): 51–67.

———. *Religious Conflict in Social Context: The Resurgence of Orthodox Judaism in Frankfurt am Main, 1838–1877.* Westport: Greenwood Press, 1985.

———. "Was There a Jewish Movement for Emancipation in Germany?" *Leo Baeck Institute Year Book* 31 (1986): 35–49.

Lichtheim, George. *The Origins of Socialism.* London: Weidenfeld and Nicolson, 1969.

———. "Socialism and the Jews." *Dissent* July–August (1968): 314–342.

Liebeschütz, Hans. "German Radicalism and the Formation of Jewish Political Attitudes during the Earlier Part of the Nineteenth Century." In *Studies in Nineteenth-Century Jewish Intellectual History,* edited by Alexander Altmann, 141–170. Cambridge, Mass.: Harvard University Press, 1964.

———. "Jewish Thought and Its German Background." *Leo Baeck Institute Year Book* 1 (1956): 217–236.

———. *Das Judentum in deutschen Geschichtsbild von Hegel bis Max Weber.* Tübingen: J. C. B. Mohr, 1967.

———. "Max Wiener's Reinterpretation of Liberal Judaism." *Leo Baeck Institute Year Book* 5 (1960): 35–57.

———. "Treitschke and Mommsen on Jewry and Judaism." *Leo Baeck Institute Year Book* 7 (1962): 153–182.

Louth, Andrew. "Return to Allegory." In *Discerning the Mystery: An Essay on the Nature of Theology,* 96–131. Oxford: Clarendon Press, 1983.

Löw-Beer, Martin. "Living a Life and the Problem of Existential Impossibility." *Inquiry* 34/2 (1991): 217–236.

Lowenstein, Steven. "The 1840s and the Creation of the German Jewish Religious Reform Movement." In *Revolution and Evolution: 1848 in German-Jewish History,* edited by Werner Mosse, Arnold Paucker, and Reinhard Rurup, 255–297. Tübingen: J. C. B. Mohr, 1981.

——. *The Mechanics of Change: Essays in the Social History of German Jewry.* Atlanta: Scholars Press, 1992.

——. "The Pace of Modernisation of German Jewry in the Nineteenth Century." *Leo Baeck Institute Year Book* 21 (1976): 41–56.

Lukács, Georg. *Moses Hess und die Probleme in der idealistischen Dialektik.* Leipzig: C. L. Hirschfeld, 1926.

——. "Moses Hess and the Problems of the Idealist Dialectic." *Telos* 10 (1971): 3–34.

Lundgren, Svante. *Moses Hess on Religion, Judaism and the Bible.* Aobo: Aobo Akademis Förlag, 1992.

MacIntyre, Alasdair. *After Virtue.* Notre Dame: University of Notre Dame Press, 1981.

——. "Bernstein's Distorting Mirrors: A Rejoinder." *Soundings* 67/1 (1984): 30–41.

——. "Epistemological Crisis, Dramatic Narrative and the Philosophy of Science." *The Monist* 60/4 (1977): 453–472.

Mayer, Gustav. "Early German Socialism and Jewish Emancipation." *Jewish Social Studies* 1 (1939): 409–422.

McLellan, David. *The Young Hegelians and Karl Marx.* New York: Frederick A. Praeger, 1969.

Mendelssohn, Moses. *Jerusalem.* Hanover, N.H.: University Press of New England, 1983.

Meyer, Michael. "The Emergence of Jewish Historiography: Motives and Motifs." *History and Theory* 27/4 (1988): 160–175.

——. *German Political Pressure and Jewish Religious Response in the Nineteenth Century.* New York: Leo Baeck Institute, 1981.

——. "Jewish Religious Reform and Wissenschaft des Judentums: The Positions of Zunz, Geiger and Frankel." *Leo Baeck Institute Year Book* 26 (1971): 19–41.

——. *The Origins of the Modern Jew: Jewish Identity and European Culture in Germany, 1749–1824.* Detroit: Wayne State University Press, 1967.

——. "Recent Historiography on the Jewish Religion in Modern Germany." *Leo Baeck Institute Year Book* 35 (1990): 3–16.

——. *Response to Modernity: A History of the Reform Movement in Judaism.* Oxford: Oxford University Press, 1988.

Michael, Reuven. "The Contribution of *Sulamith* to Modern Jewish Historiography" [Hebrew]. *Zion* 39 (1974): 86–113.

——. "Graetz and Hess." *Leo Baeck Institute Year Book* 9 (1964): 91–121.

——, ed. *Heinrich Graetz: Tagebuch und Briefe.* Tübingen: J. C. B. Mohr, 1977.

——. "Vier unveröffentlichte Manuskripte von Moses Hess." *Bulletin des Leo Baeck Instituts* 7 (1964): 312–344.

Mitchell, W. J. T., ed. *On Narrative.* Chicago: University of Chicago Press, 1981.

Mönke, Wolfgang. *Neue Quellen zur Hess Forschung.* Berlin: Akademie Verlag, 1964.

Mordechai, Frankel. "On the Relations between Moses Hess and Rabbi Natonek" [Hebrew]. *Shragai* 4 (1993): 205–217.

Mosse, George. *Confronting the Nation: Jewish and Western Nationalism.* Hanover, N.H.: University Press of New England, 1993.

——. *The Crisis of German Ideology: Intellectual Origins of the Third Reich.* New York: Grosset and Dunlap, 1964.

——. *German Jews Beyond Judaism.* Cincinnati: Hebrew Union College Press, 1985.

——. "German Socialists and the Jewish Question in the Weimar Republic." *Leo Baeck Institute Year Book* 16 (1971): 123–151.

——. *Toward the Final Solution: A History of European Racism.* New York: Howard Fertig, 1978.

Mosse, Werner, Arnold Paucker, and Reinhard Rurup, eds. *Revolution and Evolution: 1848 in German-Jewish History.* Tübingen: J. C. B. Mohr, 1981.

Na'aman, Shlomo. *Emanzipation und Messianismus: Leben und Werk des Moses Hess.* Frankfurt/Main: Campus Verlag, 1982.

——. "Moses Hess and the Needs of Zionist Ideology Today: A Re-examination of 'Rome and Jerusalem'" [Hebrew]. *Kivunim* 14 (1982): 21–35.

——. "Moses Hess Explains His 'Rome and Jerusalem' to the Public" [Hebrew]. *Ha-Tzionut* 17 (1993): 9–37.

Nadler, Steven. *Spinoza: A Life.* Cambridge: Cambridge University Press, 1999.

Navon, Ephraim. "The Relationship of Religious Thought and Liberal Politics in the Writings of Abraham Geiger, Zacharias Frankel, and Samson Raphael Hirsch: 1830–1851." In *Jüdische Integration und Identität in Deutschland und Österreich, 1848–1918,* edited by Walter Grab. Tel Aviv: Jahrbuch des Instituts für deutsche Geschichte, 1983.

Nussbaum, Martha. *The Fragility of Goodness: Luck and Ethics in Greek Tragedy and Philosophy.* Cambridge: Cambridge University Press, 1986.

——. *Love's Knowledge: Essays on Philosophy and Literature.* New York: Oxford University Press, 1990.

——. "Non-Relative Virtues: An Aristotelian Approach." In *The Quality of Life,* edited by Martha Nussbaum and Amartya Sen, 242–269. Oxford: Clarendon Press, 1993.

——. *The Therapy of Desire: Theory and Practice in Hellenistic Ethics.* Princeton: Princeton University Press, 1994.

Olney, James, ed. *Autobiography: Essays Theoretical and Critical.* Princeton: Princeton University Press, 1980.

O'Regan, Cyril. *The Heterodox Hegel.* Albany: State University of New York Press, 1994.

Ozer, C. L. "Jewish Education in the Transition from Ghetto to Emancipation." *Historia Judaica* 9/1, 2 (1947): 75–94, 137–158.

Parkinson, G. H. R. "Hegel, Pantheism, and Spinoza." *Journal of the History of Ideas* 38/3 (1977): 449–459.

Parzen, Herbert. "The Centenary of a Book: Moses Hess' Rome and Jerusalem." *Jewish Book Annual* 19 (1961/62): 75–79.

Pazi, Margarita. "Berthold Auerbach and Moritz Hartmann: Two Jewish Writers of the Nineteenth Century." *Leo Baeck Institute Year Book* 18 (1973): 201–218.

Pelli, Moshe. "The Attitude of the First Maskilim in Germany Towards the Talmud." *Leo Baeck Institute Year Book* 27 (1982): 243–260.

Petuchowski, Jakob. "Manuals and Catechisms of the Jewish Religion in the Early Period of Emancipation." In *Studies in Nineteenth-Century Jewish Intellectual History,* edited by Alexander Altmann, 47–64. Cambridge, Mass.: Harvard University Press, 1964.

——. *Prayerbook Reform in Europe: The Liturgy of European Liberal and Reform Judaism.* New York: The World Union for Progressive Judaism, 1968.

Philippson, Johanna. "Ludwig Philippson und die Allgemeine Zeitung des Judentums." In *Das Judentum in der deutschen Umwelt, 1800–1850,* edited by Hans and Paucker Liebeschütz, 249–291. Tübingen: J. C. B. Mohr, 1977.

——. "The Philippsons, a German-Jewish Family, 1775–1933." *Leo Baeck Institute Year Book* 7 (1962): 95–118.

Philipson, David. *The Reform Movement in Judaism*. New York: Ktav Publishing House, 1967.

Poliakov, Leon. *The Aryan Myth: A History of Racist and Nationalist Ideas in Europe*. London: Sussex University Press, 1974.

Pratt, Mary Louise. "Interpretive Strategies/Strategic Interpretations: On Anglo-American Reader Response Criticism." In *Postmodernism and Politics*, edited by Jonathan Arac, 26–54. Minneapolis: University of Minnesota Press, 1986.

Prawer, S. S. *Heine: The Tragic Satirist*. Cambridge: Cambridge University Press, 1961.

Proudfoot, Wayne. *Religious Experience*. Berkeley: University of California Press, 1985.

Rawidowicz, S. *Ludwig Feuerbachs Philosophie: Ursprung und Schicksal*. Berlin: Reuther & Reichard, 1931.

Reinharz, Jehuda, and Walter Schatzberg, eds. *The Jewish Response to German Culture: From the Enlightenment to the Second World War*. Hanover, N.H.: University Press of New England, 1985.

Richarz, Monika. *Der Eintritt der Juden in akademischen Berufe*. Tübingen: J. C. B. Mohr, 1974.

———. "Jewish Social Mobility in Germany During the Time of Emancipation (1790–1871)." *Leo Baeck Institute Year Book* 20 (1975): 69–77.

———, ed. *Jüdisches Leben in Deutschland: Selbstzeugnisse zur Sozialgeschichte, 1780–1871*. Stuttgart: Deutsche Verlags-Anstalt, 1976.

Richter, David H., ed. *The Critical Tradition*. New York: Bedford Books, 1989.

Ricoeur, Paul. *Time and Narrative*. 3 vols. Chicago: University of Chicago Press, 1984–1988.

Rinott, Moshe. "Gabriel Riesser: Fighter for Jewish Emancipation." *Leo Baeck Institute Year Book* 7 (1962): 11–38.

Rorty, Richard. "Taylor on Truth." In *Philosophy in an Age of Pluralism: The Philosophy of Charles Taylor in Question*, edited by James Tully, 20–33. Cambridge: Cambridge University Press, 1994.

Rosen, Zevi. *Moses Hess und Karl Marx: Ein Beitrag zur Entstehung der Marxschen Theorie*. Hamburg: Christians, 1983.

Rosenbloom, Noah. *Luzzatto's Ethico-Psychological Interpretation of Judaism*. New York: Balshon Printing and Offset Co., 1965.

———. *Tradition in an Age of Reform: The Religious Philosophy of Samson Raphael Hirsch*. Philadelphia: The Jewish Publication Society of America, 1976.

Rotenstreich, Nathan. "The Bruno Bauer Controversy." *Leo Baeck Institute Year Book* 4 (1959): 3–36.

———. *Jewish Philosophy in Modern Times: From Mendelssohn to Rosenzweig*. New York: Holt, Rinehart and Winston, 1968.

———. *Jews and German Philosophy*. New York: Schocken Books, 1984.

———. *Ha-mahashavah ha-yehudit be-et ha-hadashah* [Hebrew]. 2nd ed. Vol. 1. Tel-Aviv: Am Oved, 1966.

———. "Moses Hess and Karl Ludwig Michelet." *Leo Baeck Institute Year Book* 7 (1962): 283–286.

———. "Moses Hess—ein Jünger Spinozas?" *Archiv für Geschichte der Philosophie* 71 (1989): 231–247.

———. "Religion Within Limits of Reason Alone and Religion of Reason." *Leo Baeck Institute Year Book* 17 (1972): 179–187.

———. "Solomon Ludwig Steinheim: Philosopher of Revelation." *Judaism* 2/4 (1953): 326–338.

———. *Tradition and Reality: The Impact of History on Modern Jewish Thought.* New York: Random House, 1972.

Rurup, Reinhard. "Emancipation and Crisis: The 'Jewish Question' in Germany 1850–1890." *Leo Baeck Institute Year Book* 20 (1975): 13–25.

———. "German Liberalism and the Emancipation of the Jews." *Leo Baeck Institute Year Book* 20 (1975): 59–68.

———. "Jewish Emancipation and Bourgeois Society." *Leo Baeck Institute Year Book* 14 (1969): 67–91.

———. "The Tortuous and Thorny Path to Legal Equality: 'Jew Laws' and Emancipatory Legislation in Germany from the Late Eighteenth Century." *Leo Baeck Institute Year Book* 31 (1986): 3–33.

Salomon, Gotthold. "Vertrautes Schreiben an einen Rabbi." *Wissenschaftliche Zeitschrift für jüdische Theologie* 2 (1836): 417–435.

Sammons, Jeffrey. *Heinrich Heine: A Modern Biography.* Princeton: Princeton University Press, 1979.

Sanders, Ronald. "Moses Hess: the Hegelian Zionist." *Midstream* 8/1 (1962): 57–69.

Schiller, Friedrich. *On the Aesthetic Education of Man.* Edited by Elizabeth Wilkinson and L. A. Willoughby. Oxford: Clarendon Press, 1982.

Schleiermacher, F. D. E. *Hermeneutics: The Handwritten Manuscripts.* Edited by Heinz Kimmerle. Missoula, Mont.: Scholars Press, 1977.

———. *On Religion: Speeches to its Cultured Despisers.* Translated by John Oman. San Francisco: Harper and Row, 1958.

———. *On the Glaubenslehre.* Translated by James Duke and Francis Fiorenza. Chico, Calif.: Scholars Press, 1981.

Schoeps, Julius H. "Moses Hess—ein Vorläufer des modernen Zionismus." *Emuna* 10 (1975): 65–71.

Schorsch, Ismar. "Art as Social History: Oppenheim and the German Jewish Vision of Emancipation." In *Moritz Oppenheim: The First Jewish Painter,* 31–61. Jerusalem: Israel Museum, 1983.

———. "Breakthrough into the Past: The Verein für Cultur und Wissenschaft der Juden." *Leo Baeck Institute Year Book* 33 (1988): 3–28.

———. "Emancipation and the Crisis of Religious Authority: The Emergence of the Modern Rabbinate." In *Revolution and Evolution: 1848 in German-Jewish History,* edited by Werner Mosse, Arnold Paucker, and Reinhard Rurup, 205–247. Tübingen: J. C. B. Mohr, 1981.

———. "The Emergence of Historical Consciousness in Modern Judaism." *Leo Baeck Institute Year Book* 28 (1983): 413–437.

———. "The Ethos of Modern Jewish Scholarship." *Leo Baeck Institute Year Book* 35 (1990): 55–71.

———. *From Text to Context: The Turn to History in Modern Judaism.* Hanover, N.H.: University Press of New England, 1994.

———. "From Wolfenbüttel to Wissenschaft: The Divergent Paths of Israel Markus Jost and Leopold Zunz." *Leo Baeck Institute Year Book* 22 (1977): 109–128.

———. "History as Consolation." *Leo Baeck Institute Year Book* 37 (1992): 33–43.

———. "Ideology and History in the Age of Emancipation." In *Heinrich Graetz: The Struc-*

ture of Jewish History and Other Essays, edited by Ismar Schorsch, 1–62. New York: Jewish Theological Seminary of America, 1975.

———. "The Myth of Sephardic Supremacy." *Leo Baeck Institute Year Book* 34 (1989): 47–66.

———. "The Religious Parameters of Wissenschaft: Jewish Academics at Prussian Universities." *Leo Baeck Institute Year Book* 25 (1980): 3–19.

———. "Scholarship in the Service of Reform." *Leo Baeck Institute Year Book* 35 (1990): 73–101.

———. "Zacharias Frankel and the European Origins of Conservative Judaism." *Judaism* 30/ 119 (1981): 344–354.

Schuffenland, Werner. "Zur Entwicklung von Moses Hess zum 'wahren' Sozialismus." *Deutsche Zeitschrift für Philosophie* 14/5 (1968).

Schulman, Mary. *Moses Hess, Prophet of Zionism.* New York: Thomas Yoseloff, 1963.

Schweid, Eliezer. *A History of Jewish Thought in Modern Times* [Hebrew]. Jerusalem: Keter, 1977.

Sheehan, James. *German Liberalism in the Nineteenth Century.* Atlantic Highlands, N.J.: Humanities Press, 1978.

———. "The Problem of the Nation in German History." In *Die Rolle der Nation in der Deutschen Geschichte und Gegenwart,* edited by James Sheehan and Otto Busch, 3–20. Berlin: Colloquium Verlag, 1985.

———. "What Is German History? Reflections on the Role of the *Nation* in German History and Historiography." *Journal of Modern History* 1/53 (1981): 1–23.

Shils, Edward. *Tradition.* Chicago: University of Chicago Press, 1981.

Silberner, Edmund. "Heinrich Graetz' Briefe an Moses Hess 1861– 1872." *Annali* 4 (1961): 326–400.

———. "Moses Hess." *Historia Judaica* 13 (1951): 3–28.

———. *Moses Hess: An Annotated Bibliography.* New York: B. Franklin, 1951.

———, ed. *Moses Hess Briefwechsel.* Gravenhage: Mouton and Co, 1959.

———. *Moses Hess: Geschichte Seines Lebens.* Leiden: E. J. Brill, 1966.

———. "Was Marx an Anti-Semite?" *Historica Judaica* 11/1 (1949): 3–52.

———. *The Works of Moses Hess.* Leiden: E. J. Brill, 1958.

———. "Zwei unbekannte Briefe von Moses Hess an Heinrich Heine." *International Review of Social History* 6/3 (1961): 456–462.

Silberstein, Laurence, and Robert Cohn, eds. *The Other in Jewish Thought and History: Constructions of Jewish Culture and Identity.* New York: New York University Press, 1994.

Sorkin, David. "The Genesis of the Ideology of Emancipation: 1806–1840." *Leo Baeck Institute Year Book* 32 (1987): 11–40.

———. *The Transformation of German Jewry, 1780–1840.* Oxford: Oxford University Press, 1987.

———. "Wilhelm von Humboldt: The Theory and Practice of Self-Formation (*Bildung*), 1791–1810." *Journal of the History of Ideas* 44 (January 1983): 55–73.

Spinoza, Benedict de. *Ethics.* Translated by Amelia Hutchinson. Edited by James Gutmann. New York: Hafner Press, 1949.

———. *Opera.* Edited by Carl Gebhardt. IV vols. Heidelberg: Carl Winters, 1925.

———. *A Theologico-Political Treatise.* Translated by R. H. M. Elwes. New York: Dover Publications, 1951.

Stampfer, Joshua. "The Religious Zionism of Kalisher." *Judaism* 2/3 (1953): 261–268.

Stepelevich, Lawrence, ed. *The Young Hegelians.* Cambridge: Cambridge University Press, 1983.

Sterling, Eleonore. "Jewish Reactions to Jew-Hatred." *Leo Baeck Institute Year Book* 3 (1958): 103–121.

Szajkowski, Zosa. "The Jewish Saint-Simonians and Socialist Antisemites in France." *Jewish Social Studies* 9 (1947): 33–60.

Talmage, Frank. "Apples of Gold: The Inner Meaning of Sacred Texts in Medieval Judaism." In *Jewish Spirituality,* edited by Arthur Green, 314–355. New York: Crossroad Publishing Co., 1987.

Taylor, Charles. "The Concept of a Person." In *Human Agency and Language: Philosophical Papers,* 97–114. Cambridge: Cambridge University Press, 1985.

———. "The Diversity of Goods." In *Utilitarianism and Beyond,* edited by Bernard Williams, 129–144. Cambridge: Cambridge University Press, 1982.

———. *The Ethics of Authenticity.* Cambridge, Mass.: Harvard University Press, 1991.

———. "Explanation and Practical Reason." In *The Quality of Life,* edited by Martha Nussbaum and Amartya Sen, 208–231. Oxford: Clarendon Press, 1993.

———. *Hegel and Modern Society.* Cambridge: Cambridge University Press, 1979.

———. *Human Agency and Language.* Vol. I. Cambridge: Cambridge University Press, 1985.

———. *Philosophical Arguments.* Cambridge, Mass.: Harvard University Press, 1995.

———. *Philosophy and the Human Sciences.* Vol. II. Cambridge: Cambridge University Press, 1985.

———. "The Politics of Recognition." In *Multiculturalism: Examining the Politics of Recognition,* edited by Amy Gutmann, 25–73. Princeton: Princeton University Press, 1994.

———. "Responsibility for Self." In *The Identities of Persons,* edited by Amelie Rorty, 281–299. Berkeley: University of California Press, 1969.

———. "Self-Interpreting Animals." In *Human Agency and Language,* 45–76. Cambridge: Cambridge University Press, 1985.

———. *Sources of the Self: The Making of Modern Identity.* Cambridge: Cambridge University Press, 1989.

———. "The Validity of Transcendental Arguments." *Proceedings of the Aristotelian Society* 79 (1978–79): 151–165.

———. "What Is Human Agency?" In *Human Agency and Languages,* 15–44. Cambridge: Cambridge University Press, 1985.

Todorov, Tzvetan. *Theories of the Symbol.* Translated by Catherine Porter. Ithaca: Cornell University Press, 1982.

Toews, John Edward. *Hegelianism: The Path toward Dialectical Humanism, 1805–1841.* Cambridge: Cambridge University Press, 1980.

Tully, James, ed. *Philosophy in an Age of Pluralism: The Philosophy of Charles Taylor in Question.* Cambridge: Cambridge University Press, 1994.

Vallee, G. *The Spinoza Conversations between Lessing and Jacobi: Text with Excerpts from the Ensuing Controversy.* Translated by G. Vallee, J. B. Lawson, and C. G. Chapple. Lanham, Md.: University Press of America, 1988.

Vital, David. *The Origins of Zionism.* Oxford: Clarendon Press, 1975.

Vogel, Manfred. "Does Samuel Hirsch Anthropologize Religion?" *Modern Judaism* 1 (1981): 298–322.

Volkov, Shulamit. "Moses Hess: Problems of Religion and Faith." *Zionism* 3 (1981): 1–15.

———. "Religion and Faith in the Thought of Moses Hess." *Zionism* 2/1 (1981): 1–16.

Walther, Manfred. *Spinoza und der deutsche Idealismus.* Würzburg: Königshausen & Neumann, 1991.

Wartofsky, Marx. *Feuerbach.* Cambridge: Cambridge University Press, 1977.

Weinstock, Daniel. "The Political Theory of Strong Evaluation." In *Philosophy in an Age of Pluralism: The Philosophy of Charles Taylor in Question,* edited by James Tully, 171–193. Cambridge: Cambridge University Press, 1994.

Weiss, John. *Moses Hess, Utopian Socialist.* Detroit: Wayne State University Press, 1960.

Weltsch, Felix. "'Rom und Jerusalem'—nach 100 Jahren." *Bulletin des Leo Baeck Instituts* 5/20 (1962): 225–266.

White, Hayden. *The Historical Imagination in Nineteenth-Century Europe.* Baltimore and London: Johns Hopkins University Press, 1973.

———. "The Value of Narrativity in the Representation of Reality." In *On Narrative,* edited by W. J. T. Mitchell, 1– 23. Chicago: University of Chicago Press, 1981.

Wiener, Max. *Jüdische Religion im Zeitalter der Emanzipation.* Berlin: Philo Verlag, 1933.

Williams, Bernard. *Ethics and the Limits of Philosophy.* Cambridge, Mass.: Harvard University Press, 1985.

———. *Shame and Necessity.* Berkeley: University of California Press, 1993.

Winer, Gershon. *The Founding Fathers of Israel.* New York: Bloch Publishing, 1971.

Wistrich, Robert. "Karl Marx, German Socialists and the Jewish Question, 1880–1914." *Soviet Jewish Affairs* 3/1 (1973): 92–97.

———. *Socialism and the Jews: The Dilemmas of Assimilation in Germany and Austria-Hungary.* London and Toronto: Associated University Press, 1982.

Wolf, Immanuel. "On the Concept of a Science of Judaism (1822)." *Leo Baeck Institute Year Book* 2 (1957): 194–204.

Yerushalmi, Yosef Hayim. *Zakhor: Jewish History and Jewish Memory.* Seattle and London: University of Washington Press, 1982.

Zlocisti, Theodor. *Moses Hess Jüdische Schriften.* Berlin: Louis Lamm, 1905.

———. *Moses Hess: Socialistische Aufsätze (1841–1847).* Berlin: Welt-Verlag, 1921.

———. *Moses Hess: der Vorkämpfer des Sozialismus und Zionismus 1812–1875; eine Biographie.* Berlin: Welt-Verlag, 1921.

INDEX

KEN KOLTUN-FROMM is Assistant Professor of Religion at Haverford College.